THE IRWIN SERIES IN
INSURANCE AND ECONOMIC SECURITY

DAVIS W. GREGG

Consulting Editor

THE
THEORY OF INTEREST

THE
THEORY OF INTEREST

By
STEPHEN G. KELLISON
Fellow of the Society of Actuaries
University of Nebraska

1970
RICHARD D. IRWIN, INC., Homewood, Illinois   60430

Irwin-Dorsey Limited. Georgetown, Ontario   L7G 4B3

Library of Congress Catalog Card No. 79-98251

Printed in the United States of America

Foreword for the
Society of Actuaries

For a number of years the Education and Examination Committee of the Society of Actuaries has felt the need for a new textbook on compound interest which would reflect the underlying mathematical theory of the subject as well as practices in the United States and Canada. The use of compound interest is fundamental to the work of the actuary in financial calculations of present values.

This textbook has been accepted by the Education and Examination Committee of the Society of Actuaries as the reference on compound interest for students taking the examinations required for admission to membership in the Society. In addition, it should be useful to practicing actuaries and others in the financial field who are concerned with this subject. Anticipating a wider interest in this new textbook beyond that of actuarial students alone, the Society is pleased that Richard D. Irwin, Inc. has undertaken to publish this text.

The Board of Governors and the Education and Examination Committee of the Society of Actuaries appreciate the great amount of work undertaken by Mr. Kellison in preparing his book, and express their gratitude for this important contribution to the literature on compound interest.

WENDELL A. MILLIMAN
President, Society of Actuaries

EDWIN B. LANCASTER
Advisory Committee on Education and Examination

WILLIAM A. SPARE
Education and Examination Committee

Author's preface

This book is a thorough treatment of the mathematical theory and practical applications of compound interest, or mathematics of finance. The book is designed to serve as a textbook for students preparing for the examination of the Society of Actuaries covering compound interest and as a reference for practicing actuaries. The notation used is consistent with the International Actuarial Notation. However, its usefulness is not restricted to actuaries, but includes anyone engaged in financial transactions in which interest is involved.

The study of compound interest has undergone a marked decline in colleges and universities on the North American continent in recent years. This has resulted in a shortage of modern textbooks on the subject. However, the theory of interest is still quite significant in most types of financial management, and this textbook provides a modern treatment of the subject.

A working knowledge of elementary calculus is essential for a thorough understanding of all the material, since the continuous nature of interest is stressed throughout the book. However, a large portion of the book can be read by those without a calculus background by omitting the sections dependent upon calculus. Also in a very few places a knowledge of finite differences is assumed. A review of all the finite difference relationships required is given in Appendix IV. The portions of the book involving finite differences can readily be omitted without loss of continuity for those readers without such a background.

The book is designed to be appropriate for both classroom use with an instructor and for self-study by those learning the subject without the aid of an instructor. The amount of material is sufficient to comprise a one-semester university course without the need for outside supplementation.

Since a thorough knowledge of the subject can only be gained by working numerous exercises, each chapter includes a large number of examples and exercises. The answers to the exercises are given at the end of the book. Most other textbooks on compound interest have tended to have either a scarcity of exercises or else a large number of repetitious, computational exercises. This book contains a blend of both theoretical and practical exercises with each exercise illustrating a slightly different point, so that little repeti-

ix

Author's preface

tion in the exercises appears. In practice the subject of compound interest involves much numerical computation and many of the examples and exercises do proceed to numerical answers. However, the author is keenly aware that many readers will not have the aid of even a desk calculator, so that the amount of numerical computation is kept at a minimum in a large number of exercises. Throughout the book alternate approaches to the solution of problems is emphasized, with modern computer techniques playing a significant role.

Chapters 1 and 2 introduce the student to the various measures of interest and the solution of problems in interest. These chapters include essentially all the fundamental principles of the subject, with the later chapters extending these principles to more complex financial transactions. Chapters 3 and 4 give a thorough treatment to annuities-certain. Chapter 5 discusses amortization schedules and sinking funds, with an emphasis on the close relationship of the amortization method and the sinking fund method of repaying a loan. Chapter 6 discusses bonds in detail and also includes material on other securities, such as preferred and common stock. Chapter 7 includes several miscellaneous topics; namely, valuation of securities, interest measurement of a fund, construction of tables, life insurance settlement options, installment loans, and depreciation, depletion, and capitalized cost. Appendixes I and II are standard compound interest tables. Appendix III is a table of five-place logarithms. It is assumed that the reader is familiar with the use of such a table. Appendix IV is a brief mathematical review of techniques of algebra and finite differences used in the book.

The author is deeply indebted to Charles B. H. Watson, F.S.A., and John A. Fibiger, F.S.A., both of whom reviewed drafts of the book and made numerous helpful suggestions increasing the clarity of exposition. The author is also grateful to the University of Nebraska students who used a rough draft of the book under classroom conditions during the spring semester of the 1968–69 academic year. As a result of this classroom experience numerous improvements were incorporated into the book. The author wishes to thank the several insurance companies which provided most of the expenses and the secretarial help so valuable in preparing the manuscript. Finally, the author wishes to express his gratitude to the Education and Examination Committee of the Society of Actuaries for their acceptance of this textbook for use on the actuarial examination covering compound interest.

December, 1969   STEPHEN G. KELLISON

Contents

CHAPTER 1. The measurement of interest

1.1. INTRODUCTION

Interest may be defined as the consideration that a borrower of capital pays to a lender of capital for its use. This consideration can be viewed as a form of rent that the borrower pays to the lender to compensate for the loss of use of the capital by the lender while it is loaned to the borrower. In theory, capital and interest need not be expressed in terms of the same commodity. For example, Farmer A may lend a tractor to Farmer B for use in harvesting B's wheat crop in return for a percentage of the wheat harvested. In this example, the tractor is capital and the portion of wheat that B gives to A is interest. However, for almost all applications, both capital and interest are expressed in terms of money. The theory of interest is concerned with various methods by which interest is calculated and by which capital and interest are repaid by the borrower to the lender.

In Chapter 1 the various quantitative measures of interest are analyzed. This chapter includes essentially all the basic principles involved in the theory of interest. Succeeding chapters elaborate and extend these basic principles to more complex financial transactions.

1.2. THE ACCUMULATION AND AMOUNT FUNCTIONS

A common financial transaction is the investment of an amount of money at interest. For example, a man may invest in a savings account at a bank in which case the man is the lender and the bank is the borrower. The initial amount of money (capital) invested is called the *principal* and the total amount received after a period of time is called the *accumulated value*. The difference between the accumulated value and the principal is the *amount of interest*, or just *interest*, earned during the period of investment.

1

For the moment, assume that given the original principal invested, the accumulated value at any point in time can be determined. We will assume that no principal is added or withdrawn during the period of investment, i.e., that any change in the fund is due strictly to the effect of interest.

Let t measure time from the date of investment. In theory, time may be measured in many different units, e.g., days, months, decades, etc. Most commonly, t is measured in years, and this will be assumed unless stated otherwise.

Consider the investment of one unit of principal. We can define an *accumulation function*, $a(t)$, which gives the accumulated value at time $t \geq 0$ of an original investment of 1.

What properties does this function possess? First, it is clear that $a(0) = 1$. Second, $a(t)$ is generally an increasing function. A decrease in the functional values for increasing t would imply negative interest. Although negative interest would be possible mathematically, it is not relevant to most situations encountered in practice. Constant functional values would imply zero interest, a situation occurring occasionally. Third, if interest accrues continuously, as is often the case, the function will be continuous.

In general, the original principal invested will not be 1 but will be some amount $k > 0$. We now define an *amount function*, $A(t)$, which gives the accumulated value at time $t \geq 0$ of an original investment of k. Then we have

$$A(t) = k \cdot a(t) \tag{1.1}$$

and

$$A(0) = k\,.$$

The second and third properties of $a(t)$ listed above clearly also hold for $A(t)$.

We can denote the amount of interest earned during the nth year from the date of investment by I_n. Then

$$I_n = A(n) - A(n-1) \text{ for } n \geq 1\,. \tag{1.2}$$

It should be noted that I_n involves the effect of interest over a period of time, whereas $A(n)$ is an amount at a moment of time.

Actually, the accumulation function is a special case of the amount function for which $k = 1$. However, the accumulation function will be significant enough in the rest of this chapter to warrant a separate definition. In many cases, the accumulation function and the amount function can be used interchangeably.

Figure 1.1 shows four examples of amount functions. Figure (*a*) is a linear amount function. Figure (*b*) is nonlinear, in this case an exponential curve. Figure (*c*) is an amount function which is horizontal, i.e., the slope is zero. This figure represents an amount function in which the principal is accruing no interest. Figure (*d*) is an amount function in which interest is not accruing continuously but is accruing in finite segments with no interest accruing between interest payment dates.

FIGURE 1.1

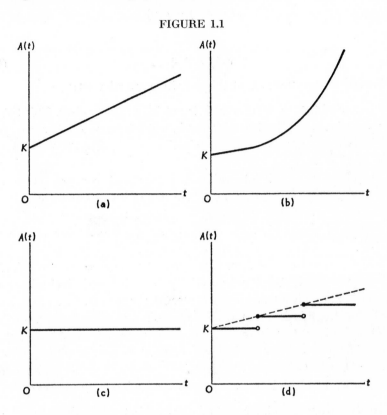

In the following sections, various measures of interest will be developed from the accumulation function. In practice, two particular accumulation functions will handle most situations which arise. However, the student should understand the properties of a general accumulation function as defined in this section and be able to work with it.

1.3. THE EFFECTIVE RATE OF INTEREST

The first measure of interest is called the *effective rate of interest* and is denoted by *i*. A precise definition is:

The effective rate of interest, i, is the amount of money that 1 invested at the beginning of a year will earn during the year, where interest is paid at the end of the year.

Note that in terms of the accumulation function, this definition is equivalent to saying that

$$i = a(1) - a(0)$$

or

$$a(1) = 1 + i. \tag{1.3}$$

Several observations about this definition are relevant:

1. The use of the word "effective" is not immediately clear. This term is reserved for annual rates of interest in which interest is paid once a year. This will be contrasted with "nominal" rates of interest to be considered in Section 1.8.
2. The effective rate of interest is often expressed as a percentage, e.g., $i = 5\%$. The concept of the effective rate of interest as a percentage is not inconsistent with the definition above, which states that it is an amount of money, since 5% can be looked upon as .05 per unit of principal.
3. The amount of principal remains constant throughout the year, i.e., no new principal is added and no principal is withdrawn during the year.
4. The definition is restricted to an interval of one year. As we shall see in Section 1.8, this definition can be generalized to other intervals of time.
5. The effective rate of interest is a measure in which interest is paid at the end of the year. The significance of this statement is not immediately clear, but it will become evident in Section 1.7, where a situation is described in which interest is paid at the beginning of the year.

The effective rate of interest can be defined in terms of the amount function as follows:

$$i = \frac{(1 + i) - 1}{1} = \frac{a(1) - a(0)}{a(0)} = \frac{A(1) - A(0)}{A(0)} = \frac{I_1}{A(0)}. \tag{1.4a}$$

Thus, an alternate definition is:

The effective rate of interest, i, is the ratio of the amount of interest earned during the year to the amount of principal invested at the beginning of the year.

The same five observations made above also apply to this alternate definition.

Effective rates of interest can be calculated over any one-year period. Let i_n be the effective rate of interest during the nth year from the date of investment. Then we have

$$i_n = \frac{A(n) - A(n - 1)}{A(n - 1)} = \frac{I_n}{A(n - 1)} \text{ for } n \geq 1. \tag{1.4b}$$

Within this framework, the "i" in formula (1.4a) might more properly be labeled "i_1."

Although formula (1.4b) allows the various effective rates of interest, i_n, to be different for different n, it will be demonstrated in Section 1.5 that for one very important accumulation function, the effective rate of interest, i_n, is constant over any one-year period, i.e., for all $n \geq 1$.

1.4. SIMPLE INTEREST

It was shown in the preceding sections that $a(0) = 1$ and $a(1) = 1 + i$. There are an infinite number of accumulation functions that pass through these two points. Two of these are most significant in practice. The first, simple interest, will be discussed in this section; and the second, compound interest, will be discussed in Section 1.5.

Consider the investment of 1 such that the amount of interest earned during each year is constant. The accumulated value of 1 at the end of the first year is $1 + i$; at the end of the second year it is $1 + 2i$, etc. Thus, in general, we have a linear accumulation function

$$a(t) = 1 + it \text{ for } t \geq 0. \tag{1.5}$$

The accruing of interest according to this pattern is called *simple interest.*

Strictly speaking, the accumulation function for simple interest has been defined only for integral values of t. However, it is natural to extend the definition to nonintegral values of t as well. This is equivalent to the crediting of interest proportionally over any fraction of a year. If this is the case, then the amount function can be represented by Figure 1.1 (a). If interest is accrued only for completed years with no credit for fractional years, then the amount function can be represented by Figure 1.1 (d). Unless stated otherwise, it will be assumed that interest is accrued over fractional periods.

There would appear to be no ambiguity in calculating simple interest over fractional periods. However, in practice, different methods have arisen when the period of time involved is a given number of days. The first method is to use the exact number of days in the numerator and to use 365 days in the denominator. Interest computed on this basis is called *exact simple interest.* The second method is to use an approximate number of days, assuming 30 days per month, in the numerator and to use 360 days in the denominator. Interest computed on this basis is called *ordinary simple interest*. A third method is to use the exact number of days in the numerator and to use 360 days in the denominator. This method is often called the *Banker's Rule*. A fourth possibility would be to use the approximate number of days in the numerator and to use 365 days in the denominator, but this method is rarely used in practice.

It can be shown that a constant rate of simple interest does not imply a constant effective rate of interest. Let i be the rate of simple interest and let i_n be the effective rate of interest for the nth year, as defined in Section 1.3. Then, we have

$$i_n = \frac{a(n) - a(n-1)}{a(n-1)} = \frac{[1+in] - [1+i(n-1)]}{1+i(n-1)} = \frac{i}{1+i(n-1)},$$

which is a decreasing function of n. Thus, a constant rate of simple interest implies a decreasing effective rate of interest.

Example 1.1.   Find the accumulated value of $200 invested for three years if the rate of simple interest is 3% per annum.

The answer is

$$200[1 + (.03)(3)] = \$218 .$$

Note that the amount of interest earned is $218 - \$200 = \$18$. This could also have been obtained as $200(.03)(3)$, or, in general, as $A(0) \cdot it$. In different notation, this becomes the familiar result from elementary and secondary school,

$$I = Prt ,$$

which states that the amount of interest is equal to the product of the amount of principal, the rate of interest, and the period of time.

1.5. COMPOUND INTEREST

Simple interest has the property that the interest is not reinvested to earn additional interest. For example, if a man invests $100 for two years at 5% simple interest, he will receive $5 at the end of each of the two years. However, in reality, for the second year he has $105 which he could have invested had he started anew. Clearly, it would be to his advantage to invest the $105 at 5%, since he would then receive $5.25 in interest for the second year instead of $5.

The theory of *compound interest* handles this problem by assuming that the interest earned is automatically reinvested. The word "compound" refers to the process of interest being reinvested to earn additional interest.

With compound interest the total investment of principal and interest earned to date is kept invested at all times.

It is now necessary to find the accumulation function for compound interest. Consider the investment of 1 which accumulates to $1 + i$ at the end of the first year. This balance of $1 + i$ can be considered as principal at the beginning of the second year and will earn interest of $i(1 + i)$ during the second year. The balance at the end of the second year is $(1 + i) + i(1 + i) = (1 + i)^2$. Similarly, the balance of $(1 + i)^2$ can be considered as principal at the beginning of the third year and will earn interest of $i(1 + i)^2$ during the third year. The balance at the end of the third year is $(1 + i)^2 + i(1 + i)^2 = (1 + i)^3$. Continuing this process indefinitely, we obtain

$$a(t) = (1 + i)^t \text{ for } t \geq 0 . \tag{1.6}$$

Strictly speaking, the accumulation function for compound interest has been defined only for integral values of t. However, it is natural to assume that interest is accruing continuously and, therefore, to extend the definition to nonintegral values of t. Unless stated otherwise, it will be assumed that interest is accrued over fractional periods. Thus the amount function is exponential and can be represented by Figure 1.1 (*b*). The exponential form of the amount function should not be unexpected, since many growth curves encountered in the natural sciences are exponential.

Many students are troubled, on one hand, by the statement that interest is paid at the end of the year and, on the other hand, by the statement that interest is accruing continuously. At first glance, the two statements appear contradictory. However, there is no inconsistency as long as interest is accrued over fractional years as well as completed years. When this is the case, the accumulated values at any point in time are equal from either perspective.

It can be shown that a constant rate of compound interest implies a constant effective rate of interest and, moreover, that the two are equal. Let i be the rate of compound interest and let i_n be the effective rate of interest for the nth year, as defined in Section 1.3. Then, we have

$$i_n = \frac{a(n) - a(n - 1)}{a(n - 1)} = \frac{(1 + i)^n - (1 + i)^{n-1}}{(1 + i)^{n-1}} = \frac{(1 + i) - 1}{1} = i,$$

which is independent of n. Thus, although defined differently, a rate of compound interest and an effective rate of interest are identical.

The result just derived can be compared with the result obtained in Section 1.4; namely, that a constant rate of simple interest implies a decreasing effective rate of interest. This result should be intuitively clear, since simple interest becomes progressively less favorable to the investor as the period of investment increases.

It is clear that simple and compound interest produce the same result over a one-year period. Over a longer period, compound interest produces a larger accumulated value than simple interest; whereas, the opposite is true over a shorter period. The proofs of these results are left as exercises.

Compound interest is used almost exclusively for financial transactions covering a period of one year or more and is often used for shorter term transactions as well. Simple interest is occasionally used for short-term transactions and as an approximation for compound interest over fractional periods. This latter use of simple interest will be examined in more detail in Section 2.2. Hereafter, unless stated otherwise, we will use compound interest instead of simple interest.

Example 1.2.   Rework Example 1.1 using compound interest instead of simple interest.

The answer is

$$200(1.03)^3 = \$218.55 \ .$$

This answer is in contrast with the answer of \$218 using simple interest. The extra \$0.55 is the result of compounding of interest.

In this example, the numerical answer can be obtained directly by multiplication. In general, if the exponent is large or nonintegral, this method is impractical. Various methods of obtaining numerical answers for such problems are discussed in Section 2.2. However, until these methods have been discussed, answers to examples and exercises in Chapter 1, for which it is impractical to obtain numerical answers directly, will be left in exponential form.

1.6. PRESENT VALUE

We have seen that an investment of 1 will accumulate to $1 + i$ at the end of one year. The term $1 + i$ is often called an *accumulation factor*, since it accumulates the value of an investment at the beginning of a year to its value at the end of the year.

It is often necessary to determine how much a person must invest initially so that he will have 1 at the end of one year. The answer is $(1 + i)^{-1}$, since this amount will accumulate to 1 at the end of one year. We now define a new symbol v, such that

$$v = \frac{1}{1 + i} \qquad (1.7)$$

The term v is often called a *discount factor*, since it "discounts" the value of an investment at the end of a year to its value at the beginning of the year.

We can generalize the above result to periods of time other than one year, i.e., to find the amount which a man must invest in order to accumulate an amount of 1 at the end of t years. The answer is the reciprocal of the accumulation function, $a^{-1}(t)$, since the accumulated value of this amount at the end of t years is $a^{-1}(t) \cdot a(t) = 1$. We shall call $a^{-1}(t)$ the *discount function*. Thus, we obtain the following results for $t \geq 0$:

Simple Interest: $a^{-1}(t) = \dfrac{1}{1 + it}$. $\qquad$ (1.8)

Compound Interest: $a^{-1}(t) = \dfrac{1}{(1 + i)^t} = v^t$. $\qquad$ (1.9)

As specified before, we will use compound interest unless stated otherwise.

In a sense, *accumulating* and *discounting* are opposite processes. The term $(1 + i)^t$ is said to be the *accumulated value* of 1 at the end of t years. The term v^t is said to be the *present value* (or *discounted value*) of 1 to be paid at the end of t years.

The term "accumulated value" as defined above seems to refer strictly to payments made in the past, whereas the term "present value" seems to refer strictly to payments to be made in the future. This is the sense in which we shall use the terms. Some writers have used "present value" to refer to either past or future payments. We shall use the term *current value* for this purpose.

It is interesting to relate v^t to the accumulation function for compound interest from an alternate viewpoint. It is immediately clear that the values of v^t extend the definition of the accumulation function to negative values of t. Thus, the accumulation function for compound interest has meaning for all values of t. The graph of this function is shown in Figure 1.2.

FIGURE 1.2

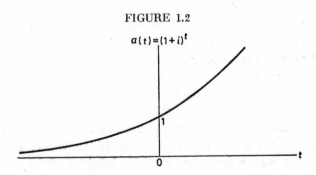

Example 1.3. Find the amount which must be invested at a rate of simple interest of 5% per annum in order to accumulate $1000 at the end of three years.

The answer is

$$\frac{1000}{1 + (.05)(3)} = \frac{1000}{1.15} = \$869.57 \, .$$

Example 1.4.   Rework Example 1.3 using compound interest instead of simple interest.

The answer is

$$1000v^3 = \frac{1000}{(1.05)^3} = \$863.84 \, .$$

From general reasoning, the student should justify the relative magnitudes of the answers to Examples 1.3 and 1.4.

1.7. THE EFFECTIVE RATE OF DISCOUNT

In Section 1.3 the effective rate of interest was defined as a measure of interest paid at the end of the year. In this section we define the *effective rate of discount*, denoted by d, as a measure of interest paid at the beginning of the year.

A numerical example will help make this distinction clear. If A goes to a bank and borrows \$100 for one year at an effective rate of interest of 6%, then the bank will give him \$100. At the end of the year, A will repay the bank the original loan of \$100, plus interest of \$6, or a total of \$106.

However, if A borrows \$100 for one year at an effective rate of discount of 6%, then the bank will collect its interest of 6% in advance and will give A only \$94. At the end of the year, A will repay \$100.

Thus, it is clear that an effective rate of interest of 6% is not the same as an effective rate of discount of 6%. In the above example, A paid \$6 interest in both cases. However, in the case of interest paid at the end of the year, he had the use of \$100 principal for the year; whereas, in the case of interest paid at the beginning of the year, he had the use of only \$94 principal for the year.

Looking at the above example in a slightly different manner, in the case of an effective rate of interest, the 6% is taken as a percentage of the balance at the beginning of the year; whereas, in the case of an effective rate of discount, the 6% is taken as a percentage of the balance at the end of the year. Thus, we can formulate a precise definition of the effective rate of discount as follows:

The effective rate of discount, d, is the ratio of the amount of interest (usually called the "amount of discount" or just "discount") earned during the year to the amount invested at the end of the year.

This definition is analogous to the alternate definition of the effective rate of interest given in Section 1.3.

Several observations about the above definition are relevant:

1. Observations 1, 2, 3, and 4 in Section 1.3 on the definition of the effective rate of interest also apply to the definition of the effective rate of discount.
2. The phrase *amount of discount* is normally used instead of "amount of interest" in situations involving rates of discount.
3. The definition does not use the word "principal," since the definition of principal refers to the amount invested at the beginning of the year and not at the end of the year.
4. The key distinction between the effective rate of interest and the effective rate of discount can be summarized as follows:
   a) Interest—paid at the end of the year on the balance at the beginning of the year.
   b) Discount—paid at the beginning of the year on the balance at the end of the year.

Effective rates of discount can be calculated over any one-year period. Let d_n be the effective rate of discount during the nth year from the date of investment. A formula analogous to (1.4b) is:

$$d_n = \frac{A(n) - A(n-1)}{A(n)} = \frac{I_n}{A(n)} \text{ for } n \geq 1. \tag{1.10}$$

As mentioned above, I_n is commonly called the "amount of discount" instead of the "amount of interest." In general, d_n may vary from year to year. However, if we have compound interest, in which case the effective rate of interest is constant, then the effective rate of discount is also constant. The proof of this statement is left as an exercise for the student. These situations are referred to as *compound discount,* a term analogous to "compound interest."

The example discussed earlier in this section showed that an effective rate of interest of 6% is not the same as an effective rate of discount of 6%. However, there is a definite relationship between effective rates of interest and effective rates of discount.

It is necessary to find a relationship between i and d such that they are *equivalent.* Two rates of interest or discount are said to be equivalent if a given principal invested for the same length of time at each of the rates yields the same accumulated value. As we shall see in Section 1.8, this definition of "equivalent" can be extended to nominal rates of interest and discount as well as effective rates.

Assume that a man borrows 1 at an effective rate of discount d. Then, in effect, the original principal is $1 - d$ and the amount of interest (discount) is d. However, from the basic definition of i as the ratio of the amount of interest (discount) to the principal, we obtain

$$i = \frac{d}{1 - d}. \tag{1.11}$$

This formula expresses i as a function of d.

By simple algebra, it is possible to express d as a function of i.

$$i = \frac{d}{1 - d}$$
$$i - id = d$$
$$d(1 + i) = i$$
$$d = \frac{i}{1 + i}. \tag{1.12a}$$

Formula (1.12a) is obvious, since it is merely a restatement of the definition of the effective rate of discount as the ratio of the amount of interest (discount) that 1 will earn during the year to the amount invested at the end of the year.

There is a close relationship between d, a rate of discount, and v, a discount factor. One relationship is identical to (1.12a); namely,

$$d = iv. \tag{1.12b}$$

This relationship has an interesting verbal interpretation. A measure of interest paid at the beginning of the year is d. A measure of interest paid at the end of the year is i. Therefore, if we discount i from the end of the year to the beginning of the year with the discount factor v, we obtain d.

There is another relationship between d and v which is often useful:

$$d = \frac{i}{1 + i}$$
$$= \frac{1 + i}{1 + i} - \frac{1}{1 + i} \tag{1.13}$$
$$= 1 - v.$$

This relationship also can be interpreted verbally. Written in the form $v = 1 - d$, it is immediately seen that both sides of the equation represent the present value of 1 to be paid at the end of the year.

There is one other relationship between i and d which is significant:

$$d = iv$$
$$= i(1 - d)$$
$$= i - id .$$

Thus,

$$i - d = id . \tag{1.14}$$

This relationship also has an interesting verbal interpretation. A man can either borrow 1 and repay $1 + i$ at the end of the year or he can borrow $1 - d$ and repay 1 at the end of the year. The expression $i - d$ is the difference in the amount of interest he pays. This difference arises because the principal borrowed differs by d. Interest on amount d for one year at rate i is id.

The effective rate of discount, or compound discount, assumes compound interest. However, it is possible to define *simple discount* in a manner analogous to the definition of simple interest. Consider a situation in which the amount of discount earned during each year is constant. Then, the original principal which will yield an accumulated value of 1 at the end of t years is

$$a^{-1}(t) = 1 - dt . \tag{1.15}$$

This contrasts with compound discount, in which case the present value is

$$a^{-1}(t) = v^t = (1 - d)^t . \tag{1.16}$$

It should be noted that formulas (1.11), (1.12), (1.13), and (1.14) assume effective rates of interest and discount and are not valid for simple rates of interest and discount unless the period of investment happens to be exactly one year.

Simple discount has properties analogous to simple interest. The proofs of the following are left as exercises:

1. Whereas a constant rate of simple interest implies a decreasing effective rate of interest, a constant rate of simple discount implies an increasing effective rate of discount.
2. Simple and compound discount produce the same result over a one-year period. Over a longer period, simple discount produces a smaller present value than compound discount; whereas, the opposite is true over a shorter period.

As was the case with simple interest, simple discount is used only for short-term transactions and as an approximation for compound discount over fractional periods.

The word "discount" unfortunately is used in two different contexts with various shades of meaning in each. It is used in connection with present values (discount factor, discount function, discounting, discounted value) and in connection with interest paid at the beginning of the year (effective rate of discount, amount of discount, compound discount, simple discount). The student should be careful in using the term "discount" to keep the meaning completely clear.

The following examples illustrate the use of rates of discount. These examples are extensions of the examples in Section 1.6.

Example 1.5.   Rework Example 1.3 using simple discount instead of simple interest.

The answer is

$$1000[1 - (.05)(3)] = \$850 .$$

Example 1.6.   Rework Example 1.3 using compound discount instead of simple interest.

The answer is

$$1000(.95)^3 = \$857.38 .$$

From general reasoning, the student should justify the relative magnitudes of the answers to Examples 1.5 and 1.6.

1.8. NOMINAL RATES OF INTEREST AND DISCOUNT

In Sections 1.3 and 1.7 effective rates of interest and discount were discussed. The term "effective" is used for annual rates of interest and discount in which interest is paid once a year, either at the end of the year or at the beginning of the year, as the case may be. In this section, we consider situations in which interest is paid more frequently than once a year. Rates of interest and discount in these cases are called "nominal."

Most persons have encountered such situations in practice. For example, Credit Union A might charge 7% effective on loans; Savings and Loan B might charge $6\frac{3}{4}\%$ compounded quarterly; while Bank C might charge $6\frac{1}{2}\%$ payable in advance and convertible monthly. Most persons probably realize that these rates are not directly comparable, but they would probably not be able to make a valid comparison among them.

Credit Union A is charging a true effective rate of interest, which has already been discussed. However, Savings and Loan B is charging what we call a nominal rate of interest, and Bank C is charging what we call a nominal rate of discount.

Various terms are used in practice to describe situations in which interest is paid more frequently than once a year. Among these are "payable," "compounded," and "convertible," as in "payable quarterly," "compounded semiannually," and "convertible monthly." The frequency with which interest is paid and reinvested to earn additional interest is called the *interest conversion period.*

The purpose of this section is to define nominal rates of interest and discount and to derive a systematic method of finding effective and nominal rates of interest and discount which are equivalent. The definition of "equivalent" was given in Section 1.7.

The symbol for a *nominal rate of interest* payable m times per year is $i^{(m)}$. By a nominal rate of interest $i^{(m)}$, we mean an annual rate payable $m$thly, i.e., the rate of interest is $\dfrac{i^{(m)}}{m}$ for each mth of a year and not $i^{(m)}$. For example, a nominal rate of 4% convertible quarterly does not mean an interest rate of 4% per quarter but rather an interest rate of 1% per quarter. In reality, we can say that a nominal rate of interest of $i^{(m)}$ per annum is identical to an effective rate of interest of $\dfrac{i^{(m)}}{m}$ per mth of a year. This use of the word "effective" requires a slight generalization to periods of time other than one year, as was discussed in observation 4 on the definition of "effective rate of interest" in Section 1.3.

The nominal rate of interest, $i^{(m)}$, is a measure of interest paid at the end of $m$ths of a year in much the same manner as i was a measure of interest paid at the end of the year. By an argument similar to the one used in developing the accumulation function for compound interest, it is possible to develop a formula relating $i^{(m)}$ and i such that they are equivalent.

Consider the investment of 1 for one year at a nominal rate of interest $i^{(m)}$. During the first mth of a year the initial balance is 1 and the amount of interest is $\dfrac{i^{(m)}}{m} \cdot 1$, forming a balance at the end of the first mth of a year of $1 + \dfrac{i^{(m)}}{m}$. During the second mth of a year, the initial balance is $1 + \dfrac{i^{(m)}}{m}$ and the amount of interest is $\dfrac{i^{(m)}}{m}\left(1 + \dfrac{i^{(m)}}{m}\right)$, forming a balance at the end of the second mth of a year of $\left(1 + \dfrac{i^{(m)}}{m}\right) + \dfrac{i^{(m)}}{m}\left(1 + \dfrac{i^{(m)}}{m}\right) = \left(1 + \dfrac{i^{(m)}}{m}\right)^2$. This process is continued until at the end of the year the balance is $\left(1 + \dfrac{i^{(m)}}{m}\right)^m$. However, the balance at the end of the year must also be $1 + i$. Thus,

$$1 + i = \left(1 + \frac{i^{(m)}}{m}\right)^m, \tag{1.17a}$$

which gives

$$i = \left(1 + \frac{i^{(m)}}{m}\right)^m - 1, \qquad (1.17b)$$

and

$$i^{(m)} = m\left[(1 + i)^{\frac{1}{m}} - 1\right]. \qquad (1.17c)$$

Figure 1.3 illustrates the above argument.

FIGURE 1.3

Time:	0	$\frac{1}{m}$		$\frac{2}{m}$	$\cdots$	$\frac{m-1}{m}$		$\frac{m}{m} = 1$
Interest:		$\frac{i^{(m)}}{m} \cdot 1$		$\frac{i^{(m)}}{m}\left(1 + \frac{i^{(m)}}{m}\right)$	$\cdots$	$\frac{i^{(m)}}{m}\left(1 + \frac{i^{(m)}}{m}\right)^{m-2}$		$\frac{i^{(m)}}{m}\left(1 + \frac{i^{(m)}}{m}\right)^{m-1}$
Balance:	1	$1 + \frac{i^{(m)}}{m}$		$\left(1 + \frac{i^{(m)}}{m}\right)^2$	$\cdots$	$\left(1 + \frac{i^{(m)}}{m}\right)^{m-1}$		$\left(1 + \frac{i^{(m)}}{m}\right)^m = 1 + i$

The diagonal arrows to the right can be interpreted as plus signs and downward arrows as equal signs.

The symbol for a *nominal rate of discount* payable m times per year is $d^{(m)}$. By a nominal rate of discount, $d^{(m)}$, we mean an annual rate payable mthly, i.e., the effective rate of discount is $\frac{d^{(m)}}{m}$ for each mth of a year.

The nominal rate of discount, $d^{(m)}$, is a measure of interest paid at the beginning of mths of a year in much the same manner as d was a measure of interest paid at the beginning of the year. By an argument similar to the one used in developing the relationship between $i^{(m)}$ and i, it is possible to develop a formula relating $d^{(m)}$ and d such that they are equivalent.

Consider an investment of 1 to be repaid at the end of the year on which interest is collected in advance at the nominal rate of discount $d^{(m)}$. In this case, we work backwards from the end of the year to the beginning of the year. During the mth mth of a year the ending balance is 1 and the amount of discount is $\frac{d^{(m)}}{m} \cdot 1$, forming a balance at the beginning of the mth mth of the year of $1 - \frac{d^{(m)}}{m}$. During the $(m - 1)$th mth of a year the ending balance is $1 - \frac{d^{(m)}}{m}$ and the amount of discount is $\frac{d^{(m)}}{m}\left(1 - \frac{d^{(m)}}{m}\right)$, forming a balance at the beginning of the $(m - 1)$th mth of a year of $\left(1 - \frac{d^{(m)}}{m}\right) - \frac{d^{(m)}}{m}\left(1 - \frac{d^{(m)}}{m}\right) = \left(1 - \frac{d^{(m)}}{m}\right)^2$. This process is continued until at the beginning of the year the balance is $\left(1 - \dfrac{d^{(m)}}{m}\right)^{m}$. However, the balance at the beginning of the year must also be $1 - d$. Thus

$$1 - d = \left(1 - \frac{d^{(m)}}{m}\right)^{m}, \tag{1.18a}$$

which gives

$$d = 1 - \left(1 - \frac{d^{(m)}}{m}\right)^{m}, \tag{1.18b}$$

and

$$d^{(m)} = m[1 - (1 - d)^{\frac{1}{m}}] = m[1 - v^{\frac{1}{m}}]. \tag{1.18c}$$

Figure 1.4 illustrates the above argument.

FIGURE 1.4

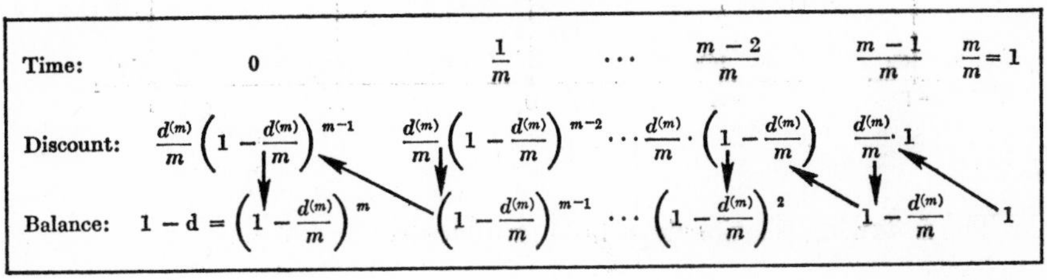

The diagonal arrows to the left can be interpreted as minus signs and downward arrows as equal signs.

There is a close relationship between nominal rates of interest and nominal rates of discount. The following relationship holds, since both sides of the equation are equal to $1 + i$,

$$\left(1 + \frac{i^{(m)}}{m}\right)^{m} = \left(1 - \frac{d^{(p)}}{p}\right)^{-p}. \tag{1.19a}$$

If $m = p$, then formula (1.19a) becomes

$$\left(1 + \frac{i^{(m)}}{m}\right) = \left(1 - \frac{d^{(m)}}{m}\right)^{-1}. \tag{1.19b}$$

If $m = 1$, then $i^{(m)} = i$, the effective rate of interest; and if $p = 1$, then $d^{(p)} = d$, the effective rate of discount. Thus formula (1.19a) can be used in general to find equivalent rates of interest or discount, either effective or nominal, convertible with any desired frequency.

Another relationship between $i^{(m)}$ and $d^{(m)}$ which is analogous to formula (1.14) is

$$\frac{i^{(m)}}{m} - \frac{d^{(m)}}{m} = \frac{i^{(m)}}{m} \cdot \frac{d^{(m)}}{m}. \tag{1.20}$$

The verbal interpretation of this result is similar to the verbal interpretation of formula (1.14). The derivation is left as an exercise.

It is interesting to relate nominal rates of interest and discount to the accumulation function, $a(t)$. An example is given in Figure 1.5 for $m = 2$. The student is encouraged to construct other examples.

FIGURE 1.5

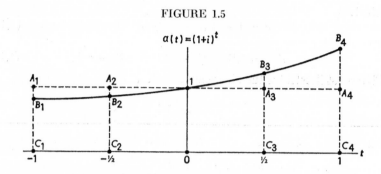

The following relationships hold graphically:

$$A_1B_1 = d \qquad\qquad B_1C_1 = v \qquad\quad = \left(1 - \frac{d^{(2)}}{2}\right)^2$$

$$A_2B_2 = \frac{d^{(2)}}{2} \qquad\qquad B_2C_2 = v^{\frac{1}{2}} \qquad = 1 - \frac{d^{(2)}}{2}$$

$$A_3B_3 = \frac{i^{(2)}}{2} \qquad\qquad B_3C_3 = (1+i)^{\frac{1}{2}} = 1 + \frac{i^{(2)}}{2}$$

$$A_4B_4 = i \qquad\qquad B_4C_4 = 1+i \qquad = \left(1 + \frac{i^{(2)}}{2}\right)^2$$

It is interesting to note that nominal rates of interest and discount are not relevant under simple interest. Since the amount of interest or discount is directly proportional to the time involved, a rate of interest or discount payable $m$thly is no different than one payable annually.

Example 1.7. Find the accumulated value of \$500 invested for five years at 8% per annum convertible quarterly.

The answer is

$$500\left(1 + \frac{.08}{4}\right)^{4\cdot5} = 500(1.02)^{20}.$$

It should be noted that this situation is identical to one in which \$500 is invested at 2% effective for 20 years.

Example 1.8.   Find the present value of $100 to be paid at the end of six years at 6% per annum payable in advance and convertible semiannually.

The answer is

$$100 \left(1 - \frac{.06}{2} \right)^{2 \cdot 6} = 100(.97)^{12}.$$

It should be noted that this situation is identical to one in which the present value of $100 to be paid at the end of 12 years is desired at an effective rate of discount of 3%.

Example 1.9.   Find the nominal rate of interest convertible quarterly which is equivalent to a nominal rate of discount of 6% per annum convertible monthly.

Using formula (1.19a),

$$\left(1 + \frac{i^{(4)}}{4} \right)^4 = \left(1 - \frac{.06}{12} \right)^{-12}$$

$$1 + \frac{i^{(4)}}{4} = (.995)^{-3}$$

$$i^{(4)} = 4[(.995)^{-3} - 1].$$

1.9. FORCES OF INTEREST AND DISCOUNT

The measures of interest defined in the preceding sections are useful for measuring interest over specified intervals of time. Effective rates of interest and discount measure interest over a one-year period, while nominal rates of interest and discount measure interest over $m$ths of a year.

It is important in many cases to be able to measure the intensity with which interest is operating at each moment of time, i.e., over an infinitesimally small interval of time. This measure of interest at individual moments of time is called the *force of interest.*

Consider the investment of a fund such that the amount in the fund at time t is given by the amount function, $A(t)$. Recall that the only factor operating on the fund is the growth of the fund through interest, i.e., no principal is added or withdrawn.

The intensity with which interest is operating at time t is dependent upon the rate of change or the slope of the $A(t)$ curve at time t. From elementary calculus, the slope of the $A(t)$ curve at time t is given by the derivative at that point, denoted by $D\,A(t)$.

However, as a measure of interest, $D\,A(t)$ is unsatisfactory, since it depends on the amount invested. If $200 and $100 are invested under identical conditions, the rate of change of the $200 fund would be twice as great as the rate of change of the $100 fund. However, interest is not operating with twice the intensity on the $200 fund; in fact, we would say that it is operating with the same intensity on both funds.

We can compensate for this by dividing $D A(t)$ by the amount in the fund at time t, namely $A(t)$. This gives a measure of the intensity with which interest is operating at time t expressed as a rate independent of the amount in the fund. Thus, the force of interest at time t, denoted by δ_t, is defined as

$$\delta_t = \frac{D A(t)}{A(t)} = \frac{D a(t)}{a(t)}. \tag{1.21}$$

The following properties of δ_t should be kept in mind:

1. δ_t is a measure of interest at exact time t.
2. δ_t expresses this interest in the form of an annual rate.

It is possible to write an expression for the value of $A(t)$ and $a(t)$ in terms of the function δ_t. It will be seen from formula (1.21) that an alternate expression for δ_t is

$$\delta_t = D \log_e A(t) = D \log_e a(t). \tag{1.22}$$

Replacing t by r and integrating both sides between the limits 0 and t,

$$\int_0^t \delta_r \, dr = \int_0^t D \log_e A(r) dr$$
$$= \log_e A(r) \Big]_0^t = \log_e \frac{A(t)}{A(0)},$$

and hence we have

$$e^{\int_0^t \delta_r \, dr} = \frac{A(t)}{A(0)} = \frac{a(t)}{a(0)} = a(t). \tag{1.23}$$

An alternate derivation can be obtained from (1.21) written as $A(t)\delta_t = D A(t)$. Integrating between the limits 0 and n, we obtain

$$\int_0^n A(t)\delta_t \, dt = \int_0^n D A(t) \, dt = A(t) \Big]_0^n = A(n) - A(0). \tag{1.24}$$

Formula (1.24) has a rather interesting verbal interpretation. The term $A(n) - A(0)$ is the amount of interest earned over the n-year period. The differential expression $A(t)\delta_t \, dt$ may be interpreted as the amount of interest earned on amount $A(t)$ at exact time t because of the force of interest δ_t. When this expression is integrated between limits 0 and n, it gives the total amount of interest earned over the n-year period.

Further insight into the nature of the force of interest may be gained by analyzing formula (1.21) in terms of the definition of the derivative. The derivative of $A(t)$ may be expressed as

$$D\,A(t) = \lim_{h \to 0} \frac{A(t+h) - A(t)}{h},$$

and δ_t from formula (1.21) may then be written

$$\delta_t = \frac{D\,A(t)}{A(t)} = \lim_{h \to 0} \frac{A(t+h) - A(t)}{h\,A(t)}. \tag{1.25}$$

Now the expression $\dfrac{A(t+h) - A(t)}{h\,A(t)}$ may be regarded as an annual rate of interest based upon interest during the interval from time t to time $t + h$. For example, if $h = 1$, we have $\dfrac{A(t+1) - A(t)}{A(t)}$, which is one year's increment in the fund divided by the amount in the fund at the beginning of the period. If $h = \frac{1}{2}$, we have $2 \cdot \dfrac{A(t+\frac{1}{2}) - A(t)}{A(t)}$, which is twice a half-year's increment in the fund divided by the amount in the fund at the beginning of the period. As h approaches 0, the limit of this expression, the force of interest, may be described as the nominal annual rate of interest based upon the intensity of interest at time t.

It is also possible to define a *force of discount* analogous to formula (1.21). For this purpose, we use the discount function, $a^{-1}(t)$ instead of the accumulation function, $a(t)$. The definition of the force of discount at time t, denoted by $\delta_t{}'$, is given by

$$\delta_t{}' = -\frac{D\,a^{-1}(t)}{a^{-1}(t)}. \tag{1.26}$$

The definition of $\delta_t{}'$ is completely analogous to the definition of δ_t except for the minus sign. The minus sign is necessary to make the force of discount a positive quantity because the denominator of formula (1.26) is positive but the numerator is negative, since $a^{-1}(t)$ is a decreasing function.

Later in this section it will be seen that the force of discount bears a relationship to nominal and effective rates of discount similar to the relationship that the force of interest bears to nominal and effective rates of interest. However, it can be shown that $\delta_t{}' = \delta_t$, so that we may dispense with $\delta_t{}'$ and use δ_t. The proof is as follows:

$$\delta_t{}' = -\frac{D\,a^{-1}(t)}{a^{-1}(t)}$$

$$= \frac{a^{-2}(t)\, D\, a(t)}{a^{-1}(t)}$$

$$= \frac{a^{-2}(t)\, a(t)\delta_t}{a^{-1}(t)} \text{ from formula (1.21)}$$

$$= \delta_t \,.$$

In theory, the force of interest may vary instantaneously. However, in practice it is often a constant. In particular, a constant effective rate of interest is equivalent to a constant force of interest.

If the effective rate of interest, i, is constant, we obtain

$$\delta_t = \frac{D\, a(t)}{a(t)} = \frac{D\,(1+i)^t}{(1+i)^t} = \frac{(1+i)^t \log_e (1+i)}{(1+i)^t} = \log_e (1+i)\,.$$

Thus, δ_t is constant for all values of t, so the t may be dropped, giving

$$\delta = \log_e (1+i)\,, \tag{1.27a}$$

which expresses δ as a function of i. Taking the antilogarithm of both sides of the equation expresses i as a function of δ,

$$1 + i = e^\delta$$
$$i = e^\delta - 1\,. \tag{1.28a}$$

This result could also have been obtained from formula (1.23), assuming a constant force of interest as follows:

$$1 + i = a(1) = e^{\int_0^1 \delta\, dr} = e^\delta\,.$$

Formulas (1.27a) and (1.28a) can also be written as series expansions:

$$\delta = \log_e (1+i) = i - \frac{i^2}{2} + \frac{i^3}{3} - \frac{i^4}{4} + \cdots . \tag{1.27b}$$

$$i = e^\delta - 1 = \delta + \frac{\delta^2}{2!} + \frac{\delta^3}{3!} + \frac{\delta^4}{4!} + \cdots . \tag{1.28b}$$

These formulas are suitable for hand calculation if a table of logarithms or a table of values of e^x is not available, since in practice i and δ are usually small positive numbers whose successive powers diminish rapidly.

Having related δ and i immediately relates δ and the other measures of interest described in this chapter. The following series of equalities is an expanded version of formula (1.19a) which summarizes much of the material contained in this chapter.

$$\left(1 + \frac{i^{(m)}}{m}\right)^m = 1 + i = v^{-1} = (1 - d)^{-1} = \left(1 - \frac{d^{(p)}}{p}\right)^{-p} = e^\delta. \tag{1.29}$$

Another interesting insight into the nature of the force of interest can be obtained by analyzing δ in terms of $i^{(m)}$. From formula (1.29),

$$\left(1 + \frac{i^{(m)}}{m}\right)^m = e^\delta$$

$$i^{(m)} = m\left[e^{\frac{\delta}{m}} - 1\right].$$

Now using a series expansion, we have

$$i^{(m)} = m\left[\frac{\delta}{m} + \frac{1}{2!}\left(\frac{\delta}{m}\right)^2 + \frac{1}{3!}\left(\frac{\delta}{m}\right)^3 + \cdots\right]$$

$$= \delta + \frac{\delta^2}{2!\,m} + \frac{\delta^3}{3!\,m^2} + \cdots.$$

and taking the limit as m approaches infinity,

$$\lim_{m \to \infty} i^{(m)} = \delta. \tag{1.30}$$

This formula has intuitive appeal. Since $i^{(m)}$ is a nominal rate of interest convertible $m$thly, we can interpret δ as a nominal rate of interest convertible continuously.

By an analogous argument, it is possible to show that

$$\lim_{m \to \infty} d^{(m)} = \delta. \tag{1.31}$$

The proof is left as an exercise. This formula also has intuitive appeal. Since $d^{(m)}$ is a nominal rate of discount convertible $m$thly, we can interpret δ as a nominal rate of discount convertible continuously. In essence, this is an alternate proof that the force of interest and the force of discount are equal. A third proof of this result is left as an exercise.

The force of interest is a useful conceptual device, making the continuous growth of money at compound interest similar to growth functions encountered in the natural sciences. In theory, the most fundamental measure of interest is the force of interest rather than the effective rate of interest. In practice, effective and nominal rates of interest and discount tend to be used more frequently because they are simpler for the layman to comprehend. This does not mean that the force of interest is devoid of practical significance. Besides being a useful conceptual and analytical tool, it can be used in practice as an approximation to interest converted very frequently, such as daily or weekly.

Example 1.10. Find the accumulated value of $100 invested for ten years if the force of interest is 5%.

The answer is

$$100e^{(.05)(10)} = 100e^{.5}.$$

1.10. VARYING INTEREST

This section is concerned with situations involving varying interest. Two types of variation are considered. Other types of variation can be analyzed from basic principles.

The first type of variation considered is a continuously varying force of interest. The basic formula for use in problems involving a varying force of interest is formula (1.23) in Section 1.9,

$$a(t) = e^{\int_0^t \delta_r dr}. \tag{1.23}$$

If the form of δ_r is readily integrable, results may be obtained directly. If the form of δ_r is not readily integrable, approximate methods of integration are necessary.

The second type of variation considered involves changes in the effective rate of interest over a period of time. This type of variation is probably the one most commonly used in practice. As before, let i_n denote the effective rate of interest during the nth year from the date of investment. Then for integral $t \geq 1$, we have

$$a(t) = (1 + i_1)(1 + i_2)(1 + i_3) \ldots (1 + i_t). \tag{1.32}$$

If $i_1 = i_2 = i_3 = \cdots = i_t = i$, the familiar result $a(t) = (1 + i)^t$ is obtained.

Example 1.11. Find the accumulated value of 1 at the end of n years if $\delta_t = \dfrac{1}{1 + t}$.

Using formula (1.23), the answer is

$$e^{\int_0^n \delta_t \, dt} = e^{\int_0^n \frac{1}{1+t} \, dt} = e^{\log_e (1+t)]_0^n} = 1 + n.$$

Example 1.12. Find the accumulated value of \$100 at the end of 15 years if the effective rate of interest is 5% for the first 5 years, $4\frac{1}{2}$% for the second 5 years, and 4% for the third 5 years.

Using formula (1.32), the answer is

$$100(1.05)^5(1.045)^5(1.04)^5.$$

1.11. SUMMARY OF RESULTS

Table 1.1 summarizes much of the material of this chapter.

TABLE 1.1

Rate of Interest or Discount	The Accumulated Value of 1 at Time t $= a(t)$	The Present Value of 1 at Time t $= a^{-1}(t)$
Compound Interest		
i	$(1+i)^t$	$v^t = (1+i)^{-t}$
$i^{(m)}$	$\left(1+\dfrac{i^{(m)}}{m}\right)^{mt}$	$\left(1+\dfrac{i^{(m)}}{m}\right)^{-mt}$
d	$(1-d)^{-t}$	$(1-d)^t$
$d^{(m)}$	$\left(1-\dfrac{d^{(m)}}{m}\right)^{-mt}$	$\left(1-\dfrac{d^{(m)}}{m}\right)^{mt}$
δ	$e^{\delta t}$	$e^{-\delta t}$
Simple Interest		
i	$1+it$	$(1+it)^{-1}$
d	$(1-dt)^{-1}$	$1-dt$

EXERCISES

1.1. Introduction; 1.2. The accumulation and amount functions

1. Consider the amount function $A(t) = t^2 + 2t + 3$.
   a) Find the corresponding accumulation function, $a(t)$.
   b) Verify that $a(t)$ satisfies the three properties of an accumulation function.
   c) Find I_n.
2. a) Prove that $A(n) - A(0) = I_1 + I_2 + \cdots + I_n$.
   b) Verbally interpret the result obtained in (a).
3. Find $A(n) - A(t)$ for $t < n$ if—
   a) $I_r = r$.
   b) $I_r = 2^r$.

1.3. The effective rate of interest

4. Assume that $A(t) = 100 + 5t$.
   a) Find i_5.
   b) Find i_{10}.

5. Assume that $A(t) = 100(1.1)^t$.
   a) Find i_5.
   b) Find i_{10}.
6. Show that $A(n) = (1 + i_n) A(n - 1)$.
7. If $A(0) = 100$ and $i_n = .01n$, use the result in Exercise 6 to find $A(3)$.

1.4. Simple interest

8. A sum of $10,000 is invested for the months of July and August at 6% simple interest. Find the amount of interest earned:
   a) Assuming exact simple interest.
   b) Assuming ordinary simple interest.
   c) Assuming the Banker's Rule.
9. Prove that the Banker's Rule is more favorable to the lender than is exact simple interest.
10. a) At what rate of simple interest will $500 accumulate to $560 in $2\frac{1}{2}$ years?
    b) In how many years will $500 accumulate to $560 at 3.6% simple interest?
11. At a certain rate of simple interest $1000 will accumulate to $1110 after a certain period of time. Find the accumulated value of $500 at a rate of simple interest three fourths as great over twice as long a period of time.

1.5. Compound interest

12. Assuming that $0 < i < 1$, show that—
    a) $(1 + i)^t < 1 + it$ $0 < t < 1$.
    b) $(1 + i)^t = 1 + it$ $t = 1$.
    c) $(1 + i)^t > 1 + it$ $t > 1$.
    This exercise verifies the relative magnitudes of accumulated values at simple and compound interest over various periods of time.
13. Show that the ratio of the accumulated value of 1, invested at rate i for n years, to the accumulated value of 1, invested at rate j for n years, $(i > j)$ is equal to the accumulated value of 1, invested for n years at rate r. Find an expression for r as a function of i and j.
14. Find the amount of interest earned between 5 and 10 years after the date of investment by an investment of $100.

1.6. Present value

15. Find an expression for the discount factor during the nth year from the date of investment, i.e., $(1 + i_n)^{-1}$, in terms of the amount function.
16. Find the current value on July 4, 1976, of payments of $1000 on July 4, 1969, and $500 on July 4, 1984.
17. The sum of the present value of 1 paid at the end of n years and 1 paid at the end of $2n$ years is 1. Find $(1 + i)^{2n}$.

1.7. The effective rate of discount

18. *a)* Find the simple interest rate, i, which is equivalent to the simple discount rate, d, over an n-year period.
    b) Find the simple discount rate, d, which is equivalent to the simple interest rate, i, over an n-year period.
    c) Show that the results in (*a*) and (*b*) are equivalent to formulas (1.11) and (1.12*a*), respectively, over a one-year period of time.

19. *a)* Assuming compound discount, show that d_n is constant for all n.
    b) Assuming simple discount, show that d_n is increasing for increasing n
    $$\left(\text{assuming } 0 < n - 1 < \frac{1}{d}\right).$$

20. Assuming that $0 < d < 1$, show that—
    a) $(1 - d)^t < 1 - dt$ $0 < t < 1.$
    b) $(1 - d)^t = 1 - dt$ $t = 1.$
    c) $(1 - d)^t > 1 - dt$ $t > 1.$
    This exercise verifies the relative magnitudes of present values at simple and compound discount over various periods of time.

21. *a)* A borrower agrees to repay \$100 at the end of n years, where the lender charges a 5% simple discount rate. Find the net amount borrowed, i.e., the present value of the \$100, if—
    (1) $n = 15$.
    (2) $n = 20$.
    (3) $n = 25$.
    b) From the answers to (*a*), what can you conclude about the practicality of using simple discount over long periods of time?

22. Find the accumulated value of \$100 at the end of two years—
    a) At a simple discount rate of 4%.
    b) At a compound discount rate of 4%.
    c) Justify from general reasoning the relative magnitudes of the answers to (*a*) and (*b*).

23. If $i = \dfrac{1}{n}$, find d.

24. Assume that $A(t) = 100 + 5t$.
    a) Find d_5.
    b) Find d_{10}.

1.8. Nominal rates of interest and discount

25. *a)* Derive formula (1.20).
    b) Verbally interpret formula (1.20).

26. Assuming a nominal annual rate of interest of 6% convertible quarterly,
    a) Find the accumulated value of \$100 at the end of two years.
    b) Find the present value of \$100 to be paid at the end of ten years.

27. Rework Exercise 26 assuming a nominal annual rate of discount of 6% convertible monthly.

28. *a)* On occasion, interest is convertible less frequently than once a year. Define $i^{\left(\frac{1}{m}\right)}$ and $d^{\left(\frac{1}{m}\right)}$ to be nominal annual rates of interest and discount convertible once every m years. Find a formula analogous to formula (1.19a) for this situation.
    b) Rework Exercise 26 assuming a nominal annual rate of discount of 6% convertible once every four years.

29. *a)* Express $d^{(4)}$ as a function of $i^{(3)}$.
    b) Express $i^{(6)}$ as a function of $d^{(2)}$.

1.9. Forces of interest and discount

30. Derive formula (1.31).

31. Use formula (1.20) to give a third proof of the result that $\delta' = \delta$.

32. Rank i, $i^{(m)}$, d, $d^{(m)}$, and δ in increasing order of magnitude.

33. Show that $D\,\delta_t = \dfrac{D^2\,A(t)}{A(t)} - \delta_t^2$.

34. *a)* Obtain an expression for δ_t if $A(t) = Ka^t b^{t^2} d^{e^t}$.
    b) Is formula (1.21) or (1.22) more convenient in this case?

35. Show that—

    a) $\displaystyle\int_0^n \delta_t\,dt = -\log_e v^n$.

    b) $\displaystyle\int_0^n A(t)\delta_t\,dt = I_1 + I_2 + \ldots + I_n$.

36. *a)* Express $i^{(6)}$ as a function of δ.
    b) Express δ as a function of $d^{(4)}$.

37. *a)* (1) Derive an expression for δ_t, assuming simple interest, expressed as a function of i and t.
       (2) Is δ_t an increasing or decreasing function of t? Justify by general reasoning.
    b) (1) Derive an expression for δ_t', assuming simple discount, expressed as a function of d and t.

       (2) Is δ_t' an increasing or decreasing function of $t\left(\text{assuming } 0 < t < \dfrac{1}{d}\right)$? Justify by general reasoning.

1.10. Varying interest; 1.11. Summary of results

38. If $\delta_t = .01t$, $0 \le t \le 2$, find the equivalent annual effective rate of interest over the interval $0 \le t \le 2$.

39. Find the accumulated value of 1 at the end of 19 years if $\delta_t = .04(1 + t)^{-2}$.

40. If $\delta_t = (1 + t)^{-2}\log_e 2$, $0 \le t \le 2$, find the equivalent effective rate of discount over the interval $0 \le t \le 2$.

41. Find the level effective rate of interest over a three-year period which is equivalent to an effective rate of discount of 4% the first year, 3% the second year, and 2% the third year.

42. Find the accumulated value of $100 at the end of 15 years if the nominal rate of interest compounded quarterly is 8% for the first 5 years, if the effective rate of discount is 7% for the second 5 years, and if the nominal rate of discount compounded semiannually is 6% for the third 5 years.

43. a) Find the accumulated value of 1 at the end of n years where the effective rate of interest for the kth year, $1 \le k \le n$, is defined by

$$i_k = (1 + r)^k(1 + i) - 1 .$$

b) Show that the answer to (a) can be written in the form $(1 + j)^n$. Find j.

Miscellaneous problems

44. a) Show that $\delta = \dfrac{i^{(m)} + d^{(m)}}{2}$, approximately.

b) Assuming $m = 1$, find an exact expression for the error in (a) expressed as a series expansion in δ.

45. Find an expression for the fraction of a year for which the excess of simple interest over compound interest is a maximum.

46. Show that

$$\sum_{m=1}^{\infty} (-1)^{m-1} i^m \left(\frac{1}{d^{(m)}} - \frac{1}{i^{(m)}} \right) = \delta .$$

47. Find the following derivatives:

a) $\dfrac{d}{di} d$.

b) $\dfrac{d}{di} \delta$.

c) $\dfrac{d}{dd} d^{(m)}$.

d) $\dfrac{d}{dv} \delta$.

e) $\dfrac{d}{d\delta} d$.

48. Find the following in the form of series expansions:
   a) i as a function of d.
   b) d as a function of i.
   c) v as a function of δ.
   d) $i^{(m)}$ as a function of i.
   e) δ as a function of d.

49. Show that

$$\delta = \frac{d+i}{2} + \frac{d^2 - i^2}{4} + \frac{d^3 + i^3}{6} + \cdots .$$

50. Show that

$$\frac{d^n}{dv^n}\,(v^{n-1}\delta) = -(1+i)\,(n-1)!$$

51. *a)* (1) Derive an expression for $a(t)$ assuming δ_r is linear and positive, i.e., $\delta_r = a + br$, where $a > 0$ and $b > 0$.

   (2) Find the accumulation factor during the nth year from the date of investment, i.e., $1 + i_n$.

   b) (1) Derive an expression for $a(t)$ assuming δ_r is exponential and positive, i.e., $\delta_r = ab^r$, where $a > 0$ and $b > 0$.

   (2) Find the accumulation factor during the nth year from the date of investment, i.e., $1 + i_n$.

52. The sum of the accumulated value of 1 at the end of three years at a certain effective rate of interest, and the present value of 1 to be paid at the end of three years at an effective rate of discount numerically equal to i is 2.0096. Find the rate.

53. A fund of money is accumulating for one year at a varying force of interest such that the amount in the fund at any time t, $0 \le t \le 1$, is a second degree polynomial in t. The nominal rate of interest convertible semiannually for the first half of the year is 4% per annum. The effective rate of interest for the year is 5% per annum. Find the force of interest half of the way through the year, i.e., find $\delta_{\frac{1}{2}}$.

CHAPTER 2. Solution of problems in interest

2.1. INTRODUCTION

The basic principles of the theory of interest are relatively few. In Chapter 1, the various quantitative measures of interest were analyzed. Chapter 2 discusses general principles to be followed in the solution of problems in interest. The purpose of this chapter is to develop a systematic approach by which the basic principles from Chapter 1 can be applied to more complex financial transactions.

With a thorough understanding of the first two chapters it is possible to solve nearly any problem in interest. Successive chapters have two main purposes:

1. To familiarize the student with more complex types of financial transactions, including definitions of terms, which occur in practice.
2. To provide a systematic analysis of these financial transactions, which will often lead to a more efficient handling of the problem than resorting to basic principles.

As a result of 2, on occasion, simplifying formulas will be derived. Fortunately, the number of formulas which the student may feel he needs to commit to memory is small. Even so, a common source of difficulty for many students is to rely blindly on formulas without an understanding of the basic principles upon which the formulas are based. It is important to realize that any problem in interest can be solved from basic principles and that in many cases resorting to basic principles is not as inefficient as it may first appear to be.

2.2. OBTAINING NUMERICAL RESULTS

In Chapter 1, answers to many of the examples and exercises involving accumulated values and present values and involving equivalent rates of interest and discount were left in exponential form. This was done to facilitate the presentation of the basic principles without the necessity of the student performing an undue amount of arithmetical computation. Naturally, in practical work, actual numerical answers are usually desired, and the purpose of this section is to discuss the various possible methods of obtaining such answers.

The advent of digital computers makes it feasible to obtain answers to all problems in interest by direct calculation. In fact, direct calculation is probably the easiest and most efficient method. However, it is often not possible to use a computer, either because one is not readily available or because the volume of the calculations to be performed does not warrant the use of a computer. The rest of this section considers obtaining numerical answers without the use of a computer.

The approach to be used varies somewhat depending upon the form of the function to be evaluated. There are three cases which we will consider: (1) evaluating $(1 + i)^n$ for integral n, (2) evaluating $(1 + i)^n$ for nonintegral n, and (3) evaluating $e^{\delta n}$.

Evaluating $(1 + i)^n$ for integral n

There are three possible methods for this case. The choice of method will depend upon the situation.

The first method is to use compound interest tables. Such tables appear in Appendix I and include values of v^n and $(1 + i)^n$, as well as other functions which will be defined in succeeding chapters, for several rates of interest and for values of n from 1 to 50. Use of these tables is the preferred method if required values appear in the tables. The student should thoroughly familiarize himself with these tables.

The second method is to calculate the numerical values directly. This is the approach that was used in several of the examples in Chapter 1. In general, this approach is impractical for hand calculation unless the exponents involved are small positive integers. With a desk calculator the situation is improved somewhat. For example, evaluating $(1.054)^{18}$ is not as difficult as it may appear at first. To evaluate $(1.054)^{18}$ we could square 1.054, then square the product to obtain the 4th power, then square the product to obtain the 8th power, then square the product to obtain the 16th power, and finally multiply by $(1.054)^2$ to obtain the answer. As mentioned previously, if a computer is available, then generation of all compound interest functions by direct calculation is probably the best method.

The third method is the use of a table of logarithms. Logarithms can be used for nearly any problem of the type under consideration, although we will use this method only for those problems not readily handled by one of the first two methods. A table of five-place logarithms to base 10 appears in Appendix III. It is assumed that the student is familiar with the use of such a table.

Evaluating $(1 + i)^n$ for nonintegral n

The situation is somewhat different in this case. Note that it is sufficient to consider the evaluation of $(1 + i)^k$ or v^k for $0 < k < 1$. Any term with nonintegral exponents can be reduced to a form which involves a factor with an integral exponent and a factor of the above form. For example,

$$(1 + i)^{8\frac{1}{4}} = (1 + i)^8(1 + i)^{\frac{1}{4}}.$$

There are four possible methods of evaluating $(1 + i)^k$ or v^k for $0 < k < 1$.

The first method is to use compound interest tables. Appendix I includes values of $(1 + i)^k$ and v^k for $k = \frac{1}{2}, \frac{1}{4}$, and $\frac{1}{12}$. Use of these tables is the preferred method if required values appear in the tables.

The second method is to use the binomial theorem, as follows:

$$(1 + i)^k = 1 + ki + \frac{k(k - 1)}{2!} i^2 + \frac{k(k - 1)(k - 2)}{3!} i^3 + \cdots. \quad (2.1)$$

This formula can be used for either positive or negative k.

The third method is to use logarithms.

The fourth method is to use simple interest as an approximation to compound interest for any fractional period. This approach is equivalent to using only the first two terms of the binomial expansion in formula (2.1), assuming $0 < k < 1$. As will be shown in the exercises, the use of simple interest for a final fractional period is also equivalent to performing a linear interpolation in the interest tables. For example, evaluating $(1 + i)^{8\frac{1}{4}}$ by a linear interpolation between $(1 + i)^8$ and $(1 + i)^9$ is equivalent to assuming simple interest during the final fractional period. The use of simple interest introduces a bias, since it was shown in Section 1.5 that simple interest produces a larger accumulated value over fractional periods than does compound interest.

Evaluating $e^{\delta n}$

There are two possible methods for this case.

The first method is to use the series expansion for $e^{\delta n}$ as follows:

$$e^{\delta n} = 1 + (\delta n) + \frac{(\delta n)^2}{2!} + \frac{(\delta n)^3}{3!} + \cdots. \qquad (2.2)$$

This formula can be used for either positive or negative n.

The second approach is to use a table of logarithms or a table of values of e^x if such a table is available.

Example 2.1.   Obtain numerical answers for Examples 1.7, 1.8, 1.9, 1.10, and 1.12.

1. *Example 1.7:*
   From the interest tables,

   $$500(1.02)^{20} = 500(1.48595) = \$742.98\,.$$

2. *Example 1.8:*
   In this case logarithms are appropriate.

   $$\log_{10} 100(.97)^{12} = \log_{10} 100 + 12 \log_{10} .97$$
   $$= 2 + 12(-.01323) = 1.84124$$
   $$\text{antilog}_{10}\, 1.\overline{8}4124 = \$69.38\,.$$

3. *Example 1.9:*
   In this case direct calculation is feasible.

   $$i^{(4)} = 4\left[\frac{1}{(.995)^3} - 1\right] = .0606, \text{ or } 6.06\%\,.$$

4. *Example 1.10:*
   Using a series expansion,

   $$100e^{.5} = 100\left[1 + .5 + \frac{(.5)^2}{2!} + \frac{(.5)^3}{3!} + \frac{(.5)^4}{4!} + \frac{(.5)^5}{5!} + \cdots\right] = \$164.87\,.$$

5. *Example 1.12:*
   From the interest tables,

   $$100(1.05)^5\,(1.045)^5\,(1.04)^5 = 100(1.27628)(1.24618)(1.21665) = \$193.51\,.$$

Example 2.2.   Find the accumulated value of $50 at the end of 30 years and 4 months at 6% per annum convertible semiannually, (1) assuming compound interest throughout, and (2) assuming simple interest during the final fractional period.

1. Assuming compound interest throughout, the answer is

$$50(1.03)^{60\frac{1}{3}}$$

which can be factored into

$$50(1.03)^{50}(1.03)^{10}(1.03)^{\frac{1}{3}} .$$

Now using the binomial theorem, we have

$$(1.03)^{\frac{1}{3}} = 1 + \tfrac{2}{3}(.03) + \frac{(\tfrac{2}{3})(-\tfrac{1}{3})}{2!} \, (.03)^2 + \cdots = 1.01990 .$$

The answer is

$$50(4.38391)(1.34392)(1.01990) = \$300.44 .$$

2. Assuming simple interest during the final fractional period, the answer is

$$50(4.38391)(1.34392)(1.02) = \$300.47 .$$

The answer to 2 is larger than 1, illustrating that simple interest produces larger accumulated values over fractional periods than compound interest does, although the difference is quite small.

2.3. THE BASIC PROBLEM

Broken down into its simplest terms, every interest problem involves four quantities:

1. The principal originally invested.
2. The period of investment.
3. The rate of interest.
4. The accumulated value of the principal at the end of the period of investment.

If any three of these quantities are known, then the fourth quantity is automatically determined. In the problems involving accumulated values considered so far, No. 4 is the unknown quantity; whereas, in the problems involving present values, No. 1 is the unknown quantity. Section 2.5 considers the case in which No. 2 is the unknown, while Section 2.6 considers the case in which No. 3 is the unknown.

The following general principles may prove helpful to the student in the solution of problems in interest.

a) The period of investment is measured in time units. It was mentioned in Chapter 1 that the fundamental time unit is assumed to be one year, and many problems are worked with this as the time unit, especially those involving effective rates of interest or discount.

However, if nominal rates of interest or discount are involved, often a time unit other than one year is most advantageous. For example, consider the problem of finding the accumulated value of $100 at the end of 10 years if the rate of interest is 4% per annum convertible semiannually. If the problem is worked with a time unit of one year, then two steps are necessary. First, the effective rate of interest, i, corresponding to $i^{(2)}$ = .04 must be found.

$$1 + i = (1.02)^2$$
$$i = .0404 .$$

Second, the answer is $100(1.0404)^{10}$. Since no interest tables are available for 4.04%, logarithms must be used to obtain a numerical answer. The problem is greatly simplified by working with a time unit of a half-year, which is the same frequency that interest is converted, instead of one year. The answer then is $100(1.02)^{20}$ = $148.59, immediately, from the interest tables.

In general, the time unit chosen must be consistent with the interest function involved. The above example shows that it is often possible to save much effort with a judicious choice of the time unit.

b) Different interest functions may be used in a problem. For nonnumerical problems, the choice of the proper interest function may lead to considerable simplification, depending upon the nature of the problem. For numerical problems, a function for which interest tables are available should be chosen if possible. The example given above in (a) illustrates this. In general, the time unit and the interest function should be chosen together.

c) Any interest problem can be viewed from two perspectives, since it involves a financial transaction between two parties, the borrower and the lender. From either perspective, the problem is essentially the same; however, the wording of a problem may be different depending upon the point of view. Examples and exercises phrased from both points of view appear, and the student should not let the different phraseology confuse him.

2.4. EQUATIONS OF VALUE

It is a fundamental principle in the theory of interest that the value of an amount of money at any given point in time depends upon the time elapsed since the money was paid in the past or upon the time which will elapse in the future before it is paid. We have already seen this in many of the examples and exercises considered thus far in the first two chapters.

As a consequence of the above principle, it is obvious that two or more amounts of money payable at different points in time cannot be compared until all the amounts are accumulated or discounted to a common date. This common date is called the *comparison date*, and the equation which accumulates or discounts each payment to the comparison date is called the *equation of value*.

One device which is often helpful in the solution of equations of value is the *time diagram*. A time diagram is a one-dimensional diagram in which units of time are measured along the one dimension and payments are placed on the diagram at the appropriate points. The comparison date is denoted by an arrow. Figure 2.1 is an example of a time diagram used in the solution of Example 2.3.

The time diagram is not necessary in the solution of equations of value; it is merely an aid in visualizing the problem. With some practice the student can usually dispense with a time diagram on simpler problems. However, time diagrams are usually helpful in the solution of more complex problems.

One of the properties of compound interest is that the choice of the comparison date makes no difference in the answer obtained. Thus, there is a different equation of value for each comparison date, but they all yield the same answer. However, the judicious choice of a comparison date will often yield a saving in the amount of arithmetical computation, as will be illustrated in Example 2.3.

The student should be aware that the problems involving accumulated values and present values already considered in the first two chapters are examples of equations of values. The following example illustrates a more general type of problem.

Example 2.3. ***In return for a promise to receive $600 at the end of 8 years, a man agrees to pay $100 at once, $200 at the end of 5 years, and to make a further payment at the end of 10 years. Find the payment at the end of 10 years if the effective rate of interest is 4% per annum.***

We shall first work the problem with a comparison date of the present. The time diagram is shown in Figure 2.1.

FIGURE 2.1

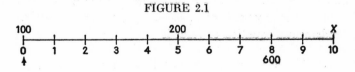

The equation of value is

$$100 + 200v^5 + xv^{10} = 600v^8 .$$

$$x = \frac{600v^8 - 100 - 200v^5}{v^{10}}$$

$$= \frac{600(.73069) - 100 - 200(.82193)}{.67556}$$

$$= \$257.61 .$$

We could also have chosen a different comparison date and obtained a different equation of value. For example, if the comparison date were chosen to be the end of the 10th year, then the arrow in the time diagram would be under 10 and the equation of value would be

$$100(1.04)^{10} + 200(1.04)^5 + x = 600(1.04)^2 .$$
$$x = 600(1.04)^2 - 100(1.04)^{10} - 200(1.04)^5$$
$$= 600(1.08160) - 100(1.48024) - 200(1.21665)$$
$$= \$257.61 .$$

Thus, the same answer is obtained. The two equations of value are equivalent. If both sides of the first one are multiplied by $(1.04)^{10}$, the second one is obtained. However, it should be noted that the second equation of value involves less arithmetical computation and, thus, is preferable for hand calculation.

2.5. UNKNOWN TIME

As discussed in Section 2.3, if any three of the four quantities entering into any interest problem are given, then the fourth can be determined. In this section we consider the situation in which the period of investment is the unknown.

There are two methods to use in approaching this type of problem. The first of these is interpolation in the interest tables, and the second is to use logarithms. These will be illustrated in Example 2.4. For most purposes we will use the method of interpolation in the interest tables.

A situation sometimes arises in which several payments made at various points in time are to be replaced by one payment numerically equal to the sum of the other payments. The problem is to find the point in time at which the one payment should be made such that it is equivalent in value to the payments made separately.

Let amounts $s_1, s_2, \ldots, s_n$ be paid at times $t_1, t_2, \ldots, t_n$ respectively. The problem is to find time t, such that $s_1 + s_2 + \cdots + s_n$ paid at time t is equivalent to the payments of $s_1, s_2, \ldots, s_n$ made separately.

The fundamental equation of value is

$$(s_1 + s_2 + \cdots + s_n)v^t = s_1 v^{t_1} + s_2 v^{t_2} + \cdots + s_n v^{t_n} , \qquad (2.3)$$

which is one equation in one unknown, t. As an exercise, the student is asked to find an exact expression for t.

As a first approximation, t is often calculated as a weighted average of the various times of payment, where the weights are the various amounts paid, i.e.,

$$t = \frac{s_1 t_1 + s_2 t_2 + \cdots + s_n t_n}{s_1 + s_2 + \cdots + s_n}. \tag{2.4}$$

This approximation to t is often called the *method of equated time*.

It is possible to prove that the value of t from formula (2.4) is always greater than the true value of t from formula (2.3), or, alternatively, that the present value using the method of equated time is smaller than the true present value.

Consider s_1 quantities equal to v^{t_1}, s_2 quantities equal to v^{t_2}, and so forth until there are s_n quantities equal to v^{t_n}. The arithmetic mean of these quantities is

$$\frac{s_1 v^{t_1} + s_2 v^{t_2} + \cdots + s_n v^{t_n}}{s_1 + s_2 + \cdots + s_n}.$$

The geometric mean of these quantities is

$$v^{\frac{s_1 t_1 + s_2 t_2 + \ldots + s_n t_n}{s_1 + s_2 + \ldots + s_n}} = v^t,$$

where t is calculated by the method of equated time. However, we know that the arithmetic mean of n positive numbers is greater than the geometric mean, and thus we have

$$\frac{s_1 v^{t_1} + s_2 v^{t_2} + \cdots + s_n v^{t_n}}{s_1 + s_2 + \cdots + s_n} > v^t,$$

or

$$s_1 v^{t_1} + s_2 v^{t_2} + \cdots + s_n v^{t_n} > (s_1 + s_2 + \cdots + s_n) v^t.$$

The left side is the true present value which exceeds the present value given by the method of equated time on the right side. Thus, the value of t from formula (2.4) is always greater than the true value of t from formula (2.3).

Example 2.4. Find the length of time necessary for $1000 to accumulate to $1500 if invested at 6% per annum compounded semiannually (1) by interpolating in the interest tables, and (2) by use of logarithms.

Let n be the number of half-years. The equation of value is

$$1000(1.03)^n = 1500$$
$$(1.03)^n = 1.5 \,.$$

1. From the interest tables, $(1.03)^{13} = 1.46853$ and $(1.03)^{14} = 1.51259$, so that $13 < n < 14$. Performing a linear interpolation,

$$n = 13 + \frac{1.50000 - 1.46853}{1.51259 - 1.46853} = 13.714 \,.$$

Thus, the number of years is 6.857. This method is equivalent to the assumption of simple interest during the final fraction of an interest conversion period. This point was discussed in more detail in Section 2.2.

2. Using logarithms,

$$n \log_{10} 1.03 = \log_{10} 1.5$$
$$n = \frac{\log_{10} 1.5}{\log_{10} 1.03} = \frac{.17609}{.01284} = 13.714 \,.$$

Thus, the number of years is 6.857, which agrees with method 1 to three decimal places.

Example 2.5. Payments of $100, $200, and $500 are due at the ends of years 2, 3, and 8, respectively. Assuming an effective rate of interest of 5% per annum, find the point in time at which a payment of $800 would be equivalent, (1) by the method of equated time, and (2) by an exact method.

1. By the method of equated time using formula (2.4),

$$t = \frac{100 \cdot 2 + 200 \cdot 3 + 500 \cdot 8}{100 + 200 + 500} = 6 \text{ years} \,.$$

2. The exact equation of value is

$$800v^t = 100v^2 + 200v^3 + 500v^8$$

or

$$v^t = \frac{100(.90703) + 200(.86384) + 500(.67684)}{800} = .75236 \,.$$

This equation can be solved by interpolation in the interest tables or by logarithms. Interpolating in the interest tables between $v^5 = .78353$ and $v^6 = .74622$, we obtain

$$t = 5 + \frac{.75236 - .78353}{.74622 - .78353} = 5.835 \text{ years} \,.$$

As expected, the true value of t is less than the value using the method of equated time.

2. *Solution of problems in interest*   **41**

2.6. UNKNOWN RATE OF INTEREST

Section 2.5 considered the case in which the period of investment is the unknown. In this section we consider the situation in which the rate of interest is the unknown.

There are three methods to use in approaching this type of problem. The first of these is interpolation in the interest tables, which is the method we will use in most cases. The second is to use logarithms. The third is to solve the equation of value, expressed by algebraic techniques, as a series in i or in $1 + i$.

The third method described above is often unwieldly for hand calculation. However, it is often quite efficient if a digital computer is available. For example, an equation of value with integral exponents on all the terms can be written as an nth degree polynomial in i or $1 + i$. It is a simple matter to find the roots of an nth degree polynomial with standard computer subroutines.

Problems involving an unknown rate of interest can best be illustrated by example.

Example 2.6. *At what interest rate convertible quarterly would $1000 accumulate to $1600 in six years?*

Let $j = \dfrac{i^{(4)}}{4}$ so that the equation of value becomes

$$1000(1 + j)^{24} = 1600$$

or

$$j = (1.6)^{\frac{1}{24}} - 1 .$$

Now using logarithms, we have

$$\log_{10} (1.6)^{\frac{1}{24}} = \tfrac{1}{24} \log_{10} 1.6 = \tfrac{1}{24} (.20412) = .008505$$
$$\text{antilog}_{10} .008505 = 1.0198 ,$$

which gives

$$j = 1.0198 - 1 = .0198$$

and

$$i^{(4)} = 4(.0198) = .0792, \text{ or } 7.92\% .$$

It should be noted that this problem can also be worked by interpolation in the interest tables.

Example 2.7. *At what interest rate convertible semiannually would an investment of $100 immediately and $200 3 years from the present accumulate to $500 10 years from the present?*

Let $j = \dfrac{i^{(2)}}{2}$ so that the equation of value becomes

$$100(1 + j)^{20} + 200(1 + j)^{14} = 500 .$$

This problem does not lend itself to logarithms, so we will interpolate in the interest tables. Define

$$f(j) = 100(1 + j)^{20} + 200(1 + j)^{14} - 500 .$$

We seek to find j, such that $f(j) = 0$. By trial and error,

$$f(.0300) = 100(1.80611) + 200(1.51259) - 500 = -16.871$$
$$f(.0350) = 100(1.98979) + 200(1.61869) - 500 = 22.717$$

and performing a linear interpolation

$$j = .0300 + .0050 \frac{0 + 16.871}{22.717 + 16.871} = .0321 ,$$

which gives

$$i^{(2)} = 2(.0321) = .0642, \text{ or } 6.42\% .$$

It should be noted that although logarithms could not be used in obtaining the answer, the accuracy of the answer can be checked using logarithms.

Example 2.8. *At what effective rate of interest is the present value of a series of payments of $1 at the end of every two years, forever, equal to $10?*

The equation of value is

$$10 = v^2 + v^4 + v^6 + \cdots = \frac{v^2}{1 - v^2} = \frac{1}{(1 + i)^2 - 1} ,$$

or

$$(1 + i)^2 = 1.1 ,$$

and taking square roots

$$1 + \imath = 1.0488$$

giving

$$i = .0488, \text{ or } 4.88\% .$$

EXERCISES

2.1. Introduction; 2.2. Obtaining numerical results

1. It is desired to find $(1 + i)^{n+k}$ for positive integral n and $0 < k < 1$. Prove that the following two methods are equivalent:

   a) Linear interpolation between $(1 + i)^n$ and $(1 + i)^{n+1}$.

   b) Assuming simple interest over the final fractional period.

2. It is desired to find v^{n+k} for positive integral n and $0 < k < 1$. Prove that the following two methods are equivalent:

   a) Linear interpolation between v^n and v^{n+1}.

   b) Assuming simple discount over the final fractional period.

2.3. The basic problem; 2.4. Equations of value

3. In return for payments of $200 at the end of 4 years and $500 at the end of 10 years, a man agrees to pay $300 immediately and to make an additional payment at the end of 3 years. Find the amount of the additional payment if $i^{(4)} = .06$.

4. In return for payments of $200 at the end of 5 years and $300 at the end of 10 years, a man agrees to pay X at the end of 3 years and $2X$ at the end of 6 years. Find X if $i = 3\frac{1}{2}\%$.

5. Whereas the choice of a comparison date has no effect on the answer obtained with compound interest, the same cannot be said of simple interest. Find the amount to be paid at the end of 10 years which is equivalent to two payments of $100 each, the first to be paid immediately and the second to be paid at the end of 5 years. Assume 5% simple interest is earned from the date each payment is made and use a comparison date of—

   a) The end of 10 years.

   b) The end of 15 years.

2.5. Unknown time

6. Solve formula (2.3) for t exactly.

7. In how many years will an amount of money double itself at an effective rate of interest i?

8. Use logarithms to find how long $100 should be left to accumulate at 6% effective in order that it may amount to twice the accumulated value of another $100 deposited at the same time at 4% effective.

9. *a*) The present value of two payments of $100 each to be made at the end of n years and $2n$ years is $100. If $i = .035$, find n by interpolation in the interest tables.

   b) Can this exercise be directly worked using a table of logarithms?

10. A payment of n is made at the end of n years, $2n$ at the end of $2n$ years, . . . , n^2 at the end of n^2 years. Find the value of t by the method of equated time.

2.6. Unknown rate of interest

11. Use interpolation in the interest tables to find the effective rate of interest at which the accumulated value of $100 at the end of 30 years is $300.

12. Find an expression for the exact effective rate of interest at which payments of $300 at the present, $200 at the end of one year, and $100 at the end of two years will accumulate to $700 at the end of two years.

13. It is known that an investment of $100 will accumulate to $182.50 at the end of 10 years. If it is assumed that the investment earns simple interest at rate i during the 1st year, $2i$ during the 2nd year, . . . , $10i$ during the 10th year, find i.

14. It is known that an amount of money will double itself in 10 years at a varying force of interest $\delta_t = kt$. Find an expression for k.

Miscellaneous problems

15. If an investment of 1 will be doubled in 51.975 years at a force of interest δ, in how many years will an investment of 1 be tripled at a nominal rate of interest numerically equal to δ and convertible once every three years? Assume $\log_e 2 = .693$.

16. A deposit of $100 is made at the beginning of each quarter for a year. Find the total interest earned during the year as a function of x, where

$$x = 1 + \frac{i^{(12)}}{12}.$$

17. Fund A accumulates at 2% effective and Fund B accumulates at 3% effective. At the end of 20 years the total of the two funds is $1000. At the end of 10 years the amount in Fund A is half that in Fund B. What is the total of the two funds at the end of five years?

18. A savings and loan association pays 4% effective on deposits at the end of each year. At the end of every three years a 2% bonus is paid on the balance at that time. Find the effective rate of interest earned by an investor if he leaves his money on deposit—
    a) Two years.
    b) Three years.
    c) Four years.

3.1. INTRODUCTION

An *annuity* may be defined as a series of payments made at equal intervals of time. Annuities are common in our economic life. House rents, mortgage payments, installment payments on automobiles, and interest payments on money invested are all examples of annuities. Originally the meaning of the word "annuity" was restricted to annual payments, but it has been extended to include payments made at other regular intervals as well.

Consider an annuity such that payments are certain to be made for a fixed period of time. An annuity with these properties is called an *annuity-certain*. The fixed period of time for which payments are made is called the *term* of the annuity. For example, mortgage payments on a home or business constitute an annuity-certain.

Not all annuities are annuities-certain. An annuity under which the payments are not certain to be made is called a *contingent annuity*. A common type of contingent annuity is one in which payments are made only if a person is alive. Such an annuity is called a *life annuity*. For example, monthly retirement benefits from a pension plan, which continue for the life of a retiree, constitute a life annuity.

In this book, we shall restrict our attention to annuities-certain. It will often be convenient to drop the word "certain" and use the term "annuity" to refer to an annuity-certain.

The frequency with which annuity payments are made is called the *payment period*. In this chapter, we consider annuities for which the payment period and the interest conversion period are equal, and for which the payments are of level amount. In Chapter 4, annuities for which payments are made more or less frequently than interest is converted and annuities with a varying series of payments are examined.

45

3.2. ANNUITY-IMMEDIATE

Consider an annuity under which payments of 1 are made at the end of each year for n years. Such an annuity is called an *annuity-immediate*. Figure 3.1 is a time diagram for such an annuity. Arrow 1 appears one year

FIGURE 3.1

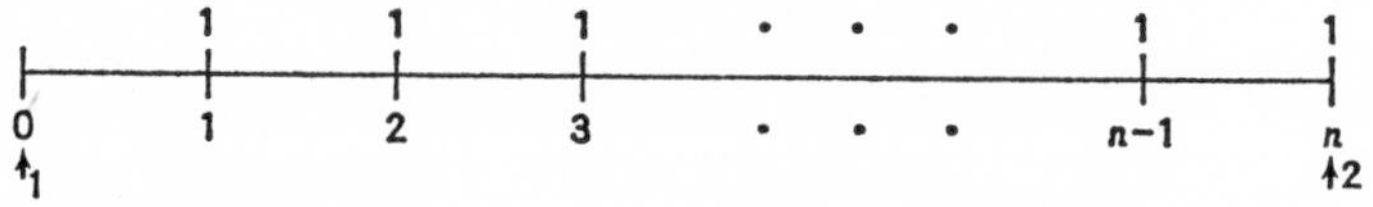

before the first payment is made. The present value of the annuity at this point in time is denoted by $a_{\overline{n}|}$. Arrow 2 appears n years after arrow 1, just after the last payment is made. The accumulated value of the annuity at this point in time is denoted by $s_{\overline{n}|}$.

We can derive an expression for $a_{\overline{n}|}$ as an equation of value at the beginning of the first year. The present value of a payment of 1 at the end of the first year is v. The present value of a payment of 1 at the end of the second year is v^2. This process is continued until the present value of a payment of 1 at the end of the nth year is v^n. The total present value, $a_{\overline{n}|}$, must equal the sum of the present values of each payment, i.e.,

$$a_{\overline{n}|} = v + v^2 + \cdots + v^{n-1} + v^n . \tag{3.1}$$

This formula could be used to evaluate $a_{\overline{n}|}$, but it would become impractical for large n. It is possible to derive a more compact expression by recognizing that formula (3.1) is a geometric progression.

$$\begin{aligned}
a_{\overline{n}|} &= v + v^2 + \cdots + v^{n-1} + v^n \\
&= v\frac{1 - v^n}{1 - v} \\
&= v\frac{1 - v^n}{iv} \\
&= \frac{1 - v^n}{i} .
\end{aligned} \tag{3.2}$$

An expression for $s_{\overline{n}|}$ can be derived in an analogous manner as an equation of value at the end of the nth year. The accumulated value of a payment of 1 at the end of the first year is $(1 + i)^{n-1}$. The accumulated value of a payment of 1 at the end of the second year is $(1 + i)^{n-2}$. This process is continued until the accumulated value of a payment of 1 at the end of the nth year is just 1. The total accumulated value, $s_{\overline{n}|}$, must equal the sum of the accumulated values of each payment, i.e.,

$$s_{\overline{n}|} = 1 + (1 + i) + \cdots + (1 + i)^{n-2} + (1 + i)^{n-1}. \qquad (3.3)$$

Again, a more compact expression can be derived by summing the geometric progression.

$$\begin{aligned} s_{\overline{n}|} &= 1 + (1 + i) + \cdots + (1 + i)^{n-2} + (1 + i)^{n-1} \\ &= \frac{(1 + i)^n - 1}{(1 + i) - 1} \\ &= \frac{(1 + i)^n - 1}{i}. \end{aligned} \qquad (3.4)$$

Values of $a_{\overline{n}|}$ and $s_{\overline{n}|}$ at several rates of interest and for values of n from 1 to 50 appear in the interest tables in Appendix I. On occasion, the interest rate is written to the lower right of the symbol, e.g., $a_{\overline{10}|.04}$ and $s_{\overline{25}|.05}$. Since this tends to clutter the symbols, we will do this only if there could be any ambiguity concerning the interest rate to be used in evaluating the function.

It is possible to give a verbal interpretation to formula (3.2) written as

$$1 = ia_{\overline{n}|} + v^n.$$

Consider the investment of 1 for n years. Each year the investment of 1 will yield interest of i paid at the end of the year. The present value of these interest payments is $ia_{\overline{n}|}$. At the end of n years the original investment of 1, whose present value is v^n, is returned. Thus, both sides of the equation represent the present value of an investment of 1 at the date of investment. A similar verbal interpretation for formula (3.4) is left as an exercise.

There is a simple relationship between $a_{\overline{n}|}$ and $s_{\overline{n}|}$,

$$s_{\overline{n}|} = a_{\overline{n}|}(1 + i)^n. \qquad (3.5)$$

This relationship is obvious from a comparison of either formulas (3.1) and (3.3) or from formulas (3.2) and (3.4). It is also obvious from the time diagram, since $s_{\overline{n}|}$ is the value of the same payments as $a_{\overline{n}|}$, only the value is taken n years later.

Another relationship between $a_{\overline{n}|}$ and $s_{\overline{n}|}$ is

$$\frac{1}{a_{\overline{n}|}} = \frac{1}{s_{\overline{n}|}} + i. \qquad (3.6)$$

This relationship can be derived as follows:

$$\frac{1}{s_{\overline{n}|}} + i = \frac{i}{(1+i)^n - 1} + i$$

$$= \frac{i + i(1+i)^n - i}{(1+i)^n - 1}$$

$$= \frac{i}{1 - v^n}$$

$$= \frac{1}{a_{\overline{n}|}} .$$

Values of $\frac{1}{s_{\overline{n}|}}$ appear in the interest tables in Appendix I. Formula (3.6) is useful in obtaining values of $\frac{1}{a_{\overline{n}|}}$ without having to perform a division. This will be illustrated in Example 3.3. (This formula will also be very significant in another context in Chapter 5.)

For simplicity, we have considered annuities in which the interest conversion period and the payment period are both one year. However, we can generalize our results to any situation in which the interest conversion period and the payment period are equal. This generalization is illustrated in Example 3.2, and it will apply throughout the rest of the chapter.

Example 3.1. Find the present value of an annuity which pays $50 at the end of each year for 20 years if the effective rate of interest is 5%.

The answer is

$$50a_{\overline{20}|} = 50(12.4622) = \$623.11.$$

Example 3.2. Find the accumulated value immediately after the last payment of an annuity which pays $25 every 2 months for 10 years if the rate of interest is 6% convertible 6 times a year.

The answer is

$$25s_{\overline{60}|.01} ,$$

since the interest conversion period and the payment period are both two months. Values of $s_{\overline{60}|}$ do not appear in the tables. However we can use formula (3.4) as follows:

$$25s_{\overline{60}|.01} = 25\frac{(1.01)^{30\cdot2} - 1}{.01}$$

$$= 25\frac{(1.34785)^2 - 1}{.01}$$

$$= 25(81.670)$$

$$= \$2041.75 .$$

Example 3.3. If a man invests $1000 at 4% per annum convertible semiannually, how much can he withdraw at the end of every six months to use up the fund exactly at the end of 20 years?

Let R be the amount of each withdrawal. The equation of value at the date of investment is

$$Ra_{\overline{40}|.02} = 1000$$
$$R = \frac{1000}{a_{\overline{40}|.02}}.$$

We can avoid performing a division by using formula (3.6).

$$R = 1000 \left(\frac{1}{a_{\overline{40}|.02}} \right)$$
$$= 1000 \left(\frac{1}{s_{\overline{40}|.02}} + .02 \right)$$
$$= 1000(.016556 + .02)$$
$$= \$36.56 .$$

3.3. ANNUITY-DUE

In Section 3.2, the annuity-immediate was defined as an annuity in which payments are made at the end of the year. In this section, we will consider the *annuity-due* in which payments are made at the beginning of the year instead of at the end of the year. The use of the terms "annuity-immediate" and "annuity-due" is unfortunate, since these terms are not descriptive of the properties of these annuities.

Figure 3.2 is a time diagram for an n-year annuity-due. Arrow 1 appears

FIGURE 3.2

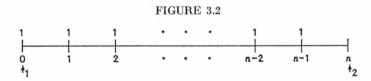

at the time the first payment is made. The present value of the annuity at this point in time is denoted by $\ddot{a}_{\overline{n}|}$. Arrow 2 appears n years after arrow 1, one year after the last payment is made. The accumulated value of the annuity at this point in time is denoted by $\ddot{s}_{\overline{n}|}$.

We can write an expression for $\ddot{a}_{\overline{n}|}$ analogous to formula (3.1).

$$\ddot{a}_{\overline{n}|} = 1 + v + v^2 + \cdots + v^{n-1}, \tag{3.7}$$

and, again, summing a geometric progression,

$$\ddot{a}_{\overline{n}|} = \frac{1 - v^n}{1 - v}$$
$$= \frac{1 - v^n}{iv} = \frac{1 - v^n}{d}, \tag{3.8}$$

which is analogous to formula (3.2).

Similarly for $\ddot{s}_{\overline{n}|}$, we have the following formulas analogous to formulas (3.3) and (3.4).

$$\ddot{s}_{\overline{n}|} = (1 + i) + (1 + i)^2 + \cdots + (1 + i)^{n-1} + (1 + i)^n \tag{3.9}$$

$$= (1 + i) \frac{(1 + i)^n - 1}{(1 + i) - 1}$$

$$= \frac{(1 + i)^n - 1}{iv} = \frac{(1 + i)^n - 1}{d}. \tag{3.10}$$

It is useful to compare formulas (3.2) and (3.8). The numerators are identical; however, the denominator of (3.2) is i and the denominator of (3.8) is d. Under the annuity-immediate, payments are made at the end of the year and i is a measure of interest payable at the end of the year. Under the annuity-due, payments are made at the beginning of the year and d is a measure of interest payable at the beginning of the year. A comparison of formulas (3.4) and (3.10) yields similar results.

The above property, relating the time annuity payments are made to the measure of interest in the denominator, greatly facilitates the memorization of annuity formulas. Moreover, this property can be generalized to the more complex annuities which are discussed in Chapter 4.

It is immediately obvious that

$$\ddot{s}_{\overline{n}|} = \ddot{a}_{\overline{n}|}(1 + i)^n, \tag{3.11}$$

a formula analogous to formula (3.5). It can also be shown that

$$\frac{1}{\ddot{a}_{\overline{n}|}} = \frac{1}{\ddot{s}_{\overline{n}|}} + d, \tag{3.12}$$

a formula analogous to formula (3.6). The derivation of (3.12) is left as an exercise.

It is possible to relate the annuity-immediate and the annuity-due. One type of relationship is

$$\ddot{a}_{\overline{n}|} = a_{\overline{n}|}(1 + i), \tag{3.13}$$

and

$$\ddot{s}_{\overline{n}|} = s_{\overline{n}|}(1 + i). \tag{3.14}$$

Formula (3.13) can immediately be derived by comparing formulas (3.1) and (3.7), or formulas (3.2) and (3.8). Since each payment under $\ddot{a}_{\overline{n}|}$ is made one year earlier than each payment under $a_{\overline{n}|}$, the total present value must be larger by one year's interest. Formula (3.14) can be derived similarly.

There is another type of relationship between the annuity-immediate and the annuity-due,

$$\ddot{a}_{\overline{n}|} = 1 + a_{\overline{n-1}|} . \tag{3.15}$$

This formula can be derived from Figure 3.2. The n payments made under $\ddot{a}_{\overline{n}|}$ can be split into the first payment and the remaining $n - 1$ payments. The present value of the first payment is 1, and the present value of the remaining $n - 1$ payments is $a_{\overline{n-1}|}$. The sum must give the total present value $\ddot{a}_{\overline{n}|}$.

Similarly, we can obtain

$$\ddot{s}_{\overline{n}|} = s_{\overline{n+1}|} - 1 . \tag{3.16}$$

This formula can also be derived from Figure 3.2. Temporarily, assume that an imaginary payment of 1 is made at the end of the nth year. Then, the total accumulated value of the $n + 1$ payments is $s_{\overline{n+1}|}$. However, we must remove the accumulated value of the imaginary payment which is just 1. The difference yields the accumulated value, $\ddot{s}_{\overline{n}|}$.

Formulas (3.15) and (3.16) are more convenient than formulas (3.13) and (3.14) for hand calculation, since they involve additions and subtractions instead of multiplications. Most compound interest tables, including those in Appendix I, do not include values for annuities-due.

Considerable confusion has often been caused by treating the annuity-immediate and the annuity-due as if they were greatly different. Actually they refer to evaluating exactly the same series of payments at different points in time. Figure 3.3 clarifies this.

FIGURE 3.3

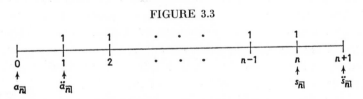

Example 3.4. A man wishes to accumulate \$1000 in a fund on July 1, 1980. To accomplish this he plans to make annual deposits on July 1, 1969, through July 1, 1979. How large should each deposit be if the fund earns 4% effective?

Since we are interested in the accumulated value one year after the last payment, the equation of value as of July 1, 1980, is

$$R\ddot{s}_{\overline{11}|} = 1000 .$$

where R is the annual deposit.

$$R = \frac{1000}{\ddot{s}_{\overline{11}|}}$$

$$= \frac{1000}{s_{\overline{12}|} - 1}$$

$$= \frac{1000}{15.0258 - 1}$$

$$= \$71.30 .$$

Alternatively, we have

$$R = \frac{1000}{s_{\overline{11}|}} \cdot \frac{1}{1.04} = \frac{74.149}{1.04} = \$71.30 .$$

This latter approach is preferable for hand calculation.

3.4. ANNUITY VALUES ON ANY DATE

Thus far we have considered evaluating annuities only at the beginning of the series of payments (either one year before, or on the date of, the first payment), or at the end of the series of payments (either on the date of, or one year after, the last payment). However, it is often necessary to evaluate annuities on other dates. We will discuss the following three cases: (1) present values more than one year before the first payment date, (2) accumulated values more than one year after the last payment date, and (3) current values between the first and last payment dates. We will assume that the evaluation date is an integral number of years from each payment date.

The value of an annuity on any date could be found by accumulating or discounting each separate payment and summing the results. However, this method would become impractical if a large number of payments are involved. We will see that it is possible to develop values for all three cases in terms of annuity symbols already defined.

The above three cases can best be illustrated by example. Consider an annuity under which seven payments of 1 are made at the end of the 3rd through the 9th years inclusive. Figure 3.4 is a time diagram for this annuity. The values at the end of the 2nd, 3rd, 9th, and 10th years are given directly, either by annuities-immediate or by annuities-due, as labeled on the time diagram.

The present value at the beginning of the 1st year is an example of case 1, the accumulated value at the end of the 12th year is an example of case 2,

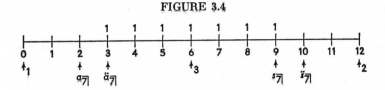

FIGURE 3.4

and the current value at the end of the 6th year is an example of case **3**. These three cases are denoted by arrows 1, 2, and 3, respectively, on the time diagram.

Present values more than one year before the first payment date

In this example, the present value of the annuity at the beginning of the 1st year is seen to be the present value at the end of the 2nd year discounted for two years, i.e.,

$$v^2 a_{\overline{7}|} .$$

It is possible to develop an alternate expression for this present value. Temporarily assume that imaginary payments of 1 are made at the end of the 1st and 2nd years. Then the present value of all nine payments is $a_{\overline{9}|}$. However, we must remove the present value of the imaginary payments, which is $a_{\overline{2}|}$. Thus, an alternate expression for the present value is

$$a_{\overline{9}|} - a_{\overline{2}|} .$$

This expression is preferable for hand calculation, since it involves a subtraction instead of a multiplication.

An annuity in case 1 is often called a *deferred annuity*, since payments commence only after a deferred period. The symbol for an m-year deferred annuity-immediate with a term of n years after the deferred period is $_m|a_{\overline{n}|}$. In the above example, the appropriate symbol would be $_2|a_{\overline{7}|}$. It should be noted that since payments are made at the end of the year, the first payment made under $_m|a_{\overline{n}|}$ is $m + 1$ years after the evaluation date, instead of m years.

In general, using the reasoning in this example, we have

$$_m|a_{\overline{n}|} = v^m a_{\overline{n}|} = a_{\overline{m+n}|} - a_{\overline{m}|} . \qquad (3.17)$$

We have used annuities-immediate instead of annuities-due, since numerical values are directly available for annuities-immediate. However, it is possible to work with a deferred annuity-due, $_m|\ddot{a}_{\overline{n}|}$. The student should verify that the answer to the above example, expressed as an annuity-due, is:

$$_3|\ddot{a}_{\overline{7}|} = v^3\ddot{a}_{\overline{7}|} = \ddot{a}_{\overline{10}|} - \ddot{a}_{\overline{3}|} .$$

Accumulated values more than one year after the last payment date

In this example, the accumulated value of the annuity at the end of the 12th year is seen to be the accumulated value at the end of the 9th year, accumulated for three years, i.e.,

$$s_{\overline{7}|}(1 + i)^3 .$$

Here it is also possible to develop an alternate expression which involves a subtraction instead of a multiplication. Temporarily, assume that imaginary payments of 1 are made at the end of the 10th, 11th, and 12th years. Then the accumulated value of all 10 payments is $s_{\overline{10}|}$. However, we must remove the accumulated value of the imaginary payments, which is $s_{\overline{3}|}$. Thus, an alternate expression for the accumulated value is

$$s_{\overline{10}|} - s_{\overline{3}|} .$$

In general, the accumulated value of an n-year annuity, m years after the last payment date, is

$$s_{\overline{n}|}(1 + i)^m = s_{\overline{m+n}|} - s_{\overline{m}|} . \tag{3.18}$$

It is also possible to work with annuities-due instead of annuities-immediate. The student should verify that the answer to the above example expressed as an annuity-due is

$$\ddot{s}_{\overline{7}|}(1 + i)^2 = \ddot{s}_{\overline{9}|} - \ddot{s}_{\overline{2}|} .$$

Current values between the first and last payment dates

In this example, the current value of the annuity at the end of the 6th year is seen to be the present value at the end of the 2nd year accumulated for four years or the accumulated value at the end of the 9th year discounted for three years, i.e.,

$$a_{\overline{7}|}(1 + i)^4 = v^3 s_{\overline{7}|} .$$

Here it is possible to develop an alternate expression which involves an addition instead of a multiplication. Separate the seven payments into the first four payments and the last three payments. The accumulated value of the first four payments is $s_{\overline{4}|}$, and the present value of the last three payments is $a_{\overline{3}|}$. Thus, an alternate expression for the current value is

$$s_{\overline{4}|} + a_{\overline{3}|} .$$

In general, the current value of an n-year annuity immediately after the mth payment has been made $(m < n)$ is

$$a_{\overline{n}|}(1 + i)^m = v^{n-m}s_{\overline{n}|} = s_{\overline{m}|} + a_{\overline{n-m}|} . \qquad (3.19)$$

It is also possible to work with annuities-due instead of annuities-immediate. The student should verify that the answer to the above example expressed as an annuity-due is

$$\ddot{a}_{\overline{7}|}(1 + i)^3 = v^4\ddot{s}_{\overline{7}|} = \ddot{s}_{\overline{3}|} + \ddot{a}_{\overline{4}|} .$$

Summary

In general, it is possible to express the value of an annuity on any date which is an integral number of years from each payment date as the sum or difference of annuities-immediate, which is the most convenient form for hand calculation. Other equivalent expressions do exist, and the student should practice translating one form of an answer into alternate forms.

The student should not try to work problems by memorizing formulas (3.17), (3.18), and (3.19). Any problem of this type can be best handled from first principles, as illustrated in this section.

If it is necessary to find the value of an annuity on a date which is not an integral number of years from each payment date, the value should be found on a date which is an integral number of years from each payment date and then the value on this date can be accumulated or discounted for the fractional period to the actual evaluation date. This situation will be illustrated in the exercises.

3.5. PERPETUITIES

A *perpetuity* is an annuity whose payments continue forever, i.e., the term of the annuity is not finite. Although it seems unrealistic to have an annuity with payments continuing forever, examples do exist in practice. The dividends on preferred stock with no redemption provision and the British consols, which are nonredeemable obligations of the British government, are examples of perpetuities.

The present value of a perpetuity-immediate is denoted by $a_{\overline{\infty}|}$, and we have

$$a_{\overline{\infty}|} = v + v^2 + v^3 + \cdots$$
$$= \frac{v}{1 - v}$$

$$= \frac{v}{iv}$$

$$= \frac{1}{i} \, . \tag{3.20}$$

Alternatively, we have

$$a_{\overline{\infty}|} = \lim_{n \to \infty} a_{\overline{n}|} = \lim_{n \to \infty} \frac{1 - v^n}{i} = \frac{1}{i} \, ,$$

since

$$\lim_{n \to \infty} v^n = 0 \, .$$

Formula (3.20) can be interpreted verbally. If principal of $\frac{1}{i}$ is invested at effective rate i, then interest of $\frac{1}{i} \cdot i = 1$ can be paid at the end of every year forever, leaving the original principal intact.

By an analogous argument, for a perpetuity-due, we have

$$\ddot{a}_{\overline{\infty}|} = \frac{1}{d} \, . \tag{3.21}$$

It should be noted that accumulated values for perpetuities do not exist, since payments continue forever.

3.6. FRACTIONAL TERMS

Thus far we have assumed that n is a positive integer in any of our annuity symbols. In fact, formula (3.1) for $a_{\overline{n}|}$ and formula (3.3) for $s_{\overline{n}|}$ do not allow any other assumption.

However, it is possible to give meaning to symbols, such as $a_{\overline{n+k}|}$ and $s_{\overline{n+k}|}$, for positive integral n and $0 < k < 1$, which are consistent with formulas (3.2) and (3.4).

Consider first $a_{\overline{n+k}|}$.

$$a_{\overline{n+k}|} = \frac{1 - v^{n+k}}{i}$$

$$= \frac{1 - v^n + v^n - v^{n+k}}{i}$$

$$= a_{\overline{n}|} + v^{n+k} \left[\frac{(1 + i)^k - 1}{i} \right] . \tag{3.22}$$

Thus, $a_{\overline{n+k}|}$ is the present value of an n-year annuity-immediate of 1 per year plus a final payment at time $n + k$ of $\dfrac{(1 + i)^k - 1}{i}$.

For simplicity, the final payment is often assumed to be k instead of $\dfrac{(1 + i)^k - 1}{i}$. As an exercise, the student will be asked to find the error involved in this assumption.

Consider now $s_{\overline{n+k}|}$.

$$
\begin{aligned}
s_{\overline{n+k}|} &= \frac{(1 + i)^{n+k} - 1}{i} \\
&= \frac{(1 + i)^{n+k} - (1 + i)^k + (1 + i)^k - 1}{i} \\
&= s_{\overline{n}|}(1 + i)^k + \left[\frac{(1 + i)^k - 1}{i}\right].
\end{aligned}
\tag{3.23}
$$

Thus, $s_{\overline{n+k}|}$ is seen to be the accumulated value after $n + k$ years of the same payments for which $a_{\overline{n+k}|}$ is the present value.

As an exercise the student will be asked to give a meaning to annuity symbols for negative n.

3.7. UNKNOWN TIME

Thus far, in any problems involving annuities, we have assumed that n and i are both known. In Section 3.7 we will consider the case in which n is unknown, and in Section 3.8 we will consider the case in which i is unknown.

In general, problems involving unknown time will not produce exact integral answers for n. These problems could be handled along the lines of Section 3.6 in which a smaller payment is made during the year following the last regular payment.

However, in practice, this often is not done because of the inconvenience and confusion of making a payment at a date which is not an integral number of years from the date all other payments are made. For example, making all regular payments on July 1 of each year for a period of years followed by a smaller payment on November 27 is not convenient for either party to the transaction.

What is usually done in practice is either to make a smaller payment at the same time as the last regular payment, in effect making a payment larger than the regular payment, called a *balloon payment*, or to make a smaller payment one year after the last regular payment, called a *drop payment*. Naturally, the smaller payments in these two situations are not equal, nor would either be equal to the smaller payment made at an intermediate point as in Section 3.6.

Problems involving unknown time can best be illustrated by example.

Example 3.5. An investment of $100 is to be used to make payments of $10 at the end of every year for as long as possible. If the fund earns an effective rate of interest of 5%, find how many regular payments can be made and find the amount of a smaller payment (1) to be paid on the date of the last regular payment, (2) to be paid one year after the last regular payment, and (3) to be paid during the year following the last regular payment, as described in Section 3.6.

The equation of value is

$$10a_{\overline{n}|} = 100$$
$$a_{\overline{n}|} = 10 .$$

By inspection of the interest tables, we have $14 < n < 15$. Thus, 14 regular payments can be made plus a smaller final payment. Figure 3.5 is a time diagram for

FIGURE 3.5

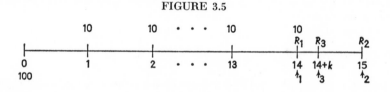

this example. In this figure R_1, R_2, and R_3 are the smaller final payments for the above three cases, arrows 1, 2, and 3 mark comparison dates for the above three cases, and k derives its meaning from Section 3.6.

1. The equation of value at the end of the 14th year is
$$10s_{\overline{14}|} + R_1 = 100(1.05)^{14} .$$
Thus,
$$R_1 = 100(1.05)^{14} - 10s_{\overline{14}|}$$
$$= 197.993 - 195.986$$
$$= \$2.01 .$$

2. The equation of value at the end of the 15th year is
$$10\ddot{s}_{\overline{14}|} + R_2 = 100(1.05)^{15}$$
Thus,
$$R_2 = 100(1.05)^{15} - 10(s_{\overline{15}|} - 1)$$
$$= 207.893 - 205.786$$
$$= \$2.11 .$$

It should be noted that $2.01(1.05) = 2.11$, or that in general $R_1(1 + i) = R_2$. The student should justify this result from general reasoning.

3. The following approach would probably be used in practice:

$$10a_{\overline{14}|} =\ \ 98.986$$
$$10a_{\overline{14+k}|} = 100.000$$
$$10a_{\overline{15}|} = 103.797\ .$$

Performing a linear interpolation,

$$k = \frac{100.000 - 98.986}{103.797 - 98.986} = .2108\ .$$

The final payment, R_3, would be $10(.2108) = \$2.11$.
This answer is approximate for two reasons:
a) The linear interpolation for k is not exact.

b) The true answer is $10\,\dfrac{(1.05)^k - 1}{.05}$ instead of $10k$.

A more exact answer can be developed as follows:

$$10 = a_{\overline{14+k}|} = \frac{1 - v^{14+k}}{.05}$$

giving

$$v^{14+k} = .5,\ \text{or}\ (1.05)^{14+k} = 2\ .$$

Using logarithms,

$$(14 + k)\log_{10} 1.05 = \log_{10} 2\ ,$$
$$k = \frac{\log_{10} 2}{\log_{10} 1.05} - 14 = \frac{.30103}{.02119} - 14 = .206\ .$$

Now the final payment is

$$R_3 = 10\,\frac{(1.05)^{.206} - 1}{.05}\ .$$

Evaluating $(1.05)^{.206}$ using logarithms,

$$\log_{10} (1.05)^{.206} = (.206)(.02119) = .00437\ ,$$
$$\text{antilog}_{10}\,.00437 = 1.0101\ .$$

Thus,

$$R_3 = 10\,\frac{1.0101 - 1}{.05} = \$2.02\ .$$

The exact answer obtained lies between the answers to 1 and 2, as we would expect. It is obvious that the method of Section 3.6 is not only inconvenient but that it is also more difficult to use if exact answers are required.

Example 3.6.   A fund of $1000 is to be accumulated by means of deposits of $100 made at the end of every year as long as necessary. If the fund earns an effective rate of interest of $2\frac{1}{2}\%$, find how *many regular deposits will be necessary and the size of a final deposit to be made one year after the last regular deposit.*

The equation of value is

$$100s_{\overline{n}|} = 1000$$
$$s_{\overline{n}|} = 10 .$$

By inspection of the interest tables, we have $9 < n < 10$. Thus, it takes nine regular deposits plus a smaller final deposit, R. The equation of value at the end of the 10th year is

$$100\ddot{s}_{\overline{9}|} + R = 1000 .$$

Thus,

$$R = 1000 - 100(s_{\overline{10}|} - 1)$$
$$= 1000 - 1020.34$$
$$= -\$20.34 .$$

What has happened here is that the last regular deposit brings the fund so close to $1000 that interest alone over the last year is sufficient to cause the fund to equal or to exceed $1000. The balance in the fund at the end of the 9th year is

$$100s_{\overline{9}|} = \$995.45 .$$

The balance in the fund at the end of the 10th year with interest only over the last year is

$$995.45(1.025) = \$1020.34 ,$$

which is in excess of the desired fund by $20.34. The result agrees with the one above. This example should not be thought of as typical, since in general a final deposit is necessary. However, it does illustrate that pitfalls do exist and that care must be used in obtaining reasonable answers.

3.8. UNKNOWN RATE OF INTEREST

In this section, we consider the case in which the rate of interest is the unknown. There are three methods to use in approaching this type of problem.

The first method is interpolation in the interest tables. This method is quite similar to that used in Section 2.6, and for most practical work is sufficiently accurate. It should be noted that interpolation in the interest tables will become significantly more accurate if interest functions are available for a larger number of interest rates than appear in Appendix I. In practical work, such tables are often available for a larger number of interest rates. The first method is the one we will use in most cases.

The second method is to use a series expansion and solve by algebraic techniques. For example,

$$a_{\overline{n}|} = v + v^2 + \cdots + v^n , \tag{3.1}$$

which is an nth degree polynomial in v. If a digital computer is available, the roots of an nth degree polynomial can be found by standard computer subroutines. Knowing v immediately determines i.

Alternatively, we can express $a_{\overline{n}|}$ or $\dfrac{1}{a_{\overline{n}|}}$ in terms of i and solve by algebraic techniques. As series expansions, we have

$$a_{\overline{n}|} = n - \frac{n(n+1)}{2!} i + \frac{n(n+1)(n+2)}{3!} i^2 - \ldots, \qquad (3.24)$$

$$\frac{1}{a_{\overline{n}|}} = \frac{1}{n}\left[1 + \frac{n+1}{2} i + \frac{n^2-1}{12} i^2 + \cdots\right]. \qquad (3.25)$$

The derivations of formulas (3.24) and (3.25) are left as exercises.

Formulas (3.24) and (3.25) can be used for hand calculation by neglecting terms of higher than the second degree in i and solving the resulting quadratic in i. If higher degree terms are included, the accuracy is improved, but the solution of the equation by hand becomes more difficult. Use of formulas (3.24) and (3.25) has not proven to be completely satisfactory in practice. Both series converge slowly, and often it is not safe to ignore third and higher degree terms, especially if n is large. Formula (3.25) does converge more rapidly than formula (3.24), and generally it produces more accurate answers.

The third method is *successive approximation* or *iteration*. Successive approximation can easily be used when an equation in the form

$$i = f(i)$$

exists. The true value of i, which is unknown, satisfies the equality exactly. Now assume some starting value, say i_0. Then generate a value i_1 by

$$i_1 = f(i_0) .$$

In general $i_1 \neq i_0$, so that another trial will be necessary. Then generate a value i_2 by

$$i_2 = f(i_1) .$$

In most cases, the successive values i_0, i_1, i_2, $\ldots$, will converge to the true value i. In practice, successive approximations will be carried out until $i_n = i_{n+1}$ to the required degree of accuracy.

If we let the given value of $a_{\overline{n}|}$ be denoted by k, then we can define

$$i = \frac{1 - (1+i)^{-n}}{k} ,$$

i.e.,

$$f(i) = \frac{1 - (1 + i)^{-n}}{k} .$$

Since each step in the successive approximation will generally involve an untabulated rate of interest, there will be a problem in evaluating $(1 + i)^{-n}$. In practice, either logarithms or direct calculation by a computer will be necessary.

The number of successive approximations necessary will be greatly reduced if the starting value i_0 is quite close to i. Good starting values for i_0 can be obtained by interpolation in the interest tables, i.e., by the first method described above.

Example 3.7. *At what rate of interest, convertible quarterly, is $16,000 the present value of $1000 paid at the end of every three months for five years? Use all three methods described here.*

Let $j = \dfrac{i^{(4)}}{4}$, so that the equation of value becomes

$$1000 a_{\overline{20}|j} = 16,000$$

or

$$a_{\overline{20}|j} = 16 .$$

1. Define $f(j) = a_{\overline{20}|j} - 16$. We seek to find j, such that $f(j) = 0$. By inspection of the interest tables,

$$f(.0200) = 16.3514 - 16 = .3514$$

and

$$f(.0225) = 15.9637 - 16 = -.0363 ,$$

and performing a linear interpolation,

$$j = .0200 + .0025 \frac{.3514 + 0}{.3514 + .0363} = .0223 ,$$

which gives

$$i^{(4)} = 4(.0223) = .0892, \text{ or } 8.92\% .$$

2. *a*) Using formula (3.24),

$$16 = 20 - \frac{20 \cdot 21}{2} j + \frac{20 \cdot 21 \cdot 22}{6} j^2$$

or

$$1540 j^2 - 210 j + 4 = 0 ,$$

and solving the quadratic,

$$j = \frac{210 \pm \sqrt{44{,}100 - 24{,}640}}{3080} = .0229 ,$$

which gives

$$i^{(4)} = 4(.0229) = .0916, \text{ or } 9.16\% .$$

b) Using formula (3.25),

$$\frac{1}{16} = \frac{1}{20}\left[1 + \frac{21}{2}j + \frac{399}{12}j^2\right]$$

or

$$532j^2 + 168j - 4 = 0 ,$$

and solving the quadratic,

$$j = \frac{-168 \pm \sqrt{28{,}224 + 8512}}{1064} = .0222 ,$$

which gives $i^{(4)} = 4(.0222) = .0888$, or 8.88%. Thus, in this example, formula (3.25) is in closer agreement with answer (1) than is formula (3.24).

3. Using successive approximation starting with $j_0 = .0225$, we have

$$j_1 = \frac{1 - (1.0225)^{-20}}{16} = \frac{1 - .64082}{16} = .0224$$

$$j_2 = \frac{1 - (1.0224)^{-20}}{16} = \frac{1 - .64207}{16} = .0224 .$$

Thus $j = .0224$ or $i^{(4)} = .0896$, or 8.96%. It should be noted that successive approximation can be carried to any desired degree of accuracy by carrying more decimal places. It should also be noted that any error made in a calculation will be corrected automatically in succeeding iterations if the work thereafter is done correctly.

3.9. VARYING INTEREST

It is possible to derive general expressions for $a_{\overline{n}|}$ and $s_{\overline{n}|}$ with varying interest in terms of the accumulation function. Any pattern of interest variation is directly reflected in the accumulation function.

The present value of an n-year annuity-immediate is equal to the sum of the present values of the individual payments. Thus, a generalized version of formula (3.1) is

$$a_{\overline{n}|} = \sum_{t=1}^{n} \frac{1}{a(t)} . \tag{3.26}$$

The accumulated value of an n-year annuity-immediate is equal to the accumulated value of $a_{\overline{n}|}$ after n years. Thus, we have

$$s_{\overline{n}|} = a(n) \sum_{t=1}^{n} \frac{1}{a(t)} . \tag{3.27}$$

Whereas the general formulas (3.26) and (3.27) can be used in finding values for an annuity with varying interest, common types of situations in practice can often best be handled using annuity symbols already defined. The following example illustrates this.

Example 3.8. ***Find the accumulated value of a 10-year annuity-immediate of \$100 per year if the effective rate of interest is 5% for the first 6 years and 4% for the last 4 years.***

The accumulated value of the first six payments after six years is
$$100 s_{\overline{6}|.05} .$$
This value is accumulated to the end of the 10 years at 4%, giving
$$100 s_{\overline{6}|.05}(1.04)^4 .$$
The accumulated value of the last four payments is
$$100 s_{\overline{4}|.04} ,$$
Thus, the answer is
$$100[s_{\overline{6}|.05}(1.04)^4 + s_{\overline{4}|.04}]$$
$$= 100[(6.8019)(1.16986) + 4.2465]$$
$$= \$1220.38 .$$

EXERCISES

3.1. Introduction; 3.2. Annuity-immediate

1. a) Find an expression for $s_{\overline{n}|}$ assuming simple interest at rate i.
   b) Find an expression for $a_{\overline{n}|}$ assuming simple discount at rate d.
2. a) Rank n, $a_{\overline{n}|}$, and $s_{\overline{n}|}$ in increasing order of magnitude.
   b) Under what conditions will equality hold for all n?
3. Verbally interpret formula (3.4).
4. Use logarithms to find $s_{\overline{40}|}$ if $i = 10\%$.
5. A man wishes to accumulate \$50,000 in a fund at the end of 20 years. If he deposits \$1000 in the fund at the end of each of the first 10 years and \$1000 + x in the fund at the end of each of the second 10 years, find x to the nearest dollar where the fund earns 4% effective.
6. a) Show that $a_{\overline{m+n}|} = a_{\overline{m}|} + v^m a_{\overline{n}|} = v^n a_{\overline{m}|} + a_{\overline{n}|}$.
   b) Show that $s_{\overline{m+n}|} = s_{\overline{m}|} + (1 + i)^m s_{\overline{n}|} = (1 + i)^n s_{\overline{m}|} + s_{\overline{n}|}$.
7. a) Show that $a_{\overline{m-n}|} = a_{\overline{m}|} - v^m s_{\overline{n}|} = (1 + i)^n a_{\overline{m}|} - s_{\overline{n}|}$ where $0 < n < m$.
   b) Show that $s_{\overline{m-n}|} = s_{\overline{m}|} - (1 + i)^m a_{\overline{n}|} = v^n s_{\overline{m}|} - a_{\overline{n}|}$ where $0 < n < m$.
8. Show that $\dfrac{1}{1 - v^{10}} = \dfrac{1}{s_{\overline{10}|}} \left(s_{\overline{10}|} + \dfrac{1}{i} \right).$
9. Show that $\dfrac{s_{\overline{2n}|}}{s_{\overline{n}|}} + \dfrac{s_{\overline{n}|}}{s_{\overline{2n}|}} - \dfrac{s_{\overline{3n}|}}{s_{\overline{2n}|}} = 1.$

3.3. Annuity-due

10. Find $\ddot{a}_{\overline{3}|}$ if the effective rate of discount is 10%.
11. Verbally interpret formula (3.8).
12. Derive formula (3.12).
13. a) Show that $\ddot{a}_{\overline{n}|} = a_{\overline{n}|} + 1 - v^n$.
    b) Show that $\ddot{s}_{\overline{n}|} = s_{\overline{n}|} - 1 + (1 + i)^n$.
14. Find the present value on January 1, 1970, of payments of $200 every six months from January 1, 1970, through January 1, 1974, inclusive, and $100 every six months from July 1, 1974, through January 1, 1980, inclusive, if $i^{(2)} = .06$.
15. A man aged 40 wishes to accumulate a fund for retirement by depositing $1000 at the beginning of each year for 25 years. Starting at age 65 he will make 15 annual withdrawals at the beginning of each year. Assuming that all payments are certain to be made, find the amount of each withdrawal starting at age 65 to the nearest dollar if the effective rate of interest is 4% during the first 25 years but only $3\frac{1}{2}\%$ thereafter.

3.4. Annuity values on any date

16. Derive formulas (3.17), (3.18), and (3.19) algebraically.
17. Payments of $100 per quarter are made from June 7, 1969, through December 7, 1980, inclusive. If the nominal rate of interest convertible quarterly is 6%—
    a) Find the present value on September 7, 1968.
    b) Find the current value on March 7, 1977.
    c) Find the accumulated value on June 7, 1981.
18. Show that $\displaystyle\sum_{t=10}^{15} (\ddot{s}_{\overline{t}|} - s_{\overline{t}|}) = s_{\overline{16}|} - s_{\overline{10}|} - 6$.
19. Find an expression for the present value of the annuity illustrated in Figure 3.4 at time $\frac{1}{4}$.
20. a) Show that $\displaystyle\sum_{t=0}^{4} {}_{10t}|a_{\overline{10}|} = a_{\overline{50}|}$.
    b) Verbally interpret the result obtained in (a).
    c) Show that a generalized version of (a) is given by

$$\sum_{t=0}^{\frac{n-k}{k}} {}_{kt}|a_{\overline{k}|} = a_{\overline{n}|}, \text{ where } \frac{n}{k} \text{ is integral.}$$

3.5. Perpetuities

21. a) Derive an expression for the present value of a deferred perpetuity in which payments commence at the end of n years and continue forever.

b) Write a symbol for the present value as a deferred perpetuity-immediate.

c) Write a symbol for the present value as a deferred perpetuity-due.

22. Deposits of $100 are placed into a fund at the beginning of each year for the next 20 years. After 30 years annual payments commence and continue forever, with the first payment at the end of the 30th year. Find an expression for the amount of each payment.

23. A man leaves an inheritance to four charities, A, B, C, and D. The total inheritance is a series of level payments at the end of each year forever. During the first n years A, B, and C share each payment equally. All payments after n years revert to D. If the present values of the shares of A, B, C, and D are all equal, find $(1 + i)^n$.

3.6. Fractional terms

24. Find an expression for the error involved in approximating

$$\frac{(1 + i)^k - 1}{i} \text{ by } k.$$

25. Derive a formula analogous to (3.22) for $\ddot{a}_{\overline{n+k}|}$.

26. Thus far annuity symbols have only been defined for positive values of n. Find expressions consistent with formulas (3.2) and (3.4) for—

   a) $a_{\overline{-n}|}$.

   b) $s_{\overline{-n}|}$.

3.7. Unknown time

27. A fund of $2000 is to be accumulated by n annual payments of $50 followed by n annual payments of $100 plus a smaller final payment made one year after the last regular payment. If the effective rate of interest is $4\frac{1}{2}\%$, find n and the amount of the final irregular payment.

28. A loan of $1000 is to be repaid by annual payments of $100 to commence at the end of the fifth year and to continue thereafter for as long as necessary. Find the duration and amount of the final payment if the final payment is to be larger than the regular payments. Assume $i = 4\frac{1}{2}\%$.

29. A loan of $1000 is to be repaid by annual payments of $50 for the first 10 years and annual payments of $100 thereafter for as long as necessary. Find the duration and amount of the final payment made one year after the last regular payment. Assume $i = 3\frac{1}{2}\%$.

3.8. Unknown rate of interest

30. A fund of $1700 is to be accumulated at the end of 10 years with payments of $100 at the end of each of the first 5 years and $200 at the end of each of the second 5 years. Find the effective rate of interest earned by the fund by interpolation in the interest tables.

31. If $a_{\overline{2}|} = 1.75$, find an exact expression for i.

32. *a*) Derive formula (3.24).
    b) Derive formula (3.25).

33. *a*) Show that $s_{\overline{n}|} = n + \dfrac{n(n-1)}{2!} i + \dfrac{n(n-1)(n-2)}{3!} i^2 + \cdots$.

    b) Show that $\dfrac{1}{s_{\overline{n}|}} = \dfrac{1}{n}\left[1 - \dfrac{n-1}{2} i + \dfrac{n^2-1}{12} i^2 - \cdots\right]$.

3.9. Varying interest

34. If $a(t) = \dfrac{1}{\log_2 (t+2) - \log_2 (t+1)}$, find an expression for $\ddot{a}_{\overline{n}|}$.

35. *a*) Find the present value of a 10-year annuity-immediate of 1 per annum if the rate of interest is 4% for the first 6 years and $3\frac{1}{2}$% for the last 4 years.

    b) Find the present value of a 10-year annuity-immediate of 1 per annum if the first 6 payments are discounted at 4% interest and the last 4 payments are discounted at $3\frac{1}{2}$% interest.

    c) Justify from general reasoning that the answer to (*b*) should be larger than the answer to (*a*).

36. A loan of P is to be repaid by 10 annual payments beginning 6 months from the date of the loan. The first payment is to be half as large as the others. For the first $4\frac{1}{2}$ years interest is i effective; for the remainder of the term interest is j effective. Find an expression for the first payment.

Miscellaneous problems

37. If $s_{\overline{n}|} = 10$ and $i = 10\%$, find $s_{\overline{n+2}|}$.

38. If $s_{\overline{2n}|} = 34$ and $i = 7\%$, find $s_{\overline{n}|}$.

39. If $\ddot{a}_{\overline{2n+1}|} = 13.5$ and $(1+i)^n = 4$, find i.

40. If $a_{\overline{n}|} = 10$ and $i = 5\%$, find $s_{\overline{3n}|} + 2s_{\overline{2n}|} + s_{\overline{n}|}$.

41. If $a_{\overline{n}|} = x$ and $a_{\overline{2n}|} = y$, express d as a function of x and y.

42. If $\ddot{a}_{\overline{p}|} = x$ and $s_{\overline{q}|} = y$, show that $a_{\overline{p+q}|} = \dfrac{vx + y}{1 + iy}$.

43. A loan of \$1000 is to be repaid by annual payments at the end of each year for the next 20 years. The first 5 years the payments are k per year; the second 5 years, $2k$ per year; the third 5 years, $3k$ per year; and the fourth 5 years, $4k$ per year. Find an expression for k.

44. The present value of an annuity-immediate which pays \$200 every 6 months during the next 10 years and \$100 every 6 months during the following 10 years is \$4000. The present value of a 10-year deferred annuity-immediate which pays \$250 every 6 months for 10 years is \$2500. Find the present value of an annuity-immediate which pays \$200 every 6 months during the next 10 years and \$300 every 6 months during the following 10 years.

4. More General Annuities

4.1. INTRODUCTION

In Chapter 3, we discussed annuities for which the payment period and the interest conversion period are equal and for which the payments are of level amount. In Chapter 4, annuities for which payments are made more or less frequently than interest is convertible and annuities with a varying series of payments will be discussed.

4.2. ANNUITIES PAYABLE LESS FREQUENTLY THAN INTEREST IS CONVERTIBLE

In this section annuities payable less frequently than interest is convertible are examined. This section will be subdivided into the following areas: (1) annuity-immediate, (2) annuity-due, and (3) other considerations.

Annuity-immediate

Let k be the number of interest conversion periods in one payment period, let n be the term of the annuity measured in interest conversion periods, and let i be the rate of interest per interest conversion period. We will assume that each payment period contains an integral number of interest conversion periods. Thus, the number of annuity payments made is $\frac{n}{k}$, which is integral.

The present value of an annuity which pays 1 at the end of each k interest conversion periods for a total of n interest conversion periods is

$$v^k + v^{2k} + \cdots + v^{\frac{n}{k} \cdot k} = \frac{v^k - v^{n+k}}{1 - v^k}$$

$$= \frac{1 - v^n}{(1 + i)^k - 1}$$

$$= \frac{a_{\overline{n}|}}{s_{\overline{k}|}} . \qquad (4.1)$$

Thus, we have an expression for the present value of this annuity in terms of annuity symbols already defined.

The accumulated value of this annuity immediately after the last payment is

$$\frac{a_{\overline{n}|}}{s_{\overline{k}|}} (1 + i)^n = \frac{s_{\overline{n}|}}{s_{\overline{k}|}} . \qquad (4.2)$$

It is possible to derive formulas (4.1) and (4.2) by an alternate argument. There is a value of R such that the series of payments of 1 at the end of each k interest conversion periods for n interest conversion periods can be replaced by a series of payments of R at the end of each interest conversion period so that the present values are equal. The present value of this series is

$$R a_{\overline{n}|} .$$

Now consider any one payment period which contains k interest conversion periods. At the end of the payment period the accumulated value of payments of R at the end of each interest conversion period must equal the payment of 1 made at that point. Thus,

$$R s_{\overline{k}|} = 1 ,$$

and substituting $R = \frac{1}{s_{\overline{k}|}}$ into $R a_{\overline{n}|}$, formula (4.1) is obtained. Formula (4.2) can be derived by a similar argument.

Figure 4.1 is a time diagram clarifying the above argument.

FIGURE 4.1

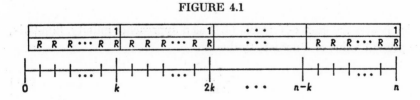

Annuity-due

The present value of an annuity which pays 1 at the beginning of each k interest conversion periods for a total of n interest conversion periods is

$$1 + v^k + v^{2k} + \cdots + v^{n-k} = \frac{1 - v^n}{1 - v^k}$$

$$= \frac{a_{\overline{n}|}}{a_{\overline{k}|}} . \tag{4.3}$$

The accumulated value of this annuity k interest conversion periods after the last payment is

$$\frac{a_{\overline{n}|}}{a_{\overline{k}|}} (1 + i)^n = \frac{s_{\overline{n}|}}{a_{\overline{k}|}} . \tag{4.4}$$

It is possible to derive formulas (4.3) and (4.4) by an alternate argument analogous to the argument used above for the annuity-immediate. The student should fill in the details for this argument. Figure 4.2 is a time diagram for this case.

FIGURE 4.2

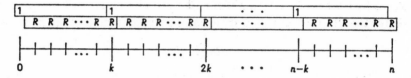

Other considerations

On occasion a perpetuity payable less frequently than interest is convertible is encountered. The present value of a perpetuity-immediate is

$$v^k + v^{2k} + \cdots = \frac{v^k}{1 - v^k}$$

$$= \frac{1}{(1 + i)^k - 1}$$

$$= \frac{1}{i s_{\overline{k}|}} , \tag{4.5}$$

which is also the limit of formula (4.1) as n approaches infinity. Similarly, the present value of a perpetuity-due is

$$\frac{1}{i a_{\overline{k}|}} . \tag{4.6}$$

It is interesting to note that Example 2.8 is an example of a perpetuity-immediate payable less frequently than interest is convertible.

A second special case occasionally encountered is to find the value of a series of payments at a given force of interest δ. Although coming under the category of annuities payable less frequently than interest is convertible, this situation is not adequately handled by the methods already discussed, since n and k are both infinite. This situation can best be handled by writing an expression for the value of the annuity as the sum of present values or accumulated values of each separate payment, replacing v^{tk} with $e^{-\delta tk}$ and $(1 + i)^{tk}$ with $e^{\delta tk}$. This expression can then be summed as a geometric progression. An example of this type appears in the exercises.

A third special case, very rarely encountered in practice, is a situation in which each payment period does not contain an integral number of interest conversion periods. Here, again, the best approach would be to resort to basic principles, i.e., to write an expression as the sum of present values or accumulated values of each separate payment, and then to sum this expression as a geometric progression. An example of this type appears in the exercises.

It should be observed that no one-symbol expressions for the annuity values given by formulas (4.1) through (4.6) are used. The only expressions are those in terms of ordinary annuity symbols given by formulas (4.1) through (4.6).

Finally, it is possible to generalize the approach to finding annuity values on any date, as discussed in Section 3.4, to annuities payable less frequently than interest is convertible. The following example illustrates this, as well as much of the rest of this section.

Example 4.1. ***Find an expression for the present value of an annuity on which there are a total of n payments of 1, the first to be made at the end of seven years, and the remaining payments at three-year intervals, at an effective rate i, expressed as (1) an annuity-immediate and (2) an annuity-due.***

Figure 4.3 is a time diagram for this example.

FIGURE 4.3

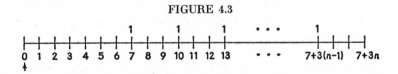

The present value of this annuity is given by

$$v^7 + v^{10} + v^{13} + \ldots + v^{3n+4}.$$

1. Summing the geometric progression, we have

$$\frac{v^7 - v^{3n+7}}{1 - v^3} = \frac{v^4 - v^{3n+4}}{(1+i)^3 - 1} = \frac{(1 - v^{3n+4}) - (1 - v^4)}{(1+i)^3 - 1}$$

$$= \frac{a_{\overline{3n+4}|} - a_{\overline{4}|}}{s_{\overline{3}|}}.$$

Note that the annuity-immediate form is characterized by the $s_{\overline{3}|}$ in the denominator.

2. Summing the geometric progression, we have

$$\frac{v^7 - v^{3n+7}}{1 - v^3} = \frac{(1 - v^{3n+7}) - (1 - v^7)}{1 - v^3}$$

$$= \frac{a_{\overline{3n+7}|} - a_{\overline{7}|}}{a_{\overline{3}|}}.$$

Note that the annuity-due form is characterized by the $a_{\overline{3}|}$ in the denominator.

With practice the student should be able to directly write down the answer to problems of this type in either the annuity-immediate form or the annuity-due form without actually summing the geometric progression.

4.3. ANNUITIES PAYABLE MORE FREQUENTLY THAN INTEREST IS CONVERTIBLE

In this section annuities payable more frequently than interest is convertible are examined. In practice annuities payable more frequently than interest is convertible are more common than annuities payable less frequently than interest is convertible. This section will be subdivided into the following areas: (1) annuity-immediate, (2) annuity-due, and (3) other considerations.

Annuity-immediate

Let m be the number of payment periods in one interest conversion period, let n be the term of the annuity measured in interest conversion periods, and let i be the interest rate per interest conversion period. We will assume that each interest conversion period contains an integral number of payment periods. Thus, the number of annuity payments made is mn, which is integral.

The present value of an annuity which pays $\dfrac{1}{m}$ at the end of each mth of an interest conversion period for a total of n interest conversion periods is denoted by $a_{\overline{n}|}^{(m)}$. We have

$$a_{\overline{n}|}^{(m)} = \frac{1}{m}\left[v^{\frac{1}{m}} + v^{\frac{2}{m}} + \cdots + v^{n - \frac{1}{m}} + v^n \right]$$

$$= \frac{1}{m}\left[\frac{v^{\frac{1}{m}} - v^{n + \frac{1}{m}}}{1 - v^{\frac{1}{m}}} \right]$$

$$= \frac{1 - v^n}{m\left[(1 + i)^{\frac{1}{m}} - 1\right]}$$

$$= \frac{1 - v^n}{i^{(m)}}. \tag{4.7}$$

The accumulated value of this annuity immediately after the last payment is made is denoted by $s_{\overline{n}|}^{(m)}$, and we have

$$s_{\overline{n}|}^{(m)} = a_{\overline{n}|}^{(m)} (1 + i)^n$$

$$= \frac{(1 + i)^n - 1}{i^{(m)}}. \tag{4.8}$$

Formulas (4.7) and (4.8) should be compared with formulas (3.2) and (3.4), respectively. They are identical except that the denominators of (4.7) and (4.8) are $i^{(m)}$ instead of i. Since $i^{(m)}$ is a measure of interest paid at the end of $m$ths of an interest conversion period, the points at which interest is paid under this measure are consistent with the points at which payments are made. This property, relating the manner in which payments are made and the measure of interest in the denominator, was originally mentioned in Section 3.3.

It is possible to write $a_{\overline{n}|}^{(m)}$ and $s_{\overline{n}|}^{(m)}$ in terms of $a_{\overline{n}|}$ and $s_{\overline{n}|}$ with an adjustment factor. The following are immediate consequences of formulas (4.7) and (4.8):

$$a_{\overline{n}|}^{(m)} = \frac{i}{i^{(m)}} a_{\overline{n}|}, \tag{4.9}$$

and

$$s_{\overline{n}|}^{(m)} = \frac{i}{i^{(m)}} s_{\overline{n}|}. \tag{4.10}$$

Formulas (4.9) and (4.10) are commonly used in obtaining numerical results. Values of $\frac{i}{i^{(m)}}$ appear in the interest tables in Appendix I. The term $\frac{i}{i^{(m)}}$ is often written as $s_{\overline{1}|}^{(m)}$, which is consistent with formula (4.8), setting $n = 1$.

One other relationship between $a_{\overline{n}|}^{(m)}$ and $s_{\overline{n}|}^{(m)}$ is

$$\frac{1}{a_{\overline{n}|}^{(m)}} = \frac{1}{s_{\overline{n}|}^{(m)}} + i^{(m)}. \tag{4.11}$$

This formula is analogous to formula (3.6), and the derivation is similar.

Annuity-due

The present value of an annuity which pays $\dfrac{1}{m}$ at the beginning of each mth of an interest conversion period for a total of n interest conversion periods is denoted $\ddot{a}_{\overline{n}|}^{(m)}$. We have

$$
\begin{aligned}
\ddot{a}_{\overline{n}|}^{(m)} &= \frac{1}{m}\left[1 + v^{\frac{1}{m}} + v^{\frac{2}{m}} + \cdots + v^{n-\frac{1}{m}} \right] \\[2mm]
&= \frac{1 - v^n}{m\left[1 - v^{\frac{1}{m}} \right]} \\[2mm]
&= \frac{1 - v^n}{m\left[1 - (1 - d)^{\frac{1}{m}} \right]} \\[2mm]
&= \frac{1 - v^n}{d^{(m)}}.
\end{aligned}
\tag{4.12}
$$

The accumulated value of this annuity one mth of an interest conversion period after the last payment is made is denoted by $\ddot{s}_{\overline{n}|}^{(m)}$, and we have

$$
\begin{aligned}
\ddot{s}_{\overline{n}|}^{(m)} &= \ddot{a}_{\overline{n}|}^{(m)} (1 + i)^n \\[2mm]
&= \frac{(1 + i)^n - 1}{d^{(m)}}.
\end{aligned}
\tag{4.13}
$$

Here, again, the relationship between the manner in which payments are made and the measure of interest in the denominator should be noted.

It is an immediate consequence of formulas (4.12) and (4.13) that

$$
\ddot{a}_{\overline{n}|}^{(m)} = \frac{i}{d^{(m)}}\, a_{\overline{n}|},
\tag{4.14}
$$

and

$$
\ddot{s}_{\overline{n}|}^{(m)} = \frac{i}{d^{(m)}}\, s_{\overline{n}|}.
\tag{4.15}
$$

Formulas (4.14) and (4.15) can be used in obtaining numerical results if values of $\dfrac{i}{d^{(m)}} = \ddot{s}_{\overline{1}|}^{(m)}$ are available. Such values do appear in Appendix I. It is also true that $\ddot{a}_{\overline{n}|}^{(m)} = \dfrac{d}{d^{(m)}}\, \ddot{a}_{\overline{n}|}$ and $\ddot{s}_{\overline{n}|}^{(m)} = \dfrac{d}{d^{(m)}}\, \ddot{s}_{\overline{n}|}$ using the relationship between the manner in which payments are made and the measure of interest in the denominator. However, formulas (4.14) and (4.15) are more frequently used, since values of $a_{\overline{n}|}$ and $s_{\overline{n}|}$ are more frequently tabulated than values of $\ddot{a}_{\overline{n}|}$ and $\ddot{s}_{\overline{n}|}$.

In practice, values of $\dfrac{i}{d^{(m)}}$ often are not available. However, there are three alternate methods of obtaining numerical results for $\ddot{a}_{\overline{n}|}^{(m)}$ and $\ddot{s}_{\overline{n}|}^{(m)}$.

The first method is to use the following:

$$\ddot{a}_{\overline{n}|}^{(m)} = \frac{1}{m} + a_{\overline{n-\frac{1}{m}|}}^{(m)}, \tag{4.16}$$

and

$$\ddot{s}_{\overline{n}|}^{(m)} = s_{\overline{n+\frac{1}{m}|}}^{(m)} - \frac{1}{m}. \tag{4.17}$$

These formulas are analogous to formulas (3.15) and (3.16), and their derivations are similar. Unfortunately, they are of little help unless values of the annuities-immediate are tabulated at $m$thly points, which often is not the case. In Appendix II the present values of annuities-immediate payable monthly are given at $2\frac{1}{2}\%$, 3%, and $3\frac{1}{2}\%$ at monthly intervals up to 240 months.

The second method is to use the following:

$$\ddot{a}_{\overline{n}|}^{(m)} = a_{\overline{n}|}^{(m)} (1 + i)^{\frac{1}{m}}, \tag{4.18}$$

and

$$\ddot{s}_{\overline{n}|}^{(m)} = s_{\overline{n}|}^{(m)} (1 + i)^{\frac{1}{m}}. \tag{4.19}$$

These formulas are analogous to formulas (3.13) and (3.14). The derivations are immediate, since each payment under $\ddot{a}_{\overline{n}|}^{(m)}$ is made one mth of an interest conversion period earlier than under $a_{\overline{n}|}^{(m)}$, and similarly for $\ddot{s}_{\overline{n}|}^{(m)}$ and $s_{\overline{n}|}^{(m)}$.

The third method is to use the following:

$$\begin{aligned}
\ddot{a}_{\overline{n}|}^{(m)} &= (1 + i)^{\frac{1}{m}} a_{\overline{n}|}^{(m)} \\
&= \left(1 + \frac{i^{(m)}}{m}\right) \frac{i}{i^{(m)}} a_{\overline{n}|} \\
&= \left(\frac{i}{i^{(m)}} + \frac{i}{m}\right) a_{\overline{n}|}, \tag{4.20}
\end{aligned}$$

and similarly,

$$\ddot{s}_{\overline{n}|}^{(m)} = \left(\frac{i}{i^{(m)}} + \frac{i}{m}\right) s_{\overline{n}|}. \tag{4.21}$$

This method is convenient if the tables necessary for one of the previous methods are not readily available.

Also, we have the following formula analogous to formula (3.12),

$$\frac{1}{\ddot{a}_{\overline{n}|}^{(m)}} = \frac{1}{\ddot{s}_{\overline{n}|}^{(m)}} + d^{(m)} . \tag{4.22}$$

Other considerations

On occasion, a perpetuity payable more frequently than interest is convertible is encountered. The following formulas are analogous to formulas (3.20) and (3.21).

$$a_{\overline{\infty}|}^{(m)} = \frac{1}{i^{(m)}} , \tag{4.23}$$

and

$$\ddot{a}_{\overline{\infty}|}^{(m)} = \frac{1}{d^{(m)}} . \tag{4.24}$$

A second special case very rarely encountered in practice is a situation in which each interest conversion period does not contain an integral number of payment periods. In this case, the best approach would be to resort to basic principles, i.e., to write an expression as the sum of present values or accumulated values of each separate payment and then to sum this expression as a geometric progression. An example of this type appears in the exercises.

Another problem which is very important in practice involves the proper coefficients for annuities payable *m*thly. Each payment made is of amount $\frac{1}{m}$, while the coefficient of the symbol is 1. In general, the proper coefficient is the amount paid during one interest conversion period and not the amount of each actual payment. The amount paid during one interest conversion period is often called the *annual rent* of the annuity. This is an appropriate term if the interest conversion period is one year, as is often the case; but it is confusing if the interest conversion period is other than one year. Sometimes the term *periodic rent* is used instead of "annual rent" to avoid this confusion.

Finally, it is possible to generalize the approach to finding annuity values on any date, as discussed in Section 3.4, to annuities payable more frequently than interest is convertible. The following example illustrates this, as well as much of the rest of this section.

Example 4.2. Payments of $10 per month are made from July 1, 1970, through June 1, 1980, inclusive. If the effective rate of interest *is 3%, find the present value of these payments (1) on June 1, 1970, and (2) on July 1, 1965.*

1. The answer is

$$120\ddot{a}_{\overline{10}|}^{(12)} = 120\,\frac{i}{i^{(12)}}\,a_{\overline{10}|}$$

$$= 120(1.013677)(8.5302) = \$1037.62\,.$$

2. The answer is

$$120\left(\ddot{a}_{\overline{15}|}^{(12)} - \ddot{a}_{\overline{5}|}^{(12)}\right) = 120\left(\frac{i}{d^{(12)}}\right)(a_{\overline{15}|} - a_{\overline{5}|})$$

$$= 120(1.016177)(11.9379 - 4.5797)$$

$$= \$897.27\,.$$

4.4. CONTINUOUS ANNUITIES

A special case of annuities payable more frequently than interest is convertible is one in which the frequency of payment becomes infinite, i.e., payments are made continuously. Although difficult to visualize in practice, a continuous annuity is of theoretical interest. Also, it is useful as an approximation to annuities payable with great frequency, such as weekly or daily.

We will denote the present value of an annuity payable continuously for n interest conversion periods, such that the total amount paid during each interest conversion period is 1, by the symbol $\bar{a}_{\overline{n}|}$. An expression for $\bar{a}_{\overline{n}|}$ is

$$\bar{a}_{\overline{n}|} = \int_0^n v^t\,dt\,, \tag{4.25}$$

since the differential expression $v^t\,dt$ is the present value of the payment made at exact moment t.

A simplified expression can be obtained by performing the integration.

$$\bar{a}_{\overline{n}|} = \int_0^n v^t\,dt$$

$$= \frac{v^t}{\log_e v}\bigg]_0^n$$

$$= \frac{1 - v^n}{\delta}\,. \tag{4.26}$$

Formula (4.26) is analogous to formula (3.2). Again, there is consistency between the manner in which payments are made and the denominator of the expression.

Also formula (4.26) could have been obtained as follows:

$$\bar{a}_{\overline{n}|} = \lim_{m \to \infty} a_{\overline{n}|}^{(m)} = \lim_{m \to \infty} \frac{1 - v^n}{i^{(m)}} = \frac{1 - v^n}{\delta},$$

or

$$\bar{a}_{\overline{n}|} = \lim_{m \to \infty} \ddot{a}_{\overline{n}|}^{(m)} = \lim_{m \to \infty} \frac{1 - v^n}{d^{(m)}} = \frac{1 - v^n}{\delta}.$$

Thus, the continuous annuity is seen to be the limiting case of annuities payable $m$thly.

It is possible to write $\bar{a}_{\overline{n}|}$ in terms of $a_{\overline{n}|}$ with an adjustment factor as follows:

$$\bar{a}_{\overline{n}|} = \frac{i}{\delta} \, a_{\overline{n}|} = \bar{s}_{\overline{1}|} \, a_{\overline{n}|}. \tag{4.27}$$

Values of $\dfrac{i}{\delta} = \bar{s}_{\overline{1}|}$ appear in the interest tables in Appendix I.

The accumulated value of a continuous annuity at the end of the term of the annuity is denoted by $\bar{s}_{\overline{n}|}$. The following relationships hold:

$$\bar{s}_{\overline{n}|} = \lim_{m \to \infty} s_{\overline{n}|}^{(m)} = \lim_{m \to \infty} \ddot{s}_{\overline{n}|}^{(m)}$$

$$= \int_0^n (1 + i)^t \, dt \tag{4.28}$$

$$= \frac{(1 + i)^t}{\log_e (1 + i)} \bigg]_0^n$$

$$= \frac{(1 + i)^n - 1}{\delta} \tag{4.29}$$

$$= \frac{i}{\delta} \, s_{\overline{n}|} = \bar{s}_{\overline{1}|} \, s_{\overline{n}|}. \tag{4.30}$$

If we have a continuous annuity and if interest is convertible continuously, then formula (4.26) can be written as

$$\bar{a}_{\overline{n}|} = \frac{1 - e^{-n\delta}}{\delta}, \tag{4.31}$$

and formula (4.29) can be written as

$$\bar{s}_{\overline{n}|} = \frac{e^{n\delta} - 1}{\delta}. \tag{4.32}$$

In a sense, this is a case of an annuity in which the payment period and interest conversion period are equal but which was not considered in Chapter 3.

Example 4.3. Money is placed into a fund continuously for 20 years at the rate of \$1 per annum for the first 10 years and \$2 per annum for the second 10 years. The fund earns an effective rate of interest of 5%. At the end of 20 years, the amount in the fund is used to buy an annuity payable at the beginning of every year for another 10 years. Find the amount of the annuity payment if money is worth 4% over the final 10-year period.

Let R be the annuity payment. Then the equation of value at the end of 20 years is

$$\bar{s}_{\overline{20}|.05} + \bar{s}_{\overline{10}|.05} = R\ddot{a}_{\overline{10}|.04}.$$

Therefore,

$$
\begin{aligned}
R &= \frac{\dfrac{i}{\delta}\left(s_{\overline{20}|.05} + s_{\overline{10}|.05}\right)}{1 + a_{\overline{9}|.04}} \\[2mm]
&= \frac{(1.024797)(33.0660 + 12.5779)}{1 + 7.4353} \\[2mm]
&= \$5.55.
\end{aligned}
$$

4.5. UNKNOWN TIME AND UNKNOWN RATE OF INTEREST

Thus far, in any problems involving annuities payable more or less frequently than interest is convertible, we have assumed that n and i are both known. In this section we will consider the cases in which one or the other is unknown. Much of the material contained in Sections 3.7 and 3.8 applies here.

Unknown time

As in Chapter 3, problems involving unknown time will generally not produce exact integral answers for n. Again a smaller payment will be made either at the same time as the last regular payment or will be made one payment period later.

One problem that immediately appears is that n is the number of interest conversion periods and not the number of payments. After n is obtained, it must be translated into a number of payments.

The case of annuities payable less frequently than interest is convertible presents no difficulty and can be handled along the lines of Section 3.7.

The case of annuities payable more frequently than interest is convertible does present a problem. As before, we can find the two integers between which n lies. However, this is not enough information for a complete solution. For example, if interest is convertible annually and payments are made monthly, then finding that $5 < n < 6$ merely means that the number of payments lies between 60 and 72. By interpolating for n it is usually possible to come close to the number of payments. An exact solution for this type of problem requires the use of annuity tables with values at $m$thly intervals. The tables in Appendix II can be used for monthly annuities.

Unknown rate of interest

For problems involving an unknown rate of interest it is usually best to first solve for the rate of interest per payment period. This can be done as in Section 3.8. Then a rate of interest convertible with the desired frequency, equivalent to the rate per payment period, can be found by the method described in Section 1.8. This approach will work equally well for annuities payable more or less frequently than interest is convertible.

Example 4.4.   An investment of $1000 is used to make payments of $100 at the end of each year for as long as possible with a smaller final payment to be made at the time of the last regular payment. If interest is 7% convertible semiannually, find the number of payments and the amount of the total final payment.

The equation of value is

$$100 \frac{a_{\overline{n}|.035}}{s_{\overline{2}|.035}} = 1000$$

or

$$a_{\overline{n}|.035} = 10s_{\overline{2}|.035} = 20.35 .$$

By inspection of the interest tables, we have $36 < n < 37$. Thus, 18 regular payments and a smaller final payment can be made. Let the smaller final payment be R. Then an equation of value at the end of 18 years is

$$R + 100 \frac{s_{\overline{36}|.035}}{s_{\overline{2}|.035}} = 1000(1.035)^{36}$$

or

$$R = 1000(3.45027) - 100 \frac{70.0076}{2.0350}$$

$$= \$10.09 .$$

The total final payment would thus be $110.09.

Example 4.5.   An investment of $10,000 is used to make payments of $100 at the beginning of each month for as long as possible, with a smaller final payment to be made one month after the last regular payment. If the effective rate of interest is 3%, find the number of payments and the amount of the smaller final payment.

The tables in Appendix II are applicable to this example. Let n be the number of monthly payments. The equation of value is

$$1200\ddot{a}^{(12)}_{\frac{n}{12}} = 10,000$$

or

$$12\ddot{a}^{(12)}_{\frac{n}{12}} = 100$$

or

$$12a^{(12)}_{\frac{n-1}{12}} = 99 .$$

By inspection of the interest tables, we have $113 < n - 1 < 114$ or $114 < n < 115$. Thus, there are 114 regular monthly payments and a smaller final payment.

Now

$$v^{\frac{114}{12}} = 12a^{(12)}_{\frac{114}{12}} - 12a^{(12)}_{\frac{113}{12}} = 99.27022 - 98.51505 = .75517 .$$

Let the smaller final payment be R. Then an equation of value is

$$1200\ddot{a}^{(12)}_{\frac{114}{12}} + Rv^{\frac{114}{12}} = 10,000 .$$

$$R = \frac{10,000 - 100\left(1 + 12a^{(12)}_{\frac{113}{12}}\right)}{v^{\frac{114}{12}}}$$

$$= \frac{10,000 - 100(1 + 98.51505)}{.75517}$$

$$= \$64.22 .$$

As a check the student should remember that the answer to this type of problem should be less than \$100. If the result is more than \$100, an error obviously has been made.

Example 4.6. **At what effective rate of interest will payments of \$100 at the end of every quarter accumulate to \$2500 at the end of five years?**

Let j be the interest rate per quarter which accomplishes the above. Then the equation of value at the end of five years is

$$100s_{\overline{20}|j} = 2500, \text{ or } s_{\overline{20}|j} = 25 .$$

Define $f(j) = s_{\overline{20}|j} - 25$. We seek to find j, such that $f(j) = 0$. By inspection of the interest tables,

$$f(.0225) = 24.9115 - 25 = -.0885$$
$$f(.0250) = 25.5447 - 25 = .5447,$$

and performing a linear interpolation,

$$j = .0225 + .0025 \frac{0 + .0885}{.5447 + .0885} = .0228.$$

Then the effective rate i can be found by

$$i = (1.0228)^4 - 1 = .0944, \text{ or } 9.44\%.$$

4.6. ELEMENTARY VARYING ANNUITIES

Thus far all the annuities considered have had a level series of payments. We now remove this restriction and consider annuities with a varying series of payments. In Section 4.6, it will be assumed that the payment period and interest conversion period are equal.

Naturally, any type of *varying annuity* can be evaluated by taking the present value or the accumulated value of each payment separately and summing the results. On occasion, this may be the only feasible approach. However, there are several types of varying annuities for which relatively simple expressions are possible, and we will consider these.

The following types of varying annuities will be discussed in this section: (1) payments varying in arithmetic progression, (2) payments varying in geometric progression, and (3) other payment patterns.

Payments varying in arithmetic progression

Consider a general annuity-immediate with a term of n years in which payments begin at P and increase by Q per year thereafter. Figure 4.4 is a time diagram for this annuity. It should be noted that P must be positive but that Q can be either positive or negative as long as $P + (n - 1)Q > 0$.

$$A = Pv + (P + Q)v^2 + (P + 2Q)v^3$$
$$+ \cdots + [P + (n - 2)Q] v^{n-1} + [P + (n - 1)Q]v^n$$

and

$$(1 + i)A = P + (P + Q)v + (P + 2Q)v^2 + (P + 3Q)v^3$$
$$+ \cdots + [P + (n - 1)Q] v^{n-1}.$$

Now subtracting the first equation from the second,

$$iA = P + Q(v + v^2 + v^3 + \cdots + v^{n-1}) - Pv^n - (n-1)Qv^n$$
$$= P(1 - v^n) + Q(v + v^2 + v^3 + \cdots + v^{n-1} + v^n) - Qnv^n .$$

FIGURE 4.4

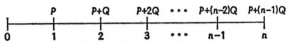

Thus,

$$A = P\frac{1 - v^n}{i} + Q\frac{a_{\overline{n}|} - nv^n}{i}$$
$$= Pa_{\overline{n}|} + Q\frac{a_{\overline{n}|} - nv^n}{i} . \tag{4.33}$$

The accumulated value is given by

$$Ps_{\overline{n}|} + Q\frac{s_{\overline{n}|} - n}{i} , \tag{4.34}$$

since it must be the present value accumulated for n years.

Formulas (4.33) and (4.34) can be used in solving any problem in which payments vary in arithmetic progression. However, there are two special cases which often appear and have special notation.

The first of these is the *increasing annuity* in which $P = 1$ and $Q = 1$. Figure 4.5 is a time diagram for this annuity. The present value of this annuity, denoted by $(Ia)_{\overline{n}|}$, is

$$(Ia)_{\overline{n}|} = a_{\overline{n}|} + \frac{a_{\overline{n}|} - nv^n}{i}$$
$$= \frac{1 - v^n + a_{\overline{n}|} - nv^n}{i}$$
$$= \frac{\ddot{a}_{\overline{n+1}|} - (n + 1)v^n}{i}$$
$$= \frac{\ddot{a}_{\overline{n}|} - nv^n}{i} . \tag{4.35}$$

The accumulated value of this annuity, denoted by $(Is)_{\overline{n}|}$, is

$$(Is)_{\overline{n}|} = (Ia)_{\overline{n}|}(1 + i)^n$$
$$= \frac{\ddot{s}_{\overline{n}|} - n}{i} = \frac{s_{\overline{n+1}|} - (n + 1)}{i} . \tag{4.36}$$

FIGURE 4.5

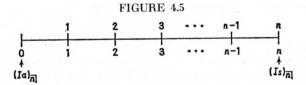

The second of these is the *decreasing annuity* in which $P = n$ and $Q = -1$. Figure 4.6 is a time diagram for this annuity. The present value of this annuity, denoted by $(Da)_{\overline{n}|}$, is

$$(Da)_{\overline{n}|} = na_{\overline{n}|} - \frac{a_{\overline{n}|} - nv^n}{i}$$

$$= \frac{n - nv^n - a_{\overline{n}|} + nv^n}{i}$$

$$= \frac{n - a_{\overline{n}|}}{i}. \qquad (4.37)$$

The accumulated value of this annuity, denoted by $(Ds)_{\overline{n}|}$, is

$$(Ds)_{\overline{n}|} = (Da)_{\overline{n}|}(1 + i)^n$$

$$= \frac{n(1 + i)^n - s_{\overline{n}|}}{i}. \qquad (4.38)$$

All the above formulas are for annuities-immediate. However, we may use the previously mentioned relationship between the manner in which payments are made and the denominator of the expression for the annuity value to find formulas for annuities-due. Changing i in the denominator of any of the above to d will produce values for annuities-due.

Also, it is possible to have varying perpetuities. We can find the general form for a perpetuity by taking the limit of formula (4.33) as n approaches infinity, obtaining

$$\frac{P}{i} + \frac{Q}{i^{\cdot}}, \qquad (4.39)$$

since

$$\lim_{n \to \infty} a_{\overline{n}|} = \frac{1}{i} \text{ and } \lim_{n \to \infty} nv^n = 0 \,.$$

Note that P and Q must both be positive to avoid negative payments.

FIGURE 4.6

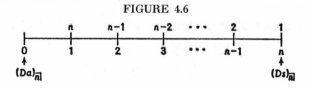

Payments varying in geometric progression

Consider a general annuity-immediate with a term of n years in which the first payment is 1 and successive payments increase in geometric progression with common ratio $(1 + k)$. The present value of this annuity is

$$v + v^2(1 + k) + \cdots + v^n(1 + k)^{n-1} \,.$$

However, this is a geometric progression whose sum is

$$v\left[\frac{1 - \left(\dfrac{1+k}{1+i}\right)^n}{1 - \left(\dfrac{1+k}{1+i}\right)}\right] = \frac{1 - \left(\dfrac{1+k}{1+i}\right)^n}{i - k}. \tag{4.40}$$

In general, this expression will have to be evaluated by logarithms or by direct calculation. However, on occasion, either $\dfrac{1+k}{1+i}$ or $\dfrac{1+i}{1+k}$ may equal $1 + j$ for some j with tabular interest functions, in which case tabular values can be used directly. This will be illustrated in Example 4.9. If $k = i$, formula (4.40) is undefined. However, then the present value is just nv.

Formulas for annuities-due can be handled in an analogous manner, since their present value is also a geometric progression.

The present value of a perpetuity will exist if $0 < \dfrac{1+k}{1+i} < 1$, in which case the sum of the geometric progression exists. If $\dfrac{1+k}{1+i} \geq 1$, then the geometric progression diverges and the present value of the perpetuity does not exist.

Other payment patterns

It is possible to derive a general expression for an annuity-immediate with a term of n years by the use of finite differences. The student is referred to Appendix IV for a brief review of finite differences.

Let u_t be the payment made at the end of the tth year. Recall that

$$\Delta u_t = u_{t+1} - u_t.$$

Then from finite differences we have the following summation formula which gives the present value of the annuity:

$$\sum_{t=1}^{n} v^t u_t = \left[\frac{v^t}{v-1}\left\{1 - \frac{v\Delta}{v-1} + \frac{v^2\Delta^2}{(v-1)^2} - \frac{v^3\Delta^3}{(v-1)^3} + \cdots\right\}u_t\right]_{t=1}^{t=n+1}$$

$$= \left[\frac{v^{t-1}}{i}\left\{1 + \frac{\Delta}{i} + \frac{\Delta^2}{i^2} + \frac{\Delta^3}{i^3} + \cdots\right\}u_t\right]_{t=n+1}^{t=1} \tag{4.41}$$

Formula (4.41) will yield practical results whenever higher order differences past a certain point can be safely ignored. In particular, if u_t is a polynomial of degree m, then $(m + 1)$th and higher differences are all zero.

Example 4.7. *Find the present value of a perpetuity-immediate whose successive payments are 1, 2, 3, 4, . . . , at an effective rate of interest of 5%.*

An appropriate symbol would be $(Ia)_{\overline{\infty}|}$. Substituting $P = 1$ and $Q = 1$ into formula (4.39), we obtain

$$\frac{1}{i} + \frac{1}{i^2} = \frac{1}{.05} + \frac{1}{.0025} = 420 .$$

Example 4.8. *Find the present value of an annuity-immediate such that payments start at 1, increase by annual amounts of 1 to a payment of n, and then decrease by annual amounts of 1 to a final payment of 1.*

The present value is

$$(Ia)_{\overline{n}|} + v^n (Da)_{\overline{n-1}|} = \frac{\ddot{a}_{\overline{n}|} - nv^n}{i} + v^n \frac{(n-1) - a_{\overline{n-1}|}}{i}$$

$$= \frac{1}{i} [a_{\overline{n-1}|} + 1 - nv^n + nv^n - v^n - v^n a_{\overline{n-1}|}]$$

$$= \frac{1}{i} [a_{\overline{n-1}|}(1 - v^n) + (1 - v^n)]$$

$$= \frac{1}{i} (1 - v^n)(a_{\overline{n-1}|} + 1)$$

$$= a_{\overline{n}|} \ddot{a}_{\overline{n}|} .$$

Example 4.9. *An annuity provides for 20 annual payments, the first payment a year hence being $100. The payments increase in such a way that each payment is 2% greater than the preceding payment. Find the present value of this annuity at 5.06% effective interest per annum.*

Using formula (4.40) we have

$$100 \frac{1 - \left(\frac{1.02}{1.0506}\right)^{20}}{.0506 - .02} = 100 \cdot \frac{.03}{.0306} \cdot \frac{1 - (1.03)^{-20}}{.03}$$

$$= \frac{100}{1.02} a_{\overline{20}|.03}$$

$$= \frac{100}{1.02} (14.8775)$$

$$= \$1458.58 .$$

Example 4.10. ***Use formula (4.41) to derive formula (4.35).***

In this case $u_t = t$ and $\Delta u_t = 1$.

$$(Ia)_{\overline{n}|} = \sum_{t=1}^{n} tv^t = \left[\frac{v^{t-1}}{i}\left\{ t + \frac{1}{i}\right\} \right]_{t=n+1}^{t=1}$$

$$= \frac{1}{i}\left(1 + \frac{1}{i}\right) - \frac{v^n}{i}\left(n + 1 + \frac{1}{i}\right)$$

$$= \frac{1}{i} \cdot \frac{1+i}{i} - \frac{v^n}{i} \cdot \frac{1+i}{i} - \frac{nv^n}{i}$$

$$= \frac{1 - v^n}{id} - \frac{nv^n}{i}$$

$$= \frac{\ddot{a}_{\overline{n}|} - nv^n}{i}.$$

Example 4.11. ***A rather novel method of solving varying annuity problems in which payments vary in arithmetic progression is to make use of the following three quantities:***

a) $F_n = v^n$ ***The present value of a payment of 1 at the end of n years.***

b) $G_n = \dfrac{v^n}{d}$ ***The present value of a level perpetuity of 1 per year, first payment at the end of n years.***

c) $H_n = \dfrac{v^n}{d^2}$ ***The present value of an increasing perpetuity of 1, 2, 3, . . . , first payment at the end of n years.***

By appropriately describing the pattern of payments, expressions for the annuity value can be immediately written down. This will be illustrated by two examples.

1. Derive formula (4.35) by this method.

The payments can be represented by

$$H_1 - H_{n+1} - n \cdot G_{n+1} ,$$

and substituting, we obtain

$$\frac{v}{d^2} - \frac{v^{n+1}}{d^2} - n\frac{v^{n+1}}{d} = \frac{1}{di} - \frac{v^n}{di} - \frac{nv^n}{i}$$

$$= \frac{\ddot{a}_{\overline{n}|} - nv^n}{i}.$$

2. Obtain the answer to Example 4.8 by this method.

The payments can be represented by

$$(H_1 - H_{n+1}) - (H_{n+1} - H_{2n+1}) = H_1 - 2H_{n+1} + H_{2n+1} .$$

and substituting, we obtain

$$\frac{v}{d^2} - \frac{2v^{n+1}}{d^2} + \frac{v^{2n+1}}{d^2} = \frac{1 - 2v^n + v^{2n}}{id} = \frac{(1 - v^n)^2}{id} = a_{\overline{n}|}\ddot{a}_{\overline{n}|}\ .$$

4.7. MORE GENERAL VARYING ANNUITIES

The varying annuities considered in Section 4.6 assumed that the payment period and the interest conversion period are equal. In Section 4.7 this restriction is removed. In practice, varying annuities with payments made more or less frequently than interest is convertible occur infrequently.

Consider first the case in which payments are made less frequently than interest is convertible. Let k be the number of interest conversion periods in one payment period, let n be the term of the annuity measured in interest conversion periods, let i be the rate of interest per interest conversion period, and let the payments begin at P and increase by Q per payment period thereafter. The number of payments is $\frac{n}{k}$, which is integral.

A generalized version of formula (4.33) for this case is

$$P\frac{a_{\overline{n}|}}{s_{\overline{k}|}} + Q\frac{\dfrac{a_{\overline{n}|}}{s_{\overline{k}|}} - \dfrac{n}{k}v^n}{is_{\overline{k}|}}\ . \tag{4.42}$$

The derivation is as follows:

Let A be the present value of the annuity, then

$$A = Pv^k + (P + Q)v^{2k} + (P + 2Q)v^{3k} + \cdots + \left[P + \left(\frac{n}{k} - 2\right)Q\right]v^{n-k}$$
$$+ \left[P + \left(\frac{n}{k} - 1\right)Q\right]v^n$$

and

$$(1 + i)^k A = P + (P + Q)v^k + (P + 2Q)v^{2k} + (P + 3Q)v^{3k} + \cdots$$
$$+ \left[P + \left(\frac{n}{k} - 1\right)Q\right]v^{n-k}\ .$$

Now subtracting the first equation from the second,

$$A[(1 + i)^k - 1] = P + Q(v^k + v^{2k} + \cdots + v^{n-k}) - Pv^n - \left(\frac{n}{k} - 1\right)Qv^n$$
$$= P(1 - v^n) + Q(v^k + v^{2k} + \cdots + v^{n-k} + v^n) - Q\frac{n}{k}v^n\ .$$

Thus,

$$A = \frac{P(1 - v^n) + Q\frac{a_{\overline{n}|}}{s_{\overline{k}|}} - Q\frac{n}{k}v^n}{(1 + i)^k - 1}$$

$$= P\frac{a_{\overline{n}|}}{s_{\overline{k}|}} + Q\frac{\frac{a_{\overline{n}|}}{s_{\overline{k}|}} - \frac{n}{k}v^n}{is_{\overline{k}|}} \,.$$

Consider next the case in which payments are made more frequently than interest is convertible. Two different cases arise depending on whether the rate of payment is constant or varies during each interest conversion period.

Consider first the situation in which the rate of payment is constant during each interest conversion period with increases or decreases occurring only once per interest conversion period. We can utilize the relationship between the manner in which payments are made and the measure of interest in the denominator to obtain the following generalized version of formula (4.33):

$$Pa_{\overline{n}|}^{(m)} + Q\frac{a_{\overline{n}|} - nv^n}{i^{(m)}} \,. \tag{4.43}$$

As a special case, we have the following generalized version of formula (4.35):

$$(Ia)_{\overline{n}|}^{(m)} = \frac{\ddot{a}_{\overline{n}|} - nv^n}{i^{(m)}} \,. \tag{4.44}$$

Formula (4.44) gives the present value of an n-year annuity-immediate, payable $m$thly, in which each payment during the first year is $\frac{1}{m}$, each payment during the second year is $\frac{2}{m}$, and so forth, until each payment during the nth year is $\frac{n}{m}$.

Consider next the situation in which the rate of payment changes with each payment period. Suppose that an increasing annuity is payable at the nominal rate of $\frac{1}{m}$ per interest conversion period at the end of the first mth of an interest conversion period, $\frac{2}{m}$ per interest conversion period at the end of the second mth of an interest conversion period, and so forth. Then the first payment will be $\frac{1}{m^2}$, the second will be $\frac{2}{m^2}$, and so forth. Denoting the present value of such an annuity by $(I^{(m)}a)_{\overline{n}|}^{(m)}$, we have

$$(I^{(m)}a)_{\overline{n}|}^{(m)} = \frac{1}{m^2}\left[v^{\frac{1}{m}} + 2v^{\frac{2}{m}} + \cdots + nmv^{\frac{nm}{m}} \right]$$

$$= \frac{\ddot{a}_{\overline{n}|}^{\cdot(m)} - nv^n}{i^{(m)}} \cdot \qquad (4.45)$$

The derivation of formula (4.45) is left as an exercise.

Example 4.12.   Find the present value of a perpetuity which pays 1 at the end of the third year, 2 at the end of the sixth year, 3 at the end of the ninth year, . . .

Denote the present value of this perpetuity by A. Then

$$A = v^3 + 2v^6 + 3v^9 + \cdots$$

and

$$v^3 A = \qquad v^6 + 2v^9 + \cdots$$

Now subtracting the second equation from the first,

$$A(1 - v^3) = v^3 + v^6 + v^9 + \cdots = \frac{v^3}{1 - v^3}$$

or

$$A = \frac{v^3}{(1 - v^3)^2} \cdot$$

4.8. CONTINUOUS VARYING ANNUITIES

The last type of varying annuity we will consider is one in which payments are being made continuously at a varying rate. Such annuities are primarily of theoretical interest.

Consider an increasing annuity in which payments are being made continuously at the rate of t per annum at exact moment t. The present value of this annuity is denoted by $(\bar{I}\bar{a})_{\overline{n}|}$, and an expression for it would be

$$(\bar{I}\bar{a})_{\overline{n}|} = \int_0^n tv^t \, dt , \qquad (4.46)$$

since the differential expression $tv^t \, dt$ is the present value of the payment made at exact moment t.

A simplified expression can be obtained by performing an integration by parts.

$$(\bar{I}\bar{a})_{\overline{n}|} = \int_0^n tv^t \, dt$$

$$= \frac{tv^t}{\log_e v} \Big]_0^n - \int_0^n \frac{v^t}{\log_e v} \, dt$$

$$= \frac{tv^t}{\log_e v}\Bigg]_0^n - \frac{v^t}{(\log_e v)^2}\Bigg]_0^n$$

$$= -\frac{nv^n}{\delta} - \frac{v^n}{\delta^2} + \frac{1}{\delta^2}$$

$$= \frac{1 - v^n}{\delta^2} - \frac{nv^n}{\delta}$$

$$= \frac{\bar{a}_{\overline{n}|} - nv^n}{\delta} . \tag{4.47}$$

It should be noted that formula (4.47) can also be derived from formula (4.45).

$$(\bar{I}\bar{a})_{\overline{n}|} = \lim_{m \to \infty}(I^{(m)}a)_{\overline{n}|}^{(m)} = \lim_{m \to \infty}\frac{\ddot{a}_{\overline{n}|}^{(m)} - nv^n}{i^{(m)}} = \frac{\bar{a}_{\overline{n}|} - nv^n}{\delta} .$$

In general, if the amount of the payment being made at exact moment t is $f(t)\,dt$, then an expression for the present value of an n-year continuous varying annuity would be

$$\int_0^n f(t)\, v^t\, dt . \tag{4.48}$$

The most general continuous varying annuity possible would be one in which not only are the payments made continuously and the variations occur continuously but also one in which the force of interest is varying continuously. In this case, a generalized version of formula (4.48) would be

$$\int_0^n f(t)\, e^{-\int_0^t \delta_r dr}\, dt . \tag{4.49}$$

Example 4.13. *Find an expression for the present value of a continuously increasing annuity with a term of n years if the force of interest is δ and if the rate of payment at time t is t^2 per annum.*

The answer is obtained by performing an integration by parts.

$$\int_0^n t^2 e^{-\delta t}\, dt = -\frac{t^2}{\delta} e^{-\delta t}\Bigg]_0^n + \frac{2}{\delta}\int_0^n t e^{-\delta t}\, dt$$

$$= -\frac{n^2}{\delta} e^{-\delta n} - \frac{2t}{\delta^2} e^{-\delta t}\Bigg]_0^n + \frac{2}{\delta^2}\int_0^n e^{-\delta t}\, dt$$

$$= -\frac{n^2}{\delta} e^{-\delta n} - \frac{2n}{\delta^2} e^{-\delta n} - \frac{2}{\delta^3} e^{-\delta t}\Bigg]_0^n$$

$$= -\frac{n^2}{\delta} e^{-\delta n} - \frac{2n}{\delta^2} e^{-\delta n} - \frac{2}{\delta^3} e^{-\delta n} + \frac{2}{\delta^3}$$

$$= \frac{2}{\delta^3} - e^{-\delta n} \left(\frac{n^2}{\delta} + \frac{2n}{\delta^2} + \frac{2}{\delta^3} \right).$$

EXERCISES

4.1. Introduction; 4.2. Annuities payable less frequently than interest is convertible

1. Give an expression in terms of functions assuming a rate of interest per half year for the accumulated value, 18 years after the first payment is made, of an annuity on which there are 8 payments of $100 at 2-year intervals:
   a) Expressed as an annuity-immediate.
   b) Expressed as an annuity-due.

2. Give an expression in terms of functions assuming a rate of interest per month for the present value, 3 years before the first payment is made, of an annuity on which there are payments of $200 every 4 months for 12 years:
   a) Expressed as an annuity-immediate.
   b) Expressed as an annuity-due.

3. A man makes annual deposits at the beginning of each year for 10 years in order to provide 40 semiannual payments of $500, the first payment to be made at the end of 10 years. Find an expression for the annual deposit in terms of annuities-due, assuming a rate of interest per half year.

4. A perpetuity of $750 payable at the end of every year and a perpetuity of $750 payable at the end of every 20 years are to be replaced by an annuity of R payable at the end of every year for 30 years. If $i^{(2)} = .04$, show that

$$R = 37,500 \left(\frac{1}{s_{\overline{2}|}} + \frac{v^{40}}{a_{\overline{40}|}} \right) \frac{s_{\overline{2}|}}{a_{\overline{60}|}}$$

   where all functions are evaluated at 2% interest.

5. Find an expression for the present value of an annuity-due of $600 per annum payable semiannually for 10 years if $d^{(12)} = .06$.

6. Find an expression for the present value of an annuity on which payments are $10 per quarter for five years, just before the first payment is made, if $\delta = .05$.

7. A perpetuity paying 1 at the beginning of each year has a present value of 20. If this is exchanged for another perpetuity paying R at the beginning of every two years, find R so that the values of the two perpetuities are equal.

8. Find an expression for the present value of an annuity on which payments are 1 at the beginning of each 4-month period for 12 years, assuming a rate of interest per 3-month period.

4.3. Annuities payable more frequently than interest is convertible

9. *a)* If $i = 4\%$, find the present value on March 20, 1973, of payments of $25 per quarter; the first payment is June 20, 1975, and the last payment is March 20, 1985.

b) Rework (a) assuming $i^{(4)} = 4\%$.

c) By general reasoning, justify the relative magnitudes of the answers to (a) and (b).

10. Express $\ddot{a}_{\overline{n}|}^{(12)}$ in terms of $a_{\overline{n}|}^{(2)}$ with an adjustment factor.

11. A man deposits \$50 at the end of each quarter for 10 years. Find the total amount of interest that he has accumulated at the end of 10 years if $i = .045$ for the first five years and $i^{(2)} = .05$ for the second five years.

12. Show algebraically and verbally that

$$a_{\overline{n}|}^{(m)} = \frac{1}{m} \sum_{t=1}^{m} \left. \frac{t}{m} \right| \ddot{a}_{\overline{n}|} .$$

13. Show algebraically and verbally that

$$a_{\overline{n}|}^{(4)} = \tfrac{1}{2} \left[a_{\overline{n}|}^{(2)} + \tfrac{1}{4} \left| \ddot{a}_{\overline{n}|}^{(2)} \right. \right] .$$

14. Use Appendix II to find values to three decimals for the following if $i = .03$:

a) $v^{\frac{100}{12}}$.

b) $(1 + i)^{\frac{100}{12}}$.

c) $12a_{\frac{100}{12}|}^{(12)}$.

d) $12\ddot{a}_{\frac{100}{12}|}^{(12)}$.

e) $12s_{\frac{100}{12}|}^{(12)}$.

f) $12\ddot{s}_{\frac{100}{12}|}^{(12)}$.

15. Find an expression for the present value of an annuity which pays 1 at the beginning of each 3-month period for 12 years, assuming a rate of interest per 4-month period.

4.4. Continuous annuities

16. a) Find an expression for $\bar{a}_{\overline{n}|}$ analogous to formula (3.26).

    b) Find an expression for $\bar{s}_{\overline{n}|}$ analogous to formula (3.27).

17. Find the value of t, $0 < t < 1$, such that \$100 paid at time t is equivalent to \$100 paid continuously throughout a one-year period of time.

18. a) Show that $\dfrac{d}{dn} \bar{s}_{\overline{n}|} = 1 + \delta\bar{s}_{\overline{n}|}$.

    b) Verbally interpret the result obtained in (a).

19. *a)* Find an expression for $\bar{a}_{\overline{n}|}$, assuming simple interest.

   b) Find an expression for $\bar{a}_{\overline{n}|}$ if $\delta_t = \dfrac{1}{1+t}$.

20. Show algebraically and verbally that $a_{\overline{n}|} < a_{\overline{n}|}^{(m)} < \bar{a}_{\overline{n}|} < \ddot{a}_{\overline{n}|}^{(m)} < \ddot{a}_{\overline{n}|}$.

4.5. Unknown time and unknown rate of interest

21. A man has \$40,000 in a fund which is accumulating at 4% per annum convertible continuously. If he withdraws money continuously at the rate of \$2400 per annum, how long will the fund last? Assume $\log_e 3 = 1.1$.

22. A sum of \$1000 is used to buy a deferred perpetuity-due paying \$50 every six months forever. Find an expression for the deferred period expressed as a function of d.

23. A sum of \$100 is placed into a fund at the beginning of every other year for eight years. If the fund balance at the end of eight years is \$520, find the rate of simple interest earned by the fund.

4.6. Elementary varying annuities

24. Simplify $\displaystyle\sum_{t=1}^{20} (t+5)v^t$.

25. Under an annuity the first payment of n is made after one year, the second payment of $n-1$ after two years, and so forth, until a payment of p is made, after which payments cease. Show that the present value of the annuity is

$$pa_{\overline{n-p+1}|} + \frac{(n-p) - a_{\overline{n-p}|}}{i}.$$

26. Find the present value of a perpetuity under which a payment of 1 is made at the end of the first year, 2 at the end of the second year, increasing until a payment of n is made at the end of the nth year, and thereafter payments are level at n per year forever.

27. The following payments are made under an annuity: \$10 at the end of the fifth year, \$9 at the end of the sixth year, decreasing by \$1 each year until nothing is paid. Show that the present value is

$$\frac{10 - a_{\overline{14}|} + a_{\overline{4}|}(1 - 10i)}{i}.$$

28. Find an expression for the amount which must be placed into a fund at the beginning of every five-year period for the next 20 years to provide for a 10-year increasing annuity-due which begins at the end of 20 years for \$200 and increases by \$200 per year thereafter until all 10 payments have been made.

29. Derive formula (4.37) by the method of Example 4.11.

30. Find the present value to the nearest dollar at $3\frac{1}{4}$% effective of a perpetuity in which the first payment of \$1000 is due immediately and in which each successive payment is 10% less than the payment for the preceding year.

31. Find the present value to the nearest dollar at 4% effective of a 20-year annuity-immediate whose successive payments are 1, 4, 9, . . . , 400.

4.7. More general varying annuities

32. Derive formula (4.45).
33. *a*) Derive a formula for the perpetuity which is a limiting case of formula (4.42).
    b) Derive a formula for the perpetuity which is a limiting case of formula (4.43).
34. Show that the present value of a perpetuity on which payments are 1 at the end of the 5th and 6th years, 2 at the end of the 7th and 8th years, 3 at the end of the 9th and 10th years, . . . , is

$$\frac{v^4}{i - vd}.$$

35. A 10-year annuity has the following payments for calendar years 1970 through 1979:

$$
\begin{aligned}
&\text{On each January 1} \ldots\ldots\ldots\ldots\ldots\ldots\$100 \\
&\text{On each April 1} \ldots\ldots\ldots\ldots\ldots\ldots\ 200 \\
&\text{On each July 1} \ldots\ldots\ldots\ldots\ldots\ldots\ 300 \\
&\text{On each October 1} \ldots\ldots\ldots\ldots\ldots\ 400
\end{aligned}
$$

Show that the present value of this annuity on January 1, 1970, is

$$1600\ddot{a}_{\overline{10}|}(I^{(4)}\ddot{a})^{(4)}_{\overline{1}|}.$$

4.8. Continuous varying annuities

36. *a*) Find an integral expression for $(\bar{D}\bar{a})_{\overline{n}|}$.
    b) Find an expression not involving integrals for $(\bar{D}\bar{a})_{\overline{n}|}$.
37. A perpetuity is payable continuously at the annual rate of $1 + t^2$ at time t. If $\delta = .05$, find the present value of the perpetuity.
38. A one-year deferred continuous varying annuity is payable for 13 years. The rate of payment at time t is $t^2 - 1$ per annum, and the force of interest at time t is $(1 + t)^{-1}$. Find the present value of the annuity.

Miscellaneous problems

39. *a*) (1) Show that $\dfrac{d}{di} a_{\overline{n}|} = -v(Ia)_{\overline{n}|}$.

    (2) Find $\dfrac{d}{di} a_{\overline{n}|}$ evaluated at $i = 0$.

    b) (1) Show that $\dfrac{d}{di} \bar{a}_{\overline{n}|} = -v(\bar{I}\bar{a})_{\overline{n}|}$.

    (2) Find $\dfrac{d}{di} \bar{a}_{\overline{n}|}$ evaluated at $i = 0$.

40. Using the result of Exercise 39(*a*)(1) and the theory of finite differences, show that

$$(Ia)_{\overline{n}|} = -\frac{1+i}{\Delta i}\left(\Delta a_{\overline{n}|} - \tfrac{1}{2}\Delta^2 a_{\overline{n}|} + \tfrac{1}{3}\Delta^3 a_{\overline{n}|} - \cdots\right)$$

where the interval of differencing is Δi.

41. If i is a standard rate of interest for which functional values are tabulated and j is a rate of interest close to i for which functional values are not tabulated, use the result of Exercise $39(a)(1)$ to show that approximate annuity values can be obtained by

$$a_{\overline{n}|j} = a_{\overline{n}|i} - \frac{j-i}{1+i}(Ia)_{\overline{n}|i}.$$

42. Show that $\dfrac{d}{dn}\,a_{\overline{n}|} = \dfrac{v^n}{s_{\overline{1}|}}.$

43. Derive an expression for the present value of an annuity on which payments are 1, 2, 1, 2, 1, 2, etc., at the end of every year for the next 29 years.

44. Evaluate $\displaystyle\sum_{t=1}^{10} s_{\overline{t}|}$ if $s_{\overline{10}|} = 15.9$ and if $i = 10\%$.

45. a) Show that $\dfrac{i}{i^{(m)}} = \dfrac{1}{1 - \dfrac{m-1}{2m}i} = 1 + \dfrac{m-1}{2m}i,$

   where all equalities are approximate.

   b) Derive the following approximate equality:

$$a_{\overline{n}|}^{(m)} = a_{\overline{n}|} + \frac{m-1}{2m}(1-v^n).$$

46. For a given n, it is known that $\bar{a}_{\overline{n}|} = n - 4$ and $\delta = 10\%$. Find $\displaystyle\int_0^n \bar{a}_{\overline{t}|}\,dt$.

47. Given that $s_{\overline{n}|} = 20$ and $i = .05$, find $_n|\bar{a}_{\overline{n}|}$.

48. The last payment under an annuity represented by $a_{n+\frac{1}{12}|}^{(4)}$ is taken as $\dfrac{1}{12}$.

   Show that the error involved in this assumption is

$$\frac{1}{12}\left[1 - \frac{i^{(12)}}{i^{(4)}}\right].$$

49. Show that

$$i^2 \sum_{n=1}^{20}(Is)_{\overline{n}|} = (1+i)\,\ddot{s}_{\overline{20}|} - 20 - 230i.$$

50. A father wishes to provide an annuity of \$100 at the end of each month to his son now entering college. The annuity will be paid for only nine months each year for four years. Prove that the present value one month before the first payment is

$$1200\ddot{a}_{\overline{4}|}a_{\frac{9}{12}|}^{(12)}.$$

51. Show that

$$\sum_{r=1}^{h} (a_{\overline{r}|} + s_{\overline{r}|}) = \frac{1}{i}\left(\frac{s_{\overline{h}|}}{a_{\overline{1}|}} - \frac{a_{\overline{h}|}}{s_{\overline{1}|}}\right).$$

52. There are two perpetuities. The first has level payments of p at the end of each year. The second is increasing such that the payments are q, $2q$, $3q$, . . . Find the rate of interest which will make the difference in present value between these perpetuities:

   a) Zero.

   b) A maximum.

53. Fence posts set in soil last 9 years and cost \$2. Posts set in concrete last 15 years and cost \$2 + x. The posts will be needed for 35 years. Show that the break-even value of x, i.e., the value at which a buyer would be indifferent between the two types of posts, is

$$2\left(\frac{a_{\overline{36}|}\, a_{\overline{15}|}}{a_{\overline{9}|}\, a_{\overline{45}|}} - 1\right).$$

54. Show algebraically and by means of a time diagram the following relationship between $(Ia)_{\overline{n}|}$ and $(Da)_{\overline{n}|}$:

$$(Da)_{\overline{n}|} = (n+1)a_{\overline{n}|} - (Ia)_{\overline{n}|}.$$

CHAPTER 5. Amortization schedules and sinking funds

5.1. INTRODUCTION

In Chapter 5 various methods of repaying a loan are analyzed in more depth than in previous chapters. In particular, two methods of repaying a loan are discussed:

1. *The amortization method.* In this method the borrower repays the lender by means of installment payments at periodic intervals. This process is called "amortization" of the loan.
2. *The sinking fund method.* In this method the borrower repays the lender by means of one lump-sum payment at the end of a specified period of time. The borrower pays interest on the loan periodically over this period. It is also assumed that the borrower makes periodic payments into a fund, called a "sinking fund," which will accumulate to the amount of the loan to be repaid at the end of the specified period of time.

Chapter 5 also considers the following questions which are related to the repayment methods mentioned above:

1. How can the outstanding principal, i.e., the outstanding loan indebtedness, at any given point in time be determined?
2. How can any payments made by the borrower be divided into repayment of principal and payment of interest?
3. How can yield rates to an investor be calculated for the various financial transactions under consideration?

Sections 5.2 and 5.3 are restricted to a consideration of the amortization method. Section 5.4 is restricted to a consideration of the sinking fund method. Succeeding sections consider both methods in greater depth, as well as other related topics.

5.2. FINDING THE OUTSTANDING PRINCIPAL

If a loan is being repaid by the amortization method, the installment payments form an annuity whose present value is equal to the amount of principal at the inception date of the loan. Section 5.2 is concerned with determining the amount of the outstanding principal at any point in time after the inception date of the loan.

Determining the amount of the outstanding principal can be of great significance in practice. For example, if a man is buying a home with a 20-year mortgage, after making mortgage payments for 12 years, how much would he have to pay in one lump sum in order to completely repay the mortgage?

There are two approaches used in finding the amount of the outstanding principal, the prospective method and the retrospective method. The names chosen are appropriate, since the prospective method calculates the outstanding principal looking into the future, while the retrospective method calculates the outstanding principal looking into the past.

According to the *prospective method*, the outstanding principal at any point in time is equal to the present value at that date of the remaining payments. According to the *retrospective method*, the outstanding principal at any point in time is equal to the original principal accumulated to that date less the accumulated value at that date of all payments previously made.

It is possible to show that in general, the prospective and retrospective methods are equivalent. At the inception date of the loan we have the following equality:

Present Value of Payments = Amount of Loan.

We can accumulate each side of this equation to the date at which the outstanding principal is desired, obtaining:

Current Value of Payments = Accumulated Value of Loan.

However, the payments can be divided into past and future payments giving:

Accumulated Value of Past Payments + Present Value of Future Payments = Accumulated Value of Loan.

Now, rearranging, we obtain:

Present Value of Future Payments = Accumulated Value of Loan − Accumulated Value of Past Payments, or,

$$\text{Prospective Method} = \text{Retrospective Method.}$$

In specific cases it is possible to show the above result algebraically. For example, consider a loan of $a_{\overline{n}|}$ being repaid with payments of 1 at the end of each year for n years, for which the outstanding principal t years after the inception date of the loan is desired $(t < n)$. The prospective method gives

$$a_{\overline{n-t}|} \, . \tag{5.1}$$

The retrospective method gives

$$a_{\overline{n}|} \, (1 + i)^t - s_{\overline{t}|} \, . \tag{5.2}$$

We can show that the retrospective form is equal to the prospective form as follows:

$$
\begin{aligned}
a_{\overline{n}|}(1 + i)^t - s_{\overline{t}|} &= \frac{1 - v^n}{i} (1 + i)^t - \frac{(1 + i)^t - 1}{i} \\
&= \frac{(1 + i)^t - v^{n-t} - (1 + i)^t + 1}{i} \\
&= \frac{1 - v^{n-t}}{i} \\
&= a_{\overline{n-t}|} \, .
\end{aligned}
$$

In a given problem the prospective method or the retrospective method may be more efficient depending upon the nature of the problem. If the size and number of payments are known, then the prospective method is usually more efficient. If the number of payments or the size of a final irregular payment is not known, then the retrospective method is usually more efficient.

Example 5.1.   A loan is being repaid with 10 payments of $20 followed by 10 payments of $10 at the end of each year. If the effective rate of interest is 5%, find the outstanding principal after five years by both the prospective method and the retrospective method.

1. Prospectively, the outstanding principal is

$$10(a_{\overline{15}|} + a_{\overline{5}|}) = 10(10.3797 + 4.3295) = \$147.09 \, .$$

2. The original loan was

$$10(a_{\overline{20}|} + a_{\overline{10}|}) = 10(12.4622 + 7.7217) = \$201.84 \, .$$

Retrospectively, the outstanding principal is

$$
\begin{aligned}
201.84(1.05)^5 - 20s_{\overline{5}|} &= 201.84(1.27628) - 20(5.5256) \\
&= 257.60 - 110.51 = \$147.09 \, .
\end{aligned}
$$

Thus, the prospective and retrospective methods produce the same result.

Example 5.2. *A loan is being repaid with 20 payments of $100 each. At the time of the 5th payment, the borrower wishes to pay an extra $200 and then repay the balance over an additional 12 years with a revised annual payment. If the effective rate of interest is $4\frac{1}{2}\%$, find the amount of the revised annual payment.*

The balance after five years, prospectively, is

$$100a_{\overline{15}|} = 100(10.7395) = \$1073.95 .$$

If he pays an additional $200, the balance is $873.95. An equation of value for the revised payment, denoted by R, is

$$Ra_{\overline{12}|} = \$873.95 .$$
$$R = \frac{873.95}{9.1186} = \$95.84 .$$

5.3. AMORTIZATION SCHEDULES

If a loan is being repaid by the amortization method, each payment is partially repayment of principal and partially payment of interest. Section 5.3 is concerned with determining how each payment can be divided into principal and interest.

Determining the amount of principal and interest contained in each payment is important to both the borrower and lender. For example, in the United States interest payments are considered as income to the lender and are deductible on the income tax return of the borrower unless the borrower claims the standard deduction. Principal repayments are not reflected on the income tax return of either party.

An *amortization schedule* is a table which shows the division of each payment into principal and interest, together with the outstanding principal after each payment is made. Consider a loan of $a_{\overline{n}|}$ being repaid with payments of 1 at the end of each year for n years. Table 5.1 is an amortization schedule for this case.

Consider the first year of the loan. At the end of the first year the interest due on the balance at the beginning of the year is $ia_{\overline{n}|} = 1 - v^n$. The rest of the total payment of 1, i.e., v^n, must be principal repaid. The outstanding principal at the end of the year equals the outstanding principal at the beginning of the year less the principal repaid, i.e., $a_{\overline{n}|} - v^n = a_{\overline{n-1}|}$. The same reasoning applies for each successive year of the schedule.

Several additional observations are possible. First, it should be noted that the outstanding principal agrees with that obtained by the prospective method in formula (5.1). Second, the sum of the principal repayments equals the original principal. Third, the sum of the interest payments is equal to the difference in the sum of the total payments and the principal repayments. Fourth, the principal repayments form a geometric progression with common ratio $1 + i$. Thus, it is a simple matter to find any one principal repayment knowing any other principal repayment and the rate of interest.

Further insight into the nature of the amortization schedule can be gained by the following argument. The original principal of $a_{\overline{n}|}$ will accumulate to $a_{\overline{n}|}(1 + i) = \ddot{a}_{\overline{n}|}$ at the end of the first year. However, $\ddot{a}_{\overline{n}|} = 1 + a_{\overline{n-1}|}$, i.e., $\ddot{a}_{\overline{n}|}$ is sufficient to make the annuity payment of 1 and leave an outstanding balance of $a_{\overline{n-1}|}$ at the end of the first year. The same reasoning applies for each successive year of the schedule.

TABLE 5.1

Duration	Payment Amount	Interest Paid	Principal Repaid	Outstanding Principal
0				$a_{\overline{n}|}$
1	1	$ia_{\overline{n}|} = 1 - v^n$	v^n	$a_{\overline{n}|} - v^n = a_{\overline{n-1}|}$
2	1	$ia_{\overline{n-1}|} = 1 - v^{n-1}$	v^{n-1}	$a_{\overline{n-1}|} - v^{n-1} = a_{\overline{n-2}|}$
.	.	.	.	.
.	.	.	.	.
.	.	.	.	.
t	1	$ia_{\overline{n-t+1}|} = 1 - v^{n-t+1}$	v^{n-t+1}	$a_{\overline{n-t+1}|} - v^{n-t+1} = a_{\overline{n-t}|}$
.	.	.	.	.
.	.	.	.	.
$n - 1$	1	$ia_{\overline{2}|} = 1 - v^2$	v^2	$a_{\overline{2}|} - v^2 = a_{\overline{1}|}$
n	1	$ia_{\overline{1}|} = 1 - v$	v	$a_{\overline{1}|} - v = 0$
Total	n	$n - a_{\overline{n}|}$	$a_{\overline{n}|}$	

It should be noted that Table 5.1 is based on an original principal of $a_{\overline{n}|}$. If the original principal were some other amount, then all the values in the schedule would be proportional. For example, if the original principal were \$1000, then each number in the schedule would be multiplied by $\dfrac{1000}{a_{\overline{n}|}}$.

For a specific problem, the amortization schedule can be constructed from basic principles. For example, consider the construction of an amortization schedule for a \$1000 loan repaid in four annual payments if the effective rate of interest is 4%. Let R be the installment payment. Then,

$$R = \frac{1000}{a_{\overline{4}|}} = 1000\left(\frac{1}{s_{\overline{4}|}} + .04\right) = 1000(.235490 + .040000) = \$275.49 \,.$$

Table 5.2 is the amortization schedule for this example. The student should reproduce Table 5.2 making certain of the method of calculation for each entry in the table.

TABLE 5.2

Duration	Payment Amount	Interest Paid	Principal Repaid	Outstanding Principal
0				1000.00
1	275.49	40.00	235.49	764.51
2	275.49	30.58	244.91	519.60
3	275.49	20.78	254.71	264.89
4	275.49	10.60	264.89	0

It is possible to construct the amortization schedule by alternate methods utilizing the various relationships in the table. As one example, the values of outstanding principal can be calculated as in Section 5.2, and then the rest of the schedule can be deduced from these values. As a second example, the principal repaid column can be calculated using the fact that the successive values are in geometric progression, and then the rest of the schedule can be deduced from these values. In practice, one of these alternate methods may prove to be more efficient if a large number of calculations are to be performed by hand.

It should be noted that if it is desired to find the amount of principal and interest in any one payment, it is not necessary to construct the entire amortization schedule. The outstanding principal at the beginning of the period in question can be determined by the methods of Section 5.2, and then that one line of the amortization schedule can be calculated.

Several assumptions have been implicit in the preceding discussion of amortization schedules. First, we have assumed a constant rate of interest. An amortization schedule at a varying rate of interest will be considered in the exercises. Second, we have assumed that the annuity payment period and the interest conversion period are equal. The cases in which they are not equal will be considered in Section 5.5. Third, we have assumed that annuity payments are level. The situation in which they are level except for a final irregular payment will be considered in Example 5.3 and in the exercises. The general case of a varying series of payments will be considered in Section 5.6.

Example 5.3. A $1000 loan is being repaid by annual payments of $100 at the end of each year for as long as necessary, plus a smaller *final payment. If the effective rate of interest is 4%, find the amount of principal and interest in the fourth payment.*

The outstanding principal at the beginning of the fourth year (the end of the third year) is, retrospectively,

$$1000(1.04)^3 - 100s_{\overline{3}|} = 1124.86 - 312.16 = \$812.70 .$$

The interest contained in the fourth payment is

$$.04(812.70) = \$32.51 .$$

The principal contained in the fourth payment is

$$\$100.00 - \$32.51 = \$67.49 .$$

Note that it was not necessary to find the duration and amount of the smaller final payment in order to solve this example.

5.4. SINKING FUNDS

Rather than repay a loan in installments by the amortization method, a borrower may choose to repay it by means of one lump-sum payment at the end of a specified period of time. In many such cases the borrower will accumulate a fund which will be sufficient to exactly repay the loan at the end of the specified period of time. Such a fund is called a sinking fund.

The payments into a sinking fund may vary irregularly at the discretion of the borrower. However, we shall be primarily interested in those cases in which the payments follow a regular pattern, i.e., where they are some form of an annuity.

It is common in practice for the borrower to pay interest on the loan periodically over the period of the loan. Thus, the amount of the loan remains constant.

Since the balance in the sinking fund at any point could presumably be applied against the loan, the net amount of the loan is equal to the original amount of the loan minus the accumulated value of the sinking fund. This concept plays the same role for the sinking fund method that the outstanding principal discussed in Section 5.2 does for the amortization method.

It is possible to show that if the rate of interest paid on the loan equals the rate of interest earned on the sinking fund, then the sinking fund method is equivalent to the amortization method.

Recall formula (3.6),

$$\frac{1}{a_{\overline{n}|}} = \frac{1}{s_{\overline{n}|}} + i . \tag{3.6}$$

Consider a loan of amount 1 repaid over an n-year period. The expression $\dfrac{1}{a_{\overline{n}|}}$ is the amount of each payment necessary to repay the loan by the amortization method. However, the expression $\dfrac{1}{s_{\overline{n}|}}$ is the annual sinking fund deposit necessary to accumulate the amount of the loan at the end of n years, while i is the amount of interest paid on the loan each year. Thus, the two methods are clearly equivalent.

It is instructive to consider this equivalence from an alternate viewpoint. Consider a loan of amount $a_{\overline{n}|}$ being repaid with annual installments of 1 at the end of each year for n years. The amount of interest each year is $ia_{\overline{n}|}$. Thus, $1 - ia_{\overline{n}|}$ is left to go into the sinking fund each year. However, the sinking fund will accumulate to

$$(1 - ia_{\overline{n}|})s_{\overline{n}|} = v^n s_{\overline{n}|} = a_{\overline{n}|}\,,$$

which is the original amount of the loan.

At first glance it might seem that the two methods cannot be equivalent, since from Table 5.2, the interest paid in the amortization method decreases $1 - v^n, 1 - v^{n-1}, \ldots, 1 - v$; whereas, the interest paid in the sinking fund method is a constant $ia_{\overline{n}|} = 1 - v^n$ each year. However, each year the sinking fund earns interest which exactly offsets the seeming discrepancy so that the net amount of interest is the same for the sinking fund method as for the amortization method.

For example, during the tth year $(t \leq n)$ the amount of interest in the amortization schedule is

$$ia_{\overline{n-t+1}|} = 1 - v^{n-t+1}\,.$$

The net amount of interest in the sinking fund method is the amount of interest paid, $ia_{\overline{n}|}$, less the amount of interest earned on the sinking fund. The amount in the sinking fund is the accumulated value of the sinking fund deposits of $1 - ia_{\overline{n}|}$ at the end of $t - 1$ years, i.e.,

$$(1 - ia_{\overline{n}|})s_{\overline{t-1}|}\,.$$

Thus, the net amount of interest in the sinking fund method in the tth year is

$$\begin{aligned}
ia_{\overline{n}|} - i(1 - ia_{\overline{n}|})s_{\overline{t-1}|} &= (1 - v^n) - v^n\left[(1 + i)^{t-1} - 1\right] \\
&= 1 - v^n - v^{n-t+1} + v^n \\
&= 1 - v^{n-t+1}\,.
\end{aligned}$$

Therefore, the net amount of interest in the sinking fund method is equal to the amount of interest in the amortization method if the rate of interest on the loan equals the rate of interest earned on the sinking fund.

The equivalence in the methods can be seen from a consideration of a *sinking fund schedule*. Table 5.3 is a sinking fund schedule for the same example considered in Table 5.2. The sinking fund deposit is $\dfrac{1000}{s_{\overline{4}|}} =$ 1000(.235490) = \$235.49. The student should verify the entries in Table 5.3.

TABLE 5.3

Duration	Interest Paid	Sinking Fund Deposit	Interest Earned on Sinking Fund	Amount in Sinking Fund	Net Amount of Loan
0					1000.00
1	40.00	235.49	0	235.49	764.51
2	40.00	235.49	9.42	480.40	519.60
3	40.00	235.49	19.22	735.11	264.89
4	40.00	235.49	29.40	1000.00	0

The following relationships between Table 5.2 and Table 5.3 should be noted:

1. The total payment in the sinking fund method, i.e., interest paid plus the sinking fund deposit, equals the payment amount in the amortization method.
2. The net interest paid in the sinking fund method, i.e., interest paid minus interest earned on the sinking fund, equals the interest paid in the amortization method.
3. The annual increment in the sinking fund, i.e., the sinking fund deposit plus the interest earned on the sinking fund, equals the principal repaid in the amortization method.
4. The net amount of the loan in the sinking fund method, i.e., the amount of the loan minus the amount in the sinking fund, equals the outstanding principal in the amortization method.

It now remains to consider the sinking fund method where the rate of interest earned on the sinking fund differs from the rate of interest paid on the loan. The rate of interest earned on the sinking fund is sometimes called the *reproductive rate of interest* and is denoted by i. The rate of interest paid on the loan is sometimes called the *remunerative rate of interest* and is denoted by i'.

In practice i is usually less than or equal to i'. It would be unusual for a borrower to be able to accumulate money in a sinking fund at a higher rate of interest than he is paying on a loan. However, this is not necessarily the case mathematically, and the following analysis is valid if i is greater than i'.

The same basic approach will be used for the case in which $i' \neq i$ as was previously used in the case in which the two rates were equal. The total payment will be split into two parts. First, interest at rate i' will be paid on the amount of the loan. Second, the remainder of the total payment not needed for interest will be placed into a sinking fund accumulating at rate i.

Let $a_{\overline{n}|i'\&i}$ represent the present value of an annuity of 1 at the end of each year for n years under the conditions just described. Then if a loan of 1 is made, the annual installment under the amortization method will be $\dfrac{1}{a_{\overline{n}|i'\&i}}$. However, from the sinking fund method this payment must pay interest at rate i' on the loan and provide for a sinking fund deposit which will accumulate at rate i to the amount of the loan at the end of n years. Thus,

$$\frac{1}{a_{\overline{n}|i'\&i}} = \frac{1}{s_{\overline{n}|i}} + i' . \tag{5.3}$$

We can now find an expression for $a_{\overline{n}|i'\&i}$ as follows:

$$\frac{1}{a_{\overline{n}|i'\&i}} = \frac{1}{s_{\overline{n}|i}} + i'$$
$$= \frac{1}{a_{\overline{n}|i}} + (i' - i) . \tag{5.4}$$

Thus,

$$a_{\overline{n}|i'\&i} = \frac{a_{\overline{n}|i}}{1 + (i' - i)a_{\overline{n}|i}} . \tag{5.5}$$

It should be noted that if $i' = i$, then $a_{\overline{n}|i'\&i} = a_{\overline{n}|i}$, as would be expected.

An alternate expression for $a_{\overline{n}|i'\&i}$ can be derived by noticing that each sinking fund deposit is

$$\frac{1}{a_{\overline{n}|i'\&i}} - i' ,$$

which must accumulate at rate i to the loan of 1. Thus,

$$\left(\frac{1}{a_{\overline{n}|i'\&i}} - i' \right) s_{\overline{n}|i} = 1 ,$$

or

$$a_{\overline{n}|i'\&i} = \frac{s_{\overline{n}|i}}{1 + i' \, s_{\overline{n}|i}} . \tag{5.6}$$

The construction of a sinking fund schedule at two rates of interest is very similar to the construction of a sinking fund schedule at a single rate of interest. As an example, consider a $1000 loan for four years on which interest of $4\frac{1}{2}\%$ effective is charged if the borrower accumulates the principal by means of four annual sinking fund deposits in a fund earning 4% effective. The annual deposit is

$$\frac{1000}{a_{\overline{4}|.045\,\&\,.04}} = \frac{1000}{s_{\overline{4}|.04}} + 1000(.045)$$
$$= 235.49 + 45.00 = \$280.49.$$

This example is a generalization of the example considered in Table 5.3. Note that the sinking fund schedule would be identical to Table 5.3, except that each entry in the interest paid column is $45 instead of $40.

In general, the sinking fund schedule at two rates of interest is identical to the sinking fund schedule at one rate of interest which is equal to the rate of interest earned on the sinking fund, except that a constant addition of $(i' - i)$ times the amount of the loan is added to the interest paid column.

Table 5.4 is a sinking fund schedule in which a loan of 1 is being repaid with n annual installments of $\dfrac{1}{a_{\overline{n}|i'\&i}}$. All interest functions are at effective rate i unless primed. The student should verify the entries in Table 5.4.

It remains to determine how each payment of a borrower in the sinking fund method should be split between principal and interest.

The net amount of interest paid in the tth installment $(t \leq n)$ is equal to the interest paid less the interest earned on the sinking fund, i.e.,

$$i' - i\frac{s_{\overline{t-1}|}}{s_{\overline{n}|}}. \tag{5.7}$$

This expression can alternatively be derived as the amount of interest in an amortization schedule at rate i in which the original amount of the loan is 1 instead of $a_{\overline{n}|}$, plus the additional interest at rate $i' - i$ on the loan of 1. Thus, we have

$$\frac{1}{a_{\overline{n}|}}(1 - v^{n-t+1}) + (i' - i) = \frac{1 - v^{n-t+1} + i'a_{\overline{n}|} - 1 + v^n}{a_{\overline{n}|}}$$
$$= \frac{i'a_{\overline{n}|} + v^n(1 - v^{-t+1})}{a_{\overline{n}|}}$$
$$= i' - i\frac{s_{\overline{t-1}|}}{s_{\overline{n}|}}. \tag{5.7}$$

The amount of principal repaid in the tth installment $(t \leq n)$ is equal to the total payment less the amount of interest paid. Thus, we have

$$\left(\frac{1}{s_{\overline{n}|}} + i'\right) - \left(i' - i\,\frac{s_{\overline{t-1}|}}{s_{\overline{n}|}}\right) = \frac{1 + is_{\overline{t-1}|}}{s_{\overline{n}|}}$$
$$= \frac{(1+i)^{t-1}}{s_{\overline{n}|}}. \tag{5.8}$$

TABLE 5.4

Dura-tion	Interest Paid	Sinking Fund Deposit	Interest Earned on Sinking Fund	Amount in Sinking Fund	Net Amount of Loan
0					1
1	i'	$\dfrac{1}{s_{\overline{n}|}}$	0	$\dfrac{1}{s_{\overline{n}|}} = \dfrac{s_{\overline{1}|}}{s_{\overline{n}|}}$	$1 - \dfrac{s_{\overline{1}|}}{s_{\overline{n}|}}$
2	i'	$\dfrac{1}{s_{\overline{n}|}}$	$\dfrac{is_{\overline{1}|}}{s_{\overline{n}|}}$	$\dfrac{s_{\overline{1}|}(1+i)+1}{s_{\overline{n}|}} = \dfrac{s_{\overline{2}|}}{s_{\overline{n}|}}$	$1 - \dfrac{s_{\overline{2}|}}{s_{\overline{n}|}}$
.	.	.	.	.	.
.	.	.	.	.	.
.	.	.	.	.	.
t	i'	$\dfrac{1}{s_{\overline{n}|}}$	$\dfrac{is_{\overline{t-1}|}}{s_{\overline{n}|}}$	$\dfrac{s_{\overline{t-1}|}(1+i)+1}{s_{\overline{n}|}} = \dfrac{s_{\overline{t}|}}{s_{\overline{n}|}}$	$1 - \dfrac{s_{\overline{t}|}}{s_{\overline{n}|}}$
.	.	.	.	.	.
.	.	.	.	.	.
.	.	.	.	.	.
$n-1$	i'	$\dfrac{1}{s_{\overline{n}|}}$	$\dfrac{is_{\overline{n-2}|}}{s_{\overline{n}|}}$	$\dfrac{s_{\overline{n-2}|}(1+i)+1}{s_{\overline{n}|}} = \dfrac{s_{\overline{n-1}|}}{s_{\overline{n}|}}$	$1 - \dfrac{s_{\overline{n-1}|}}{s_{\overline{n}|}}$
n	i'	$\dfrac{1}{s_{\overline{n}|}}$	$\dfrac{is_{\overline{n-1}|}}{s_{\overline{n}|}}$	$\dfrac{s_{\overline{n-1}|}(1+i)+1}{s_{\overline{n}|}} = \dfrac{s_{\overline{n}|}}{s_{\overline{n}|}} = 1$	$1 - \dfrac{s_{\overline{n}|}}{s_{\overline{n}|}} = 0$
Total	ni'	$\dfrac{n}{s_{\overline{n}|}}$	$\dfrac{s_{\overline{n}|} - n}{s_{\overline{n}|}} = 1 - \dfrac{n}{s_{\overline{n}|}}$		

This expression can alternatively be derived by using the fact that the amount of principal repaid in any installment is equal to the increment in the sinking fund for that year. The increment in the sinking fund for the tth year is the balance at time t minus the balance at time $t - 1$, i.e.,

$$\frac{s_{\overline{t}|}}{s_{\overline{n}|}} - \frac{s_{\overline{t-1}|}}{s_{\overline{n}|}} = \frac{(1+i)^{t-1}}{s_{\overline{n}|}}. \tag{5.8}$$

It should be noted that formula (5.8) is independent of i', i.e., the amount of principal repaid is not dependent upon i'.

It is instructive to show that Table 5.4 is equivalent to Table 5.1 if $i' = i$. Since the amount of the loan in Table 5.1 is $a_{\overline{n}|}$, the entries from

Table 5.4 must be multiplied by $a_{\overline{n}|}$ to show this equivalence. For the tth installment $(t \leq n)$, we have the following:

Table 5.1	Table 5.4
Payment amount.......1	$a_{\overline{n}|}\left[i + \dfrac{1}{s_{\overline{n}|}} \right] = \dfrac{a_{\overline{n}|}}{a_{\overline{n}|}} = 1$
Interest paid...........$1 - v^{n-t+1}$	$a_{\overline{n}|}\left[\dfrac{is_{\overline{n}|} - is_{\overline{t-1}|}}{s_{\overline{n}|}} \right] = \dfrac{(1+i)^n - (1+i)^{t-1}}{(1+i)^n} = 1 - v^{n-t+1}$
Principal repaid........v^{n-t+1}	$a_{\overline{n}|}\left[\dfrac{(1+i)^{t-1}}{s_{\overline{n}|}} \right] = \dfrac{(1+i)^{t-1}}{(1+i)^n} = v^{n-t+1}$
Outstanding principal...$a_{\overline{n-t}|}$	$a_{\overline{n}|}\left[\dfrac{s_{\overline{n}|} - s_{\overline{t}|}}{s_{\overline{n}|}} \right] = \dfrac{(1+i)^n - (1+i)^t}{i(1+i)^n} = \dfrac{1 - v^{n-t}}{i} = a_{\overline{n-t}|}$

Example 5.4.   A man wishes to borrow $1000. One lender offers a loan in which the principal is to be repaid at the end of four years. In the meantime $4\frac{1}{2}\%$ effective is to be paid on the loan and the borrower is to accumulate the principal by means of a sinking fund earning 4% effective. Another lender offers a loan for four years in which the borrower repays the principal by the amortization method. What is the largest rate of interest that this lender can charge so that the borrower is indifferent between the two offers?

Under either method the borrower will make four equal payments at the end of each year to repay the loan. Thus, he will be indifferent between the two offers if his annual payment is equal on both of them.

On the sinking fund offer his annual payment is

$$\frac{1000}{a_{\overline{4}|.045\ \&.04}} = \$280.49 ,$$

as shown earlier in this section. Thus, on the amortization offer the lender could charge i where

$$280.49a_{\overline{4}|i} = 1000$$
$$a_{\overline{4}|i} = 3.5652 .$$

Now from the interest tables:

$$a_{\overline{4}|.045} = 3.5875$$
$$a_{\overline{4}|.05} = 3.5460$$

and performing a linear interpolation

$$i = .0450 + .0050\,\frac{3.5652 - 3.5875}{3.5460 - 3.5875} = .0477 .$$

In essence we have shown that

$$a_{\overline{4}|.045\ \&.04} = a_{\overline{4}|.0477} .$$

This example illustrates that to a borrower the total annual payment is of primary concern and that the difference between the amortization method and the sinking fund method is somewhat artificial.

The student may find the answer of .0477 surprising, since he might have expected the answer to be intermediate between .04 and .045. In general, if the equivalent rate of interest in the amortization method is denoted by i'', we have the following approximate equality:

$$i'' = i' + \tfrac{1}{2}(i' - i) .$$

This formula would produce an answer for this example of $.045 + \tfrac{1}{2}(.045 - .04) = .0475$, which is close to the true answer of .0477.

The equivalent rate i'' is greater than i' because the borrower not only is paying i' per unit borrowed but he also is investing in a sinking fund in which he is giving up interest at rate $i' - i$. Since the average balance in the sinking fund per unit borrowed is $\tfrac{1}{2}$, the extra interest cost is approximately $\tfrac{1}{2}(i' - i)$. Thus, the total interest cost per unit borrowed is approximately

$$i' + \tfrac{1}{2}(i' - i) .$$

5.5. DIFFERING PAYMENT PERIODS AND INTEREST CONVERSION PERIODS

In Sections 5.3 and 5.4 it has been assumed that all payment periods and interest conversion periods are equal. Section 5.5 examines the implications of removing this assumption.

We shall first analyze amortization schedules in which payments are made more or less frequently than interest is convertible.

Consider first a loan which is being repaid with payments of 1 at the end of each k interest conversion periods for a total of n interest conversion periods. The number of payments is $\dfrac{n}{k}$, which is integral. Table 5.5 is a generalization of Table 5.1 for this situation. The student should verify the entries in Table 5.5.

Consider next a loan which is being repaid with payments of $\dfrac{1}{m}$ at the end of each mth of an interest conversion period for a total of n interest conversion periods. The number of payments is mn, which is integral. Table 5.6 is a generalization of Table 5.1 for this situation. The student should verify the entries in Table 5.6.

The same observations made of the amortization schedules in Section 5.3 also apply to the amortization schedules in this section. The student is cautioned not to rely too heavily upon the memorization of formulas in amortization and sinking fund schedules, since the reasoning behind these schedules is of primary importance. Any amortization or sinking fund schedule can be constructed from basic principles.

TABLE 5.5

Duration	Payment Amount	Interest Paid	Principal Repaid	Outstanding Principal
0				$\dfrac{a_{\overline{n}|}}{s_{\overline{k}|}}$
k	1	$[(1+i)^k - 1]\dfrac{a_{\overline{n}|}}{s_{\overline{k}|}} = 1 - v^n$	v^n	$\dfrac{a_{\overline{n}|}}{s_{\overline{k}|}} - v^n = \dfrac{a_{\overline{n-k}|}}{s_{\overline{k}|}}$
$2k$	1	$[(1+i)^k - 1]\dfrac{a_{\overline{n-k}|}}{s_{\overline{k}|}} = 1 - v^{n-k}$	v^{n-k}	$\dfrac{a_{\overline{n-k}|}}{s_{\overline{k}|}} - v^{n-k} = \dfrac{a_{\overline{n-2k}|}}{s_{\overline{k}|}}$
$\cdot$ $\cdot$ $\cdot$	$\cdot$	$\cdot$ $\cdot$ $\cdot$	$\cdot$	
tk	1	$[(1+i)^k - 1]\dfrac{a_{\overline{n-(t-1)k}|}}{s_{\overline{k}|}} = 1 - v^{n-(t-1)k}$	$v^{n-(t-1)k}$	$\dfrac{a_{\overline{n-(t-1)k}|}}{s_{\overline{k}|}} - v^{n-(t-1)k} = \dfrac{a_{\overline{n-tk}|}}{s_{\overline{k}|}}$
$\cdot$ $\cdot$ $\cdot$	$\cdot$	$\cdot$ $\cdot$ $\cdot$	$\cdot$	$\cdot$ $\cdot$ $\cdot$
$n - k$	1	$[(1+i)^k - 1]\dfrac{a_{\overline{2k}|}}{s_{\overline{k}|}} = 1 - v^{2k}$	v^{2k}	$\dfrac{a_{\overline{2k}|}}{s_{\overline{k}|}} - v^{2k} = \dfrac{a_{\overline{k}|}}{s_{\overline{k}|}}$
n	1	$[(1+i)^k - 1]\dfrac{a_{\overline{k}|}}{s_{\overline{k}|}} = 1 - v^k$	v^k	$\dfrac{a_{\overline{k}|}}{s_{\overline{k}|}} - v^k = 0$
Total	$\dfrac{n}{k}$	$\dfrac{n}{k} - \dfrac{a_{\overline{n}|}}{s_{\overline{k}|}}$	$\dfrac{a_{\overline{n}|}}{s_{\overline{k}|}}$	

TABLE 5.6

Duration	Payment Amount	Interest Paid	Principal Repaid	Outstanding Principal
0				$a_{\overline{n}|}^{(m)}$
$\dfrac{1}{m}$	$\dfrac{1}{m}$	$\dfrac{i^{(m)}}{m}\,a_{\overline{n}|}^{(m)} = \dfrac{1}{m}\left(1 - v^{n}\right)$	$\dfrac{1}{m}\,v^{n}$	$a_{\overline{n}|}^{(m)} - \dfrac{1}{m}\,v^{n} = a_{\overline{n-\frac{1}{m}}|}^{(m)}$
$\dfrac{2}{m}$	$\dfrac{1}{m}$	$\dfrac{i^{(m)}}{m}\cdot a_{\overline{n-\frac{1}{m}}|}^{(m)} = \dfrac{1}{m}\left(1 - v^{n-\frac{1}{m}}\right)$	$\dfrac{1}{m}\,v^{n-\frac{1}{m}}$	$a_{\overline{n-\frac{1}{m}}|}^{(m)} - \dfrac{1}{m}\,v^{n-\frac{1}{m}} = a_{\overline{n-\frac{2}{m}}|}^{(m)}$
$\cdots$	$\cdots$	$\cdots$	$\cdots$	$\cdots$
$\dfrac{t}{m}$	$\dfrac{1}{m}$	$\dfrac{i^{(m)}}{m}\cdot a_{\overline{n-\frac{t-1}{m}}|}^{(m)} = \dfrac{1}{m}\left(1 - v^{n-\frac{t-1}{m}}\right)$	$\dfrac{1}{m}\,v^{n-\frac{t-1}{m}}$	$a_{\overline{n-\frac{t-1}{m}}|}^{(m)} - \dfrac{1}{m}\,v^{n-\frac{t-1}{m}} = a_{\overline{n-\frac{t}{m}}|}^{(m)}$
$\cdots$	$\cdots$	$\cdots$	$\cdots$	$\cdots$
$n - \dfrac{1}{m}$	$\dfrac{1}{m}$	$\dfrac{i^{(m)}}{m}\,a_{\overline{\frac{2}{m}}|}^{(m)} = \dfrac{1}{m}\left(1 - v^{\frac{2}{m}}\right)$	$\dfrac{1}{m}\,v^{\frac{2}{m}}$	$a_{\overline{\frac{2}{m}}|}^{(m)} - \dfrac{1}{m}\,v^{\frac{2}{m}} = a_{\overline{\frac{1}{m}}|}^{(m)}$
n	$\dfrac{1}{m}$	$\dfrac{i^{(m)}}{m}\,a_{\overline{\frac{1}{m}}|}^{(m)} = \dfrac{1}{m}\left(1 - v^{\frac{1}{m}}\right)$	$\dfrac{1}{m}\,v^{\frac{1}{m}}$	$a_{\overline{\frac{1}{m}}|}^{(m)} - \dfrac{1}{m}\,v^{\frac{1}{m}} = 0$
Total	n	$n - a_{\overline{n}|}^{(m)}$	$a_{\overline{n}|}^{(m)}$	

In the case of sinking funds the situation is a bit more complex, since the frequency of the following may differ: (1) interest payments on the loan, (2) sinking fund deposits, and (3) interest conversion period in the sinking fund.

Cases involving sinking funds with differing frequencies can be handled from basic principles. Example 5.5 is illustrative of this.

Example 5.5. A man wishes to borrow $100 for two years. Construct a sinking fund schedule if he must pay 5% effective on the loan and if he replaces the principal with semiannual deposits in a sinking fund earning 4% convertible quarterly.

In this case all three frequencies vary: (1) interest payments on the loan are made annually, (2) sinking fund deposits are made semiannually, and (3) interest on the sinking fund is convertible quarterly.

The interest payments on the loan are $5 at the end of each year. Let the sinking fund deposit be R. Then

$$R \frac{s_{\overline{8}|.01}}{s_{\overline{2}|.01}} = 100$$

$$R = 100 \frac{s_{\overline{2}|.01}}{s_{\overline{8}|.01}} = 100(2.01)(.12069) = \$24.26 .$$

The sinking fund schedule is as follows:

TABLE 5.7

Duration	Interest Paid	Sinking Fund Deposit	Interest Earned on Sinking Fund	Amount in Sinking Fund	Net Amount of Loan
0					100.00
$\frac{1}{4}$	0	0	0	0	100.00
$\frac{1}{2}$	0	24.26	0	24.26	75.74
$\frac{3}{4}$	0	0	.24	24.50	75.50
1	5.00	24.26	.25	49.01	50.99
$1\frac{1}{4}$	0	0	.49	49.50	50.50
$1\frac{1}{2}$	0	24.26	.49	74.25	25.75
$1\frac{3}{4}$	0	0	.74	74.99	25.01
2	5.00	24.26	.75	100.00	0

Example 5.6. A debt is being amortized by means of monthly payments at an effective rate of interest of 4%. If the amount of principal in the third payment is $100, find the amount of principal in the 33rd payment.

Because of the relationships in Table 5.6, the principal in the 33rd payment is

$$100(1.04)^{2\frac{1}{2}} = 100(1.04)^2(1.04)^{\frac{1}{2}} = 100(1.0816)(1.019804)$$
$$= \$110.30 .$$

5.6. VARYING SERIES OF PAYMENTS

If a loan is being repaid by the amortization method, it is possible that the borrower may repay with installments which are not level. The case in which all the payments are level except for an irregular final payment was considered in Section 5.3. In this section we consider more general patterns of variation.

If a loan L is to be repaid with n annual installments $u_1, u_2, \ldots, u_n$, then we must have

$$L = \sum_{t=1}^{n} v^t u_t .$$ (5.9)

Often the series of payments u_t follow some regular pattern so that the results of Section 4.6 can be used.

If it is desired to construct an amortization schedule, it can be constructed from basic principles as before. Alternatively, the outstanding principal column can be found prospectively or retrospectively as in Section 5.2, and then the interest paid and principal repaid columns can be found directly.

It is also possible to have a varying series of payments with the sinking fund method. We will assume that the interest paid to the lender is constant each year so that only the sinking fund deposits vary.

Assume that the varying annual payments by the borrower are $u_1, u_2, \ldots, u_n$ and that $i \neq i'$. Let the amount of the loan be denoted by L. Then the sinking fund deposit for the tth year is $u_t - i'L$. Since the accumulated value of the sinking fund at the end of n years must be L, we have

$$L = (u_1 - i'L)(1 + i)^{n-1} + (u_2 - i'L)(1 + i)^{n-2} + \cdots + (u_n - i'L)$$

$$= \sum_{t=1}^{n} u_t(1 + i)^{n-t} - i'Ls_{\overline{n}|i}$$

or

$$L = \frac{\displaystyle\sum_{t=1}^{n} u_t(1 + i)^{n-t}}{1 + i's_{\overline{n}|i}} = \frac{\displaystyle\sum_{t=1}^{n} v^t u_t}{1 + (i' - i)a_{\overline{n}|i}} .$$ (5.10)

If $u_t = 1$, then formulas (5.5) and (5.6) are obtained from formula (5.10).

If $i' = i$, then formula (5.10) becomes

$$L = \sum_{t=1}^{n} v^t u_t$$

which is formula (5.9). Thus, the amortization method and the sinking fund method are equivalent if $i' = i$.

It should be noted that we have implicitly assumed that $(u_t - i'L)$ is positive. If it were negative, then it would mean that the payment in that year is not even sufficient to pay the interest on the loan. Mathematically we would then have to have a negative sinking fund deposit, i.e., a withdrawal, for that year. However, in practice such situations are avoided if possible.

It is possible that when the amortization method is used, the interest in a payment is larger than the total payment, in which case the principal repaid would be negative, i.e., the outstanding principal would increase instead of decrease. Such situations arise infrequently in practice.

Example 5.7.   A man is repaying a loan at 5% effective with payments at the end of each year for 10 years, such that the payment the first year is $200, the second year $190, and so forth, until the 10th year it is $110. (1) Find the amount of the loan. (2) Find the principal and interest in the fifth payment.

1. The amount of the loan is

$$100a_{\overline{10}|} + 10(Da)_{\overline{10}|} = 100(7.7217) + 10\frac{10 - 7.7217}{.05} = \$1227.83 \ .$$

2. The fifth payment is $160. The outstanding balance at the end of the fourth year, prospectively, is

$$100a_{\overline{6}|} + 10(Da)_{\overline{6}|} \ .$$

The interest in the fifth payment is

$$\begin{aligned}.05[100a_{\overline{6}|} + 10(Da)_{\overline{6}|}] &= 100(1 - v^6) + 10(6 - a_{\overline{6}|}) \\ &= 100(1 - .74622) + 10(6 - 5.0757) = \$34.62 \ .\end{aligned}$$

The principal in the fifth payment is

$$\$160.00 - \$34.62 = \$125.38 \ .$$

Example 5.8.   Assuming the same payment pattern as in Example 5.7, find the amount of the loan if the borrower pays 6% effective interest and accumulates a sinking fund to replace his capital at 5% effective.

Using formula (5.10) the amount of the loan is

$$\frac{100a_{\overline{10}|.05} + 10(Da)_{\overline{10}|.05}}{1 + (.06 - .05)a_{\overline{10}|.05}} = \frac{1227.83}{1 + (.01)(7.7217)} = \$1139.82 \ .$$

This answer is less than the answer to Example 5.7(1), since these terms are less favorable to the borrower.

5.7. YIELD RATES

An investor who makes a series of expenditures at various points in time and receives payments in return at various points in time can be said to earn a *yield rate* on his investment. The yield rate is that effective rate of interest at which the present value of his expenditures is equal to the present value of his returns.

Consider a situation in which an investor makes expenditures of a_0, $a_1, \ldots, a_n$ and realizes returns of $b_0, b_1, \ldots, b_n$ at times $0, 1, \ldots, n$. Note that $a_t \geq 0$ and $b_t \geq 0$ for $t = 0, 1, \ldots, n$. Then the yield rate i is defined by

$$\sum_{t=0}^{n} v^t a_t = \sum_{t=0}^{n} v^t b_t . \tag{5.11}$$

If we define c_t to be the net investment made at time t, i.e.,

$$c_t = a_t - b_t \quad \text{for} \quad t = 0, 1, \ldots, n$$

then we have

$$\sum_{t=0}^{n} v^t c_t = 0 . \tag{5.12}$$

If $c_t > 0$, then there is a net cash flow into the investment at time t; whereas if $c_t < 0$, then there is a net cash flow out of the investment at time t.

Yield rates are not an entirely new concept; we have encountered them before. As one example, if an investor lends \$1000 to be repaid over a four-year period at $4\frac{1}{2}\%$ effective by the amortization method, then his yield rate is $4\frac{1}{2}\%$.

As a second example, assume that an investor lends \$1000 to be repaid in one sum at the end of a four-year period on which interest at $4\frac{1}{2}\%$ effective is paid and a sinking fund is accumulated at 4% effective to replace the original loan. Then the lender's yield rate is $4\frac{1}{2}\%$ if the sinking fund is invested by the borrower or by some third party. However, if the lender invests the sinking fund, then his yield rate will be higher than $4\frac{1}{2}\%$. It was shown in Example 5.4 that his yield rate would be 4.77% in this case.

The above examples have ignored the reinvestment by the lender of payments made by the borrower. This is equivalent to the assumption that the payments can be reinvested at the same yield rate as the original investment. The situation in which the payments cannot be reinvested at the same yield rate will be considered in Section 5.8.

It is unfortunately not true that yield rates are always unique. Example 5.12 illustrates an investment which produces more than one yield rate. In practice it is important to know whether a yield rate is unique or not.

Let B_t be the outstanding investment at time t. Then we have

$$B_0 = c_0$$

and

$$B_t = B_{t-1}(1 + i) + c_t \text{ for } t = 1, 2, \ldots, n$$

$$\left. \right\} \quad (5.13)$$

It is possible to show that if

1. $B_t > 0$ for $t = 0, 1, \ldots, n - 1$

and

2. $i > -1$ exists such that formula (5.12) is satisfied, then i is unique.

The proof of this result is as follows. The condition $i > -1$ is necessary to ensure that $1 + i$ is positive. Now rewrite formula (5.12) as

$$c_0(1 + i)^n + c_1(1 + i)^{n-1} + \cdots + c_{n-1}(1 + i) + c_n = 0.$$

We know that

$$
\begin{aligned}
B_0 &= & c_0 &> 0 \\
B_1 &= B_0(1 + i) &+ c_1 &> 0 \\
B_2 &= B_1(1 + i) &+ c_2 &> 0 \\
&\vdots & \vdots & \vdots \\
B_{n-1} &= B_{n-2}(1 + i) + c_{n-1} &> 0 \\
B_n &= B_{n-1}(1 + i) + c_n. &
\end{aligned}
$$

By successive substitution in the above equations we have

$$B_n = c_0(1 + i)^n + c_1(1 + i)^{n-1} + \cdots + c_{n-1}(1 + i) + c_n = 0.$$

This is the expected result, since the investment is exactly terminated at the end of n years. Note that $c_0 > 0$ and $c_n < 0$, but that c_t for $t = 1, 2, \ldots, n - 1$ may be either positive, negative, or zero.

To prove the uniqueness of i, let $j > i$ be another yield rate. Let the outstanding investment at time t for interest rate j be denoted by B'_t. Then we have

$$
\begin{aligned}
B'_0 &= & c_0 &= & c_0 &= B_0 \\
B'_1 &= B'_0(1 + j) &+ c_1 &> B_0(1 + i) &+ c_1 &= B_1 \\
B'_2 &= B'_1(1 + j) &+ c_2 &> B_1(1 + i) &+ c_2 &= B_2 \\
&\vdots & \vdots & \vdots & \vdots & \vdots
\end{aligned}
$$

$$B'_{n-1} = B'_{n-2}(1 + j) + c_{n-1} > B_{n-2}(1 + i) + c_{n-1} = B_{n-1}$$
$$B'_n = B'_{n-1}(1 + j) + c_n > B_{n-1}(1 + i) + c_n = B_n = 0.$$

But this is a contradiction, since B'_n must equal 0 if j is a yield rate. Thus j cannot be greater than i. The proof for $-1 < j < i$ is analogous. This establishes the uniqueness of i.

The student should note that although formulas (5.11), (5.12), (5.13), and the above proof assume integral periods of time, the results can easily be extended to include other regular or irregular intervals as well.

Thus, if the outstanding investment is positive at all points throughout the life of the investment, then a yield rate will be unique. However, if the outstanding investment ever becomes negative at any one point, then a yield rate is not necessarily unique.

If it is necessary to solve for an unknown yield rate, formula (5.12) can be solved as an nth degree polynomial in v by standard computer subroutines. Knowing v immediately determines i. Alternatively, successive approximation or iteration can be used in many cases.

The following examples illustrate the concept of yield rate in situations not directly considered before.

Example 5.9. A borrows $1000 from B and agrees to repay it in 10 equal installments of principal and interest at 3% effective. After five years B sells his right to future payments to C at a price which yields C 4% effective. (1) Find the price which C should pay. (2) Find the overall yield rate to B of his investment.

1. The annual installment is

$$\frac{1000}{a_{\overline{10}|.03}} = 1000(.087231 + .03) = \$117.23 .$$

C should pay

$$117.23 a_{\overline{5}|.04} = 117.23(4.4518) = \$521.88 .$$

2. An equation of value to determine B's yield rate is

$$117.23 a_{\overline{5}|} + 521.88 v^5 = 1000 .$$

Define $f(j) = 117.23 a_{\overline{5}|} + 521.88 v^5 - 1000.$

We seek to find j such that $f(j) = 0$.

$$f(.0250) = (117.23)(4.6458) + (521.88)(.88385) - 1000 = 5.8908$$
$$f(.0275) = (117.23)(4.6126) + (521.88)(.87315) - 1000 = -3.5854$$

$$j \doteq .0250 + .0025 \frac{5.8908 + 0}{5.8908 + 3.5854} = .0266, \text{ or } 2.66\% .$$

This answer is reasonable, since B would clearly have a yield rate of less than 3%.

Example 5.10.   An investor buys an n-year annuity with a present value of $1000 at 5% at a price which will allow him to accumulate a sinking fund to replace his capital at 4% and will produce an overall yield rate of 6%. Find the purchase price of the annuity.

The annual payment of the annuity is

$$\frac{1000}{a_{\overline{n}|.05}}.$$

Let P be the purchase price and let R be the sinking fund deposit. Now the total annual payment is split into interest on the purchase price, $.06P$, and the sinking fund deposit, R. Thus we have

$$R = \frac{1000}{a_{\overline{n}|.05}} - .06P\ .$$

However, we know that the accumulated value of the sinking fund after n years is P; thus,

$$P = Rs_{\overline{n}|.04}\ .$$

Thus, we have two equations in two unknowns, and solving for P:

$$P = \left(\frac{1000}{a_{\overline{n}|.05}} - .06P\right) s_{\overline{n}|.04}$$

or

$$P = \frac{1000 s_{\overline{n}|.04}}{a_{\overline{n}|.05}(1 + .06 s_{\overline{n}|.04})}.$$

Example 5.11.   A borrows $20,000 from B and agrees to repay it with 20 equal installments of principal plus interest on the unpaid balance at 3% effective. After 10 years B sells his right to future payments to C, at a price which yields C 5% effective over the next 5 years and 4% effective over the final 5 years. Find the price which C should pay to the nearest dollar.

FIGURE 5.1

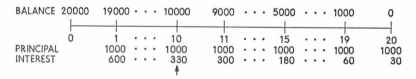

Each year A pays $1000 principal plus interest on the unpaid balance at 3%. His payments are shown in the lower portion of Figure 5.1. The price to C at the end of the 10th year is the present value of the remaining payments, i.e.,

$$1000[a_{\overline{5}|.05} + (1.05)^{-5}a_{\overline{5}|.04}] + [150a_{\overline{5}|.05} + 30(Da)_{\overline{5}|.05} + 30(1.05)^{-5}(Da)_{\overline{5}|.04}]$$

$$= 1000[4.3295 + (.78353)(4.4518)] + \left[150(4.3295) + 30 \left(\frac{5 - 4.3295}{.05} \right) \right.$$

$$\left. + 30(.78353) \left(\frac{5 - 4.4518}{.04} \right) \right]$$

$$= \$9191 .$$

The answer is less than the outstanding principal of $10,000, since C has a yield rate always in excess of 3%.

Example 5.12. *At what yield rate are payments of $100 at the present and $109.20 at the end of two years equivalent to a payment in return of $209 at the end of one year?*

An equation of value is

$$100.00(1 + i)^2 + 109.20 = 209.00(1 + i) ,$$

or

$$(1 + i)^2 - 2.09(1 + i) + 1.092 = 0 .$$

Now factoring we obtain

$$[(1 + i) - 1.04][(1 + i) - 1.05] = 0 .$$

Thus, i is equal to either 4% or 5%! This example illustrates that yield rates are not always unique. The student should verify that the outstanding investment at the end of the first year is negative at either yield rate and thus the conditions necessary for a unique yield rate are not satisfied.

5.8. REINVESTMENT RATES

In Section 5.7 it was assumed that an investor can reinvest the payments by the borrower at a *reinvestment rate* consistent with the original investment rate. In this section we consider the situation in which the reinvestment rate is different from the original investment rate.

First consider the investment of 1 for n years at effective rate i' such that the interest is reinvested at effective rate i. It is desired to find the accumulated value at the end of n years. This situation is illustrated in Figure 5.2.

FIGURE 5.2

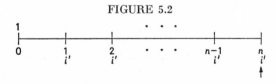

The accumulated value at the end of n years is equal to the principal plus the accumulated value of the interest, i.e.,

$$1 + i's_{\overline{n}|i} . \tag{5.14}$$

Formula (5.14) simplifies to the familiar $(1 + i)^n$ if $i' = i$.

Next consider the investment of 1 at the end of each year for n years at effective rate i' such that the interest is reinvested at effective rate i. It is desired to find the accumulated value of this annuity at the end of n years. This situation is illustrated in Figure 5.3. The accumulated value of this

FIGURE 5.3

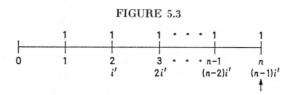

annuity is equal to the sum of the annuity payments and the accumulated value of the interest, i.e.,

$$n + i'(Is)_{\overline{n-1}|i} = n + i'\left(\frac{s_{\overline{n}|i} - n}{i}\right). \qquad (5.15)$$

Formula (5.15) simplifies to the familiar $s_{\overline{n}|}$ if $i' = i$.

Example 5.13.   Equal payments of $100 are invested at the end of each year for 10 years. The payments earn interest at 4% effective and the interest on the payments can be reinvested at 3% effective. (1) Find the amount in the fund at the end of 10 years. (2) Find the purchase price to an investor to produce a yield rate of 4%.

1. Using formula (5.15), we have

$$100\left[10 + .04\left(\frac{s_{\overline{10}|.03} - 10}{.03}\right)\right] = 100\left[10 + .04\left(\frac{11.4639 - 10}{.03}\right)\right] = \$1195.19 .$$

The answer lies between $100s_{\overline{10}|.03} = \$1146.39$ and $100s_{\overline{10}|.04} = \$1200.61$ as would be expected.

2. The purchase price is

$$1195.19(1.04)^{-10} = (1195.19)(.67556) = \$807.42 .$$

The answer is less than $100a_{\overline{10}|.04} = \$811.09$, since a purchase price of $811.09 would assume that interest could be reinvested at 4% instead of 3%.

EXERCISES

5.1. Introduction; 5.2. Finding the outstanding principal

1. A loan is being repaid by 15 annual payments. The first five installments are $400 each, the next five are $300 each, and the final five are $200 each. Find expressions for the loan balance immediately after the second $300 installment—
   a) Prospectively.
   b) Retrospectively.

2. A loan of $1000 is being repaid with quarterly payments for five years at 6% convertible quarterly. Find the outstanding loan balance at the end of the second year.

3. A loan is being repaid by annual installments of $100 at $4\frac{1}{2}\%$ effective. If the loan balance at the end of the third year is $1200, find the original loan balance.

4. A loan of $1000 is being repaid by installments of $100 at the end of each year, and a smaller final payment made one year after the last regular payment. Interest is at the effective rate of 4%. Find the amount of outstanding principal at the end of the fifth year.

5. A loan of $10,000 is to be repaid in 20 annual installments. The installments increase every five years by a uniform amount. The payment for the first five years is $400 per year. Find an expression for the principal outstanding just after the eighth payment.

6. A man is repaying a debt with 20 annual payments of $1000. At the end of the fifth year he makes an extra payment of $2500. He then shortens his payment period by two years and makes level payments until then. Find an expression for the revised annual payment.

7. A $20,000 mortgage is being repaid with 20 annual installments. The borrower makes five payments and then is temporarily unable to make payments for the next two years. Find an expression for the revised payment to start at the end of the 8th year if the loan is still to be repaid at the end of the original 20 years.

5.3. Amortization schedules

8. A loan is being repaid with semiannual installments of $100 for 10 years at 6% convertible semiannually. Find the amount of principal in the sixth installment.

9. Consider a loan which is being repaid with installments of 1 at the end of each year for n years. Find an expression at issue for the present value of the interest which will be paid over the life of the loan.

10. A loan of $1000 is being repaid with annual installments for 20 years at 5% effective. Show that the amount of interest in the 11th installment is

$$\frac{50}{1 + v^{10}}.$$

11. A loan is being repaid with 20 annual installments at 5% effective. In what installment are the principal and interest portions most nearly equal to each other?

12. A loan is being repaid with a series of 20 annual payments. If the amount of principal in the third payment is $100, find the amount of principal in the last five payments. Interest is at the effective rate of $2\frac{1}{2}\%$.

13. A loan is being repaid with 10 annual installments. The principal portion of the sixth installment is $10.13, and the interest portion is $2.20. What effective rate of interest is being paid on the loan?

14. A loan is being repaid with 20 annual installments of 1. Interest is at effective rate i for the first 10 years and effective rate j for the second 10 years. Find expressions for—

a) The amount of interest paid in the 5th installment.

b) The amount of principal repaid in the 15th installment.

15. A mortgage with original principal A is being repaid with level annual payments of K for as long as necessary plus a smaller final payment. The effective rate of interest is i.

 a) Find the amount of principal in the tth installment.

 b) Is the principal repaid column in the amortization schedule in geometric progression (excluding the irregular final payment)?

16. A borrower has a mortgage which calls for level annual payments of 1 at the end of each year for 20 years. At the time of the seventh regular payment he also makes an additional payment equal to the amount of principal that according to the original amortization schedule would have been repaid by the eighth regular payment. If payments of 1 continue to be made at the end of the eighth and succeeding years until the mortgage is fully repaid, show that the amount saved in interest payments over the full term of the mortgage is

$$1 - v^{13}.$$

5.4. Sinking funds

17. A borrower of $1000 agrees to pay interest annually at the effective rate of 5% and to build up a sinking fund which will repay the loan at the end of 10 years. If the sinking fund accumulates at 4% effective, find his total annual outlay.

18. Show that formulas (5.5) and (5.6) reduce to $a_{\overline{n}|}$ if $i' = i$.

19. A loan of $1000 is being repaid by level annual payments of $100 plus a smaller final payment made one year after the last regular payment. The effective rate of interest is 4%. Show algebraically and verbally that the principal outstanding after the fifth payment has been made is:

 a) $1000(1.04)^5 - 100s_{\overline{5}|}$.

 b) $1000 - 60s_{\overline{5}|}$.

20. A man has borrowed $1000 on which he is paying interest at 6% effective. He is accumulating a sinking fund at 5% effective to repay the loan. At the end of 10 years the balance in the sinking fund is $500. At the end of the 11th year the borrower makes a total payment of $100.

 a) How much of the $100 pays interest currently on the loan?

 b) How much of the $100 goes into the sinking fund?

 c) How much of the $100 should be considered as interest?

 d) How much of the $100 should be considered as principal?

 e) What is the sinking fund balance at the end of the 11th year?

21. A man borrows $1000 for 20 years at 5% effective. He does not pay interest currently and will pay all accrued interest at the end of 20 years together with the principal. Find the annual sinking fund deposit necessary to liquidate the loan at the end of 20 years if the sinking fund earns 4% effective.

22. A man borrows $1200 for 20 years. He annually makes payments of $100. The lender receives 6% on his investment each year for the first 10 years and 5% each year for the second 10 years. The balance of each payment is invested in a sinking fund earning 4%. Find the amount by which the sinking fund is short of repaying the loan at the end of the 20 years.

23. *a*) A man borrows \$3000 for 20 years at 4% effective. He replaces one third of the principal in a sinking fund earning $2\frac{1}{2}$% effective and the other two thirds in a sinking fund earning $3\frac{1}{2}$% effective. Find the total annual cost of the loan.

   b) Rework (*a*) if the borrower each year puts one third of his total sinking fund deposit into the $2\frac{1}{2}$% sinking fund and the other two thirds into the $3\frac{1}{2}$% sinking fund.

   c) Justify from general reasoning the relative magnitude of the answers to (*a*) and (*b*).

24. A man is repaying a loan with 10 annual payments of \$1000. Half of the loan is repaid by the amortization method at 5% effective. The other half of the loan is repaid by the sinking fund method in which the lender receives 5% effective on his investment and the sinking fund accumulates at 4% effective. Find the amount of the loan.

25. A man is repaying a \$1000 loan by the sinking fund method. His total annual outlay each year is \$100 for as long as necessary plus a smaller final payment made one year after the last regular payment. If the lender receives 6% effective on his money and the sinking fund accumulates at 4% effective—

   a) Find the duration and amount of the irregular final payment.

   b) Find the amount of principal repaid in the fourth installment.

5.5. Differing payment periods and interest conversion periods

26. An investor buys an annuity with payments of principal and interest of \$10 per half year for 20 years. Interest is at the effective rate of i per annum. How much interest does the investor receive in total over the 20-year period?

27. A man borrows \$1000 for 10 years on which he must pay interest of 6% convertible semiannually. He replaces the principal by means of deposits at the end of every year for 10 years into a sinking fund which earns 5% effective. Find the total dollar amount which he must pay over the 10-year period to completely repay the loan.

28. A man is repaying a loan with payments of \$3000 at the end of every two years over an unknown period of time. If the amount of interest in the third installment is \$2000, find the amount of principal in the sixth installment. Assume interest is 5% convertible semiannually.

5.6. Varying series of payments

29. A loan is being repaid by 10 annual payments. The first payment is equal to the interest due only, the second payment is twice the first, the third payment is three times the first, and so forth. Prove that at the rate of interest on the loan

$$(Ia)_{\overline{10}|} = a_{\overline{\infty}|} .$$

30. A loan is being repaid with 10 payments. The first payment is 10, the second 9, and so forth with the tenth payment being 1. Show that the amount of interest in the sixth payment is

$$5 - a_{\overline{5}|} .$$

31. A loan is repaid by payments which start at $20 the first year and increase by $5 per year until a payment of $100 is made, at which time payments cease. If interest is 4% effective, find the amount of principal in the fourth payment.

5.7. Yield rates

32. *a)* A man pays $100 immediately and $99 at the end of two years in return for a payment of $200 at the end of one year. Verify that the yield rate is either plus or minus 10%.

    b) A man pays $100 immediately and $101 at the end of two years in return for a payment of $200 at the end of one year. Verify that the yield rate is a complex number. (The student should be careful in using the symbol "i" to distinguish between rates of interest and $\sqrt{-1}$.)

33. A man is repaying a $1000 loan with 10 equal payments of principal. Interest at 3% effective is paid on the outstanding balance each year. Find the price to yield an investor 5% effective.

34. Find an expression for the price to be paid for an annuity of $100 per year for 10 years to yield 6% effective if the principal can be replaced with a sinking fund earning 3% effective for the first 4 years and 2% effective thereafter.

35. A 20-year immediate annuity has a present value of $1000 where interest is at 5% for the first 10 years and 4% for the second 10 years. An investor buys this annuity at a price which over the entire period yields 6% on his purchase price and further allows him to replace his capital by means of a sinking fund earning 3% for the first 10 years and 2% for the second 10 years. Find an expression for the amount that is placed in the sinking fund each year.

36. A mortgage of $8000 is repayable in 20 years by semiannual installments of $200 each plus interest on the unpaid balance at 5%. Just after the 15th payment the lender sells the mortgage at a price which yields the new lender 6% and allows him to accumulate a sinking fund to replace his capital at 4%. Assuming that all interest rates are convertible semiannually, show that the price is

$$\frac{75s_{\overline{25}|.02} + 6250}{1 + .03s_{\overline{25}|.02}}.$$

5.8. Reinvestment rates

37. It is desired to accumulate a fund of $1000 at the end of 10 years by equal deposits at the beginning of each year. If the deposits earn interest at 2% effective but the interest can be reinvested at only 1% effective, show that the deposit necessary is

$$\frac{1000}{2s_{\overline{11}|.01} - 12}.$$

38. A man invests $1000 at the beginning of each year for five years in a fund earning 5% effective. The interest from this fund can be reinvested at only 4% effective. Show that the total accumulated value at the end of 10 years is

$$1250(s_{\overline{11}|.04} - s_{\overline{6}|.04} - 1).$$

39. A loan of $10,000 is being repaid with payments of $600 at the end of each year for 20 years. If each payment of $600 is immediately reinvested at 4% effective, find the effective annual rate of interest earned over the 20-year period by interpolation in the interest tables.

Miscellaneous problems

40. A man has money invested at an effective rate i. At the end of the first year he withdraws $162\frac{1}{2}\%$ of the interest earned, at the end of the second year he withdraws 325% of the interest earned, and so forth with the withdrawal factor increasing in arithmetic progression. At the end of 16 years the fund is exhausted. Find i.

41. In order to pay off a loan of A, a man makes payments of P at the end of each year. Interest on the first B of the unpaid balance is at rate i; interest on the excess is at rate j. Find the outstanding balance at the end of the tth year, assuming it to be more than B.

42. A loan of $\bar{a}_{\overline{25}|}$ is being repaid with continuous payments at the annual rate of 1 per annum for 25 years. If $i = .05$, find the total amount of interest paid during the 6th through the 10th years inclusive.

43. The original amount of an inheritance was just sufficient at $3\frac{1}{2}\%$ effective to pay $100 at the end of each year for 10 years. The $100 payments were made as scheduled the first five years even though the fund actually earned 5% effective. How much excess interest was in the fund at the end of the fifth year?

44. A man is making level payments at the beginning of each year for 10 years to accumulate $10,000 at the end of the 10 years in a bank which is paying 5% effective. At the end of five years the bank drops its interest rate to 4% effective.
    a) Find the annual deposit for the first five years.
    b) Find the annual deposit for the second five years.

45. After having made six annual payments of $100 each on a $1000 loan at 4% effective, the borrower decides to repay the balance of the loan over the next five years by equal annual principal payments in addition to the annual interest due on the unpaid balance. If the lender insists on a yield rate of 5% over this final five-year period, find the total payment, principal plus interest, for the ninth year.

46. A man was making annual payments of R on a 5% 30-year mortgage. After making 15 payments he renegotiates to pay off the debt in five more years with the lender being satisfied with $4\frac{1}{2}\%$ effective over the entire period. Find an expression for the revised annual payment.

47. Nine years ago a man incurred a 20-year $30,000 mortgage at 4% effective on which he was making annual payments. He desires now to make a lump-sum payment of $5000 and to pay off the mortgage in nine more years. Find an expression for the revised annual payment:
    a) If the lender is satisfied with a 4% yield for the past nine years but insists on a 5% yield for the next nine years.
    b) If the lender insists on a 5% yield during the entire life of the mortgage.

CHAPTER 6. Bonds and other securities

6.1. INTRODUCTION

One of the major applications of the theory of interest is in the determination of prices and values for bonds and other securities, such as preferred stock and common stock. This chapter is mainly concerned with bonds, although brief consideration is given to preferred and common stock in Sections 6.2 and 6.10.

There are three main questions which Chapter 6 and Section 7.2 consider:

1. Given the desired yield rate of an investor, what price should he pay for a given security?
2. Given the purchase price of a security, what is the resulting yield rate to an investor?
3. What is the value of a security on a given date after it has been purchased?

It should be noted that no new basic principles are introduced in this chapter. However, several new terms and new formulas are introduced to efficiently handle the types of securities which have evolved in practice.

6.2. TYPES OF SECURITIES

Section 6.2 considers the most common types of securities which have evolved in modern financial markets. This section should not be considered as a complete discussion of these securities, since only a very brief description of the common types of securities is presented. For a more complete description of these and other types of securities, the student is encouraged to refer to any of several standard textbooks on corporate and government securities.

128

There are three main categories of securities which will be discussed. These are: (1) bonds, (2) preferred stock, and (3) common stock.

Bonds

A *bond* is an interest-bearing certificate which promises to pay a stated amount of money at some future date. It is a formal certificate of indebtedness issued by a borrower, usually for some round figure such as $500 or $1000. Bonds are commonly issued by corporations and governmental units as a means of raising capital.

Bonds are generally redeemed at the end of a fixed period of time. This fixed period of time is called the *term* of the bond. The end of the term of a bond is called the *maturity date*. On occasion, bonds with an infinite term are issued; e.g., the British consols. Also bonds may be issued with a term which varies at the discretion of the borrower. Such a bond is termed a *callable bond* and is discussed in Section 6.7. Any date prior to, or including, the maturity date on which a bond may be redeemed is termed a *redemption date*.

Bonds may be classified in several different ways. One such classification is the distinction between *accumulation bonds* and *bonds with interest payable periodically*. An accumulation bond is one in which the redemption price includes the original loan plus all accumulated interest. The Series E Savings Bonds issued by the United States Government are an example of this type of bond. However, in practice, most bonds have interest payable periodically, and this will be assumed unless stated otherwise. This chapter will largely be confined to this latter type of bond, since accumulation bonds can easily be handled with elementary compound interest methods already discussed.

A second classification is the distinction between *registered bonds* and *unregistered bonds*. A registered bond is one in which the lender is listed in the records of the borrower. If the lender decides to sell the bond, the change of ownership must be reported to the borrower. The periodic interest payments are paid by the borrower to the owners of record on each interest payment date. An unregistered bond is one in which the lender is not listed in the records of the borrower. Since the bond belongs to whomever has legal possession of it, an unregistered bond is often called a *bearer bond*. Unregistered bonds are almost always issued with coupons attached. The coupons, which are the periodic interest payments, can be detached by the holder of the bond and cashed. Such a bond is often called a *coupon bond* for this reason.

A third classification is made according to the type of security behind the bond. A *mortgage bond* is a bond secured by a mortgage on real property. A *debenture bond* is one secured only by the general credit of the borrower. Variations within these two major classifications exist. In general, mortgage bonds possess a higher degree of security than debenture bonds, since the lenders can foreclose on the collateral in the event of the default of a mortgage bond.

A type of bond with a high degree of risk to the lenders is the *income bond* or *adjustment bond*. Under this type of bond, the periodic interest payments are made only if the borrower has earned sufficient income to pay them. Income bonds were once fairly common, but they have largely disappeared in recent years.

A type of bond which is somewhat of a hybrid is a *convertible bond*. This type of bond can be converted into the common stock of the issuing corporation at some future date under certain conditions, at the option of the owner of the bond. Convertible bonds are generally debenture bonds. Such bonds offer an investor a choice between continuing his security as a bond or switching it into common stock, depending upon the performance of the corporation in the future.

A borrower in need of a large amount of funds can issue bonds with a common maturity date. However, a large volume of indebtedness falling due at one time can present problems in redeeming or refinancing the debt. For this reason, some borrowers will divide a large issue of bonds so that individual bonds will have a series of staggered redemption dates. These types of bonds are called *serial bonds* and will be discussed further in Section 6.8.

Preferred stock

Preferred stock is a type of security which earns a fixed rate of interest similar to bonds. However, it differs from a bond in that it is an ownership security rather than a debt security, i.e., the owner of preferred stock is part owner of the issuing corporation. In general, preferred stock has no maturity date, although on occasion preferred stock with a redemption provision is issued. The interest return on preferred stock is usually called a *dividend*, since it is being paid to an owner.

In terms of the degree of security, preferred stock ranks behind bonds and other debt instruments, since all payments on indebtedness must be made before the preferred stock receives a dividend. However, preferred stock ranks ahead of common stock in the degree of security involved, since preferred stock dividends must be paid before common stock dividends can be paid.

To increase the degree of security behind preferred stock, some corporations have issued *cumulative preferred stock*. This type of preferred stock has the feature that any dividends which the corporation is not able to pay are carried forward to future years when they presumably will be paid. For example, if a corporation has preferred stock on which it is paying a $5 dividend and can make only a $3 payment in one year, the $2 balance is carried forward (without interest) to future years. All arrears on preferred stock must be paid before any dividends on common stock can be paid.

Some preferred stock receives a share of earnings over and above the regular dividend if earnings are at a sufficient level. This type of preferred stock is called *participating preferred stock*, since it participates in the earnings with the common stock. Participating preferred stock is relatively uncommon at the present time.

Some preferred stock has a convertible privilege similar to convertible bonds and is called *convertible preferred stock*. Owners of this type of preferred stock have the option to convert their preferred stock to common stock under certain conditions.

Common stock

Common stock is a type of ownership security, as is preferred stock. However, it does not earn a fixed dividend rate as preferred stock does. Common stock dividends are paid only after interest payments on all bonds and other debt and dividends on preferred stock are paid. The dividend rate is completely flexible and can be set by the board of directors at its discretion. However, all residual profits after dividends to the preferred stockholders belong to the common stockholders.

6.3. PRICE OF A BOND

As mentioned in Section 6.1, one of the three primary questions under consideration in this chapter is the determination of a purchase price which will produce a given yield rate to an investor. This section considers this question for bonds.

The following assumptions are made:

1. All obligations will be paid by the borrower on the specified dates of payment. In practice the prices of bonds will vary somewhat depending upon the probability of default in payments, but we will ignore any possibility of default.
2. The bond has a fixed maturity date. Bonds with no maturity date are

mathematically equivalent to preferred stock and are considered in Section 6.10. Callable bonds with optional redemption dates are considered in Section 6.7.

3. The price of the bond is desired immediately after an interest payment date. The price of a bond between two interest payment dates is considered in Section 6.5.

The following symbols will be used in connection with bonds in this and succeeding sections:

$P =$ the *price* of a bond.

$F =$ the *par value* of a bond. This value is printed on the face of the bond and is often the amount payable at the maturity date. Its sole purpose is to define the series of payments to be made by the borrower. It is not a measure of the value or the price of a bond before maturity. It is customary to quote bond prices in terms of a par value of $100, and this will be assumed unless stated otherwise.

$C =$ the *redemption value* of a bond, i.e., the amount of money paid at a redemption date to the holder of the bond. Often C will include F as a special case; for example, the common case of a bond redeemed at its maturity date for its par value. It is possible for C to differ from F in the following cases: (1) a bond which matures for an amount not equal to its par value, or (2) a bond which has a redemption date, on which the bond can be redeemed for an amount not equal to its par value, prior to the maturity date.

$r =$ the *coupon rate* of a bond, i.e., the interest rate per payment period used in determining the amount of the coupon. It is customary to quote coupon rates as nominal rates of interest convertible semiannually, and this will be assumed unless stated otherwise. For example, a 4% bond with semiannual coupons has $r = .02$. It will also be assumed that coupons are constant. The case of varying coupons will be considered in Section 6.9.

$Fr =$ the amount of the coupon.

$g =$ the *modified coupon rate* of a bond. The rate g is defined by $Fr = Cg$ or $g = \dfrac{Fr}{C}$, i.e., g is the coupon rate per unit of redemption value instead of per unit of par value. It should be noted that g will always be convertible at the same frequency as r. In practice, g will often equal r, since C is often equal to F.

$i =$ the *yield rate* of a bond, i.e., the interest rate per interest conversion period actually earned by the investor. It is customary that yield rates are also quoted as nominal rates convertible semiannually, and this will be assumed unless stated otherwise. The case in which the payment period and the interest conversion period are not equal will be considered in Section 6.9. It will also be assumed that the yield rate is constant. The case in which this is not true is also discussed in Section 6.9.

n = the number of interest conversion periods from the date of calculation to the maturity date, or to a redemption date.

K = the present value of the redemption value at the maturity date, or a redemption date, i.e., $K = Cv^n$ at the rate i.

The student should be aware that F, C, r, g, and n are given by the terms of a bond and remain fixed throughout its life. In essence, these parameters define exactly what payments are to be made by the borrower. On the other hand, P and i will tend to vary throughout the life of the bond. The price and the yield rate have a precise inverse relationship to each other, i.e., as the price rises the yield rate falls, and vice versa. The yield rates on bonds will fluctuate with prevailing rates of interest in financial markets for securities of a similar type. Fluctuating market rates of interest will thus lead to fluctuating bond prices. However, these fluctuating bond prices do not generally reflect any increase or decrease in the degree of safety or security attributed to the bond, but rather they merely reflect changing rates of interest in the securities market. This inverse relationship between bond prices and rates of interest has not always been understood by unsophisticated bondholders, who in periods of rising rates of interest have attributed the declining prices of their bonds to a deterioration in the credit rating of the borrower, when this was not a factor at all.

There are three types of formulas which can be used to find the price of a bond. The first of these, called the *general formula*, is the most straightforward. According to this method the price must be equal to the present value of future coupons plus the present value of the redemption value,

$$P = Fra_{\overline{n}|} + Cv^n = Fra_{\overline{n}|} + K \,, \tag{6.1}$$

where the interest functions are calculated at the yield rate i.

The second formula, called the *alternate formula*, can be obtained from formula (6.1) as follows:

$$\begin{aligned} P &= Fra_{\overline{n}|} + Cv^n \\ &= Fra_{\overline{n}|} + C(1 - ia_{\overline{n}|}) \\ &= C + (Fr - Ci)a_{\overline{n}|} \end{aligned} \tag{6.2}$$

at rate i. Formula (6.2) is often more efficient than formula (6.1), since only one value from the interest tables is used instead of two.

The third formula, called the *Makeham formula* (after a famous British actuary of the 19th century), can be obtained from formula (6.1) as follows:

$$P = Cv^n + Fra_{\overline{n}|}$$
$$= Cv^n + Cg\left(\frac{1 - v^n}{i}\right)$$
$$= Cv^n + \frac{g}{i}(C - Cv^n)$$
$$= K + \frac{g}{i}(C - K). \tag{6.3}$$

It should be noted that formula (6.3) also requires only one value from the interest tables instead of two.

Example 6.1. Find the price of a \$100 par value 10-year bond with coupons at $5\frac{1}{4}\%$ convertible semiannually, which will be redeemed at \$105. The bond is bought to yield 6% convertible semiannually. Use all three formulas.

In this example we have

$$F = 100$$
$$C = 105$$
$$r = \frac{.0525}{2} = .02625$$
$$g = \frac{100}{105}(.02625) = .025$$
$$i = \frac{.06}{2} = .03$$
$$n = 20$$
$$K = 105(1.03)^{-20}$$
$$= 105(.55368) = 58.1364.$$

1. General formula:
$$P = Fra_{\overline{n}|} + K$$
$$= 2.625a_{\overline{20}|.03} + 58.1364$$
$$= (2.625)(14.8775) + 58.1364 = \$97.19.$$

2. Alternate formula:
$$P = C + (Fr - Ci)a_{\overline{n}|}$$
$$= 105 + (2.625 - 3.150)a_{\overline{20}|.03}$$
$$= 105 - (.525)(14.8775) = \$97.19.$$

3. Makeham formula:
$$P = K + \frac{g}{i}(C - K)$$

$$= 58.1364 + \frac{.025}{.03}(105 - 58.1364) = \$97.19.$$

6.4. PREMIUM AND DISCOUNT

If the purchase price of a bond exceeds its redemption value, i.e., if $P > C$, then the bond is said to sell at a *premium* and the difference between P and C is called the "premium." Similarly, if the purchase price is less than the redemption value, i.e., if $P < C$, then the bond is said to sell at a *discount*, and the difference between C and P is called the "discount."

We can derive expressions for the premium and the discount from formula (6.2):

$$\text{Premium} = P - C = (Fr - Ci)a_{\overline{n}|i} = C(g - i)a_{\overline{n}|i} \text{ if } g > i. \quad (6.4)$$
$$\text{Discount} = C - P = (Ci - Fr)a_{\overline{n}|i} = C(i - g)a_{\overline{n}|i} \text{ if } i > g. \quad (6.5)$$

It is clear that premium and discount, although bearing different names, are essentially the same concept, since discount is merely a negative premium. It should also be noted that in many cases $F = C$ and $g = r$. However, formulas (6.4) and (6.5) will handle the cases in which this is not true.

The price of a bond depends upon two quantities, the present value of the coupons and the present value of the redemption value. Since the price of a bond is generally less than or greater than the redemption value, there will be a profit (equal to the discount) or loss (equal to the premium) at the redemption date. This profit or loss is reflected in the yield rate for the bond.

However, as a result of this profit or loss at the redemption date, the amount of each coupon cannot be considered as interest income to an investor. It will be necessary to divide each coupon into interest-paid and principal-adjustment portions similar to the separation of payments into interest and principal in Chapter 5.

When this approach is used, the value of the bond will be continually adjusted from the price on the purchase date to the redemption value on the redemption date. These adjusted values of the bond are called the *book values* of the bond. The book values provide a reasonable and smooth series of values for bonds and are used by many investors in reporting the asset values of bonds for financial statements.

A *bond amortization schedule* is a table which shows the division of each coupon into its interest-paid and principal-adjustment portions, together with the book value after each coupon is paid. Consider a bond for which C is equal to 1, the coupon is equal to g, and the price is equal to $1 + p$ (where p can be either positive or negative). Table 6.1 is a bond amortization schedule for this bond.

TABLE 6.1

Duration	Coupon	Interest Paid	Principal Adjustment	Book Value
0				$1 + p = 1 + (g-i)a_{\overline{n}|i}$
1	g	$i[1+(g-i)a_{\overline{n}|i}]$	$g - i[1+(g-i)a_{\overline{n}|i}] = (g-i)v^n$	$[1+(g-i)a_{\overline{n}|i}] - (g-i)v^n = 1 + (g-i)a_{\overline{n-1}|i}$
2	g	$i[1+(g-i)a_{\overline{n-1}|i}]$	$g - i[1+(g-i)a_{\overline{n-1}|i}] = (g-i)v^{n-1}$	$[1+(g-i)a_{\overline{n-1}|i}] - (g-i)v^{n-1} = 1 + (g-i)a_{\overline{n-2}|i}$
$\cdot$	$\cdot$	$\cdot$	$\cdot$	$\cdot$
$\cdot$	$\cdot$	$\cdot$	$\cdot$	$\cdot$
l	g	$i[1+(g-i)a_{\overline{n-l+1}|i}]$	$g - i[1+(g-i)a_{\overline{n-l+1}|i}] = (g-i)v^{n-l+1}$	$[1+(g-i)a_{\overline{n-l+1}|i}] - (g-i)v^{n-l+1} = 1+(g-i)a_{\overline{n-l}|i}$
$\cdot$	$\cdot$	$\cdot$	$\cdot$	$\cdot$
$n-1$	g	$i[1+(g-i)a_{\overline{2}|i}]$	$g - i[1+(g-i)a_{\overline{2}|i}] = (g-i)v^2$	$[1+(g-i)a_{\overline{2}|i}] - (g-i)v^2 = 1+(g-i)a_{\overline{1}|i}$
n	g	$i[1+(g-i)a_{\overline{1}|i}]$	$g - i[1+(g-i)a_{\overline{1}|i}] = (g-i)v$	$[1+(g-i)a_{\overline{1}|i}] - (g-i)v(i) = 1$
Total	ng	$ng - p$	$p = (g-i)a_{\overline{n}|}$	

Consider the first coupon period of the bond. At the end of the first coupon period the interest earned on the balance at the beginning of the period is

$$i[1 + (g - i)a_{\overline{n}|i}].$$

The rest of the total coupon of g, i.e.,

$$g - i[1 + (g - i)a_{\overline{n}|i}] = (g - i)(1 - ia_{\overline{n}|i}) = (g - i)v^n,$$

must be used to amortize the book value. The book value at the end of the period equals the book value at the beginning of the period less the principal-adjustment amount, i.e.,

$$[1 + (g - i)a_{\overline{n}|i}] - (g - i)v^n = 1 + (g - i)a_{\overline{n-1}|i}.$$

The same reasoning applies for each successive period of the schedule.

Several additional observations are possible. First, it should be noted that the book values agree with the price by formula (6.2). Second, the sum of the principal adjustment column is equal to p, the amount of premium or discount, as the case may be. Third, the sum of the interest paid column is equal to the difference between the sum of the coupons and the sum of the principal adjustment column. An algebraic proof of this will be left as an exercise. Fourth, the principal adjustment column is in geometric progression with common ratio $1 + i$. Thus, it is a simple matter to find any one principal adjustment amount knowing any other principal adjustment amount and the rate of interest.

When a bond is bought at a premium, the price will gradually be adjusted downward. This process is called *amortization of premium* or *writing down*. In these cases the principal adjustment amount is often called the "amount for amortization of premium."

When a bond is bought at a discount, the price will gradually be adjusted upward. This process is called *accumulation of discount* or *writing up*. In these cases the principal adjustment amount is often called the "amount for accumulation of discount."

It should be noted that Table 6.1 is based on a value of $C = 1$. The values in the table are proportional for other values of C. In any particular case, the bond amortization schedule can be constructed from basic principles.

As an example of a bond bought at a premium, consider a $1000 par value two-year 4% bond with semiannual coupons bought to yield 3% convertible semiannually. The price of the bond is computed to be $1019.27. The semiannual coupon is $20. Table 6.2 is a bond amortization schedule for this example. The student should verify the entries in Table 6.2,

TABLE 6.2

Duration	Coupon	Interest Paid	Amount for Amortization of Premium	Book Value
0				1019.27
$\frac{1}{2}$	20.00	15.29	4.71	1014.56
1	20.00	15.22	4.78	1009.78
$1\frac{1}{2}$	20.00	15.15	4.85	1004.93
2	20.00	15.07	4.93	1000.00
Total	80.00	60.73	19.27	

As an example of a bond bought at a discount, consider the same $1000 par value two-year 4% bond with semiannual coupons bought to yield 5% convertible semiannually. The price of the bond is computed to be $981.19. The semiannual coupon is $20. Table 6.3 is a bond amortization schedule for this example. The student should verify the entries in Table 6.3.

TABLE 6.3

Duration	Coupon	Interest Paid	Amount for Accumulation of Discount	Book Value
0				981.19
$\frac{1}{2}$	20.00	24.53	4.53	985.72
1	20.00	24.64	4.64	990.36
$1\frac{1}{2}$	20.00	24.76	4.76	995.12
2	20.00	24.88	4.88	1000.00
Total	80.00	98.81	18.81	

It should be noted that the amounts for accumulation of discount are really the negatives of the numbers shown in Table 6.3, i.e., they are increments to the book value rather than decrements. However, they are usually written as positive numbers to avoid negative signs. Thus, the student should be careful to ascertain in any problem whether the bond is selling at a premium or at a discount so that the entries in the principal adjustment column can be appropriately interpreted.

It should also be noted that if it is desired to find the interest paid or principal adjustment portion of any one coupon, it is not necessary to construct the entire bond amortization schedule. The book value at the beginning of the period in question is equal to the price at that point and can be determined by the methods of Section 6.3. Then that one line of the schedule can be calculated.

The bond amortization schedule discussed in this section is intimately related to the amortization schedule described in Chapter 5. Additional insight into the bond amortization schedule can be obtained from the sinking fund method.

For example, in Table 6.2 the investor can be considered to be investing $1019.27 on which he expects a semiannual return of $15.29. This leaves $4.71 each period to place into a sinking fund to replace the premium he paid for the bond, since he will suffer the loss of the premium upon redemption. If the sinking fund can be invested at the yield rate, then the balance in the sinking fund at the end of two years is

$$4.71s_{\overline{4}|.015} = (4.71)(4.0909) = \$19.27,$$

which is the amount of premium. Example 6.2 illustrates a situation in which the sinking fund earns a rate of interest different from the yield rate.

Similarly, in Table 6.3 we have

$$4.53s_{\overline{4}|.025} = (4.53)(4.1525) = \$18.81,$$

which is the amount of discount. It should be noted that the sinking fund in this case is a negative sinking fund.

Example 6.2. ***Find the price of a $1000 par value two-year 4%
bond with semiannual coupons bought to yield 3% convertible
semiannually if the investor can replace his capital by means of a
sinking fund earning 2% convertible semiannually.***

The bond will sell at a premium, i.e., $P > 1000$. The semiannual coupon is $20, and the interest earned is $.015P$. The difference is placed into the sinking fund which must accumulate to the amount of premium. Thus, the fundamental equation of value is

$$(20 - .015P)s_{\overline{4}|.01} = P - 1000$$

or

$$P = \frac{1000 + 20s_{\overline{4}|.01}}{1 + .015s_{\overline{4}|.01}}$$

$$= \frac{1000 + (20)(4.0604)}{1 + (.015)(4.0604)} = \$1019.14.$$

This price is smaller than the bond in Table 6.2. The student should justify the relative magnitude of the two prices from general reasoning. In general, the price of a bond under these conditions is given by

$$P = \frac{C(1 + gs_{\overline{n}|i})}{1 + i's_{\overline{n}|i}}, \tag{6.6}$$

where i' is the yield rate of interest and i is the sinking fund rate of interest.

6.5. VALUATION BETWEEN INTEREST PAYMENT DATES

The preceding sections have assumed that the price or the book value of a bond is being calculated just after a coupon has been paid. It remains to consider the determination of prices and book values between interest payment dates.

Let P_t and P_{t+1} be the prices of a bond on two consecutive interest payment dates. Let Fr be the amount of the coupon. As an exercise, it will be shown that

$$P_{t+1} = P_t(1 + i) - Fr.\tag{6.7}$$

We desire to find a value for P_{t+k}, where $0 < k < 1$. The price on the interim date would be the price on the preceding coupon date accumulated with interest at the yield rate for the fractional period, i.e.,

$$P_{t+k} = P_t(1 + i)^k.\tag{6.8}$$

Alternatively, in terms of P_{t+1} we have

$$P_{t+k} = (P_{t+1} + Fr)\, v^{1-k},\tag{6.9}$$

which follows immediately from formulas (6.7) and (6.8).

Formulas (6.8) and (6.9) are exact expressions for interim prices. However, in practice, a simple interest approximation to formula (6.8) is almost always used,

$$P_{t+k} = P_t(1 + ki).\tag{6.10}$$

Another approach used is to perform a linear interpolation between the price at the beginning of the interval, P_t, and the price at the end of the interval just before the next coupon is paid, $P_{t+1} + Fr$. Then, we would have

$$P_{t+k} = [(1 - k)P_t + kP_{t+1}] + k \cdot Fr.\tag{6.11}$$

As an exercise it will be shown that formulas (6.10) and (6.11) are equivalent.

In this form it is seen that P_{t+k} is equal to a linear interpolation between P_t and P_{t+1}, plus $k \cdot Fr$. The expression $k \cdot Fr$ can be interpreted as the accrued coupon from the previous interest payment date to the date of purchase. Since the new owner will receive an entire coupon at the end of the current period, but since he did not own the bond over the entire period, his purchase price should include a proportionate part of the coupon over the period for which he did not own the bond. This proportionate part of the coupon, $k \cdot Fr$, equitably belongs to the previous owner of the bond, since he is entitled to the portion of the coupon for the period during which he owned the bond.

In commercial bond markets interim prices are calculated consistently with formulas (6.10) and (6.11). The *flat price* of a bond is the money which changes hands at the date of sale, i.e., P_{t+k}. The *market price* of the bond is equal to the interpolated price exclusive of accrued interest, i.e.,

$$(1 - k)P_t + kP_{t+1}.$$

In practice a bond price is usually quoted as market price plus accrued interest. As we shall see, this leads to a smooth progression of quoted market prices.

FIGURE 6.1

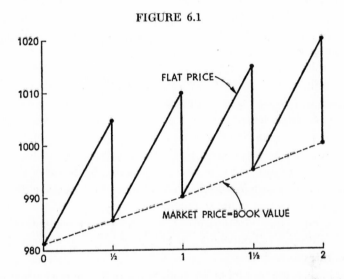

The book value of the bond is the asset value which the owner of the bond assigns to his asset. It is common practice for the book value to be equal to the market price of the bond at the original yield rate. If this is done, then any accrued interest in the financial statements of the owner of the bond must be handled as a separate item.

The relationship between the flat price and the market price and the nature of the interpolations used in this section are clarified by Figure 6.1. This figure is a graph of the prices for the same bond used in Table 6.3. The flat price is denoted by the solid line, and the market price or the book value is denoted by the dotted line. The accrued interest at any date is equal to the vertical distance between the solid line and the dotted line.

Example 6.3. *Find the market price and the flat price for the bond in Table 6.3 bought $7\frac{1}{2}$ months after its issue date.*

The market price would be quoted as a linearly interpolated value at duration $\frac{5}{8}$:

$$\tfrac{3}{4}(985.72) + \tfrac{1}{4}(990.36) = \$986.88 .$$

The flat price actually paid would equal the market price plus accrued interest:

$$986.88 + \tfrac{1}{4}(20.00) = \$991.88 .$$

As a check, the flat price should equal the price obtained from formula (6.10):

$$985.72[1 + \tfrac{1}{4}(.025)] = \$991.88 .$$

6.6. DETERMINATION OF YIELD RATES

As mentioned in Section 6.1, one of the three primary questions under consideration in this chapter is the determination of the yield rate to an investor, given the purchase price of a security. This section discusses this question for bonds.

The problem of the determination of a yield rate on a bond is similar to the determination of an unknown rate of interest for an annuity, discussed in Section 3.8. As in that section there are three main approaches: interpolation, algebraic techniques, and successive approximation.

The method most frequently used in practice is interpolation in *bond tables*, which are tables of bond prices for a wide variety of terms, coupon rates, and yield rates. These prices are calculated by means of the formulas discussed in Sections 6.3 and 6.5. Almost all bond tables make the following assumptions: (1) par value = redemption value = 100, (2) coupons are paid semiannually, and (3) yield rates are convertible semiannually. Table 6.4 is an illustrative bond table for bonds with a 10-year term at selected coupon rates and yield rates.

Bond tables are useful both in finding the purchase price when the yield rate is given and in approximating the yield rate by interpolation when the purchase price is given. In practice, bond tables much more extensive than Table 6.4 would be used, and this would significantly increase the accuracy of any interpolations. The most extensive bond tables will even include market prices between interest payment dates, as well as prices on interest payment dates.

By skillful manipulation, bond tables can often be used for situations in which the above three assumptions are not satisfied. One possible generalization would be to bonds for which the coupon rate and the yield rate are not convertible semiannually but are both convertible at some other frequency. For example, if the coupon rate and the yield rate are both convertible annually, then the bond tables can be applied by doubling the coupon rate, doubling the yield rate, and halving the term of the bond, provided these values are in the bond tables.

TABLE 6.4

TEN-YEAR BOND PRICES

Yield Rate %	Coupon Rate %				
	3	3.5	4	4.5	5
2	109.02	113.53	118.05	122.56	127.07
2.5	104.40	108.80	113.20	117.60	122.00
3	100.00	104.29	108.58	112.88	117.17
3.5	95.81	100.00	104.19	108.38	112.56
4	91.82	95.91	100.00	104.09	108.18
4.5	88.03	92.02	96.01	100.00	103.99
5	84.41	88.31	92.21	96.10	100.00
5.5	80.97	84.77	88.58	92.39	96.19
6	77.68	81.40	85.12	88.84	92.56

A second possible generalization would be to bonds for which $C \neq 100$. If the price is adjusted by dividing by $.01C$ and if the modified coupon rate, g, is used instead of the coupon rate, r, then the bond tables can be used directly. A second approach, which often appears in the instructions to bond tables, will be examined in the exercises.

When bond tables are not available, interpolation in ordinary compound interest tables can be used as an alternative. Both types of interpolation will be illustrated in Example 6.4.

The second main approach to finding yield rates is to use a series expansion and solve by algebraic techniques. For example, formula (6.1) can be written as

$$P = Fr(v + v^2 + \cdots + v^{n-1}) + (Fr + C)v^n , \qquad (6.1)$$

which is an nth degree polynomial in v. If a digital computer is available, the roots of an nth degree polynomial can be found by standard computer subroutines. Knowing v immediately determines i.

Alternatively, we can use formula (6.2),

$$P = C + (Fr - Ci)a_{\overline{n}|}$$
$$= C + C(g - i)a_{\overline{n}|} ,$$

and letting $k = \dfrac{P - C}{C}$ we have

$$(g - i)a_{\overline{n}|} = \frac{P - C}{C} = k$$

or

$$i = g - \frac{k}{a_{\overline{n}|}} \cdot \qquad (6.12)$$

To solve formula (6.12) for i, we can use formula (3.25)

$$\frac{1}{a_{\overline{n}|}} = \frac{1}{n}\left[1 + \frac{n+1}{2}i + \frac{n^2-1}{12}i^2 + \cdots\right]. \qquad (3.25)$$

If we ignore terms of higher than the first degree in i, then formula (6.12) becomes

$$i = g - \frac{k}{a_{\overline{n}|}}$$
$$= g - \frac{k}{n}\left[1 + \frac{n+1}{2}i\right],$$

and solving for i

$$i = \frac{g - \dfrac{k}{n}}{1 + \dfrac{n+1}{2n}k}. \qquad (6.13)$$

Formula (6.13) has an interesting verbal interpretation. The amount by which the value of the bond needs to be amortized is k per unit of redemption value. Since the number of periods is n, the average amount of principal adjustment each period is $\dfrac{k}{n}$. Thus, the portion of each coupon which is true interest is approximately $g - \dfrac{k}{n}$. Per unit of redemption value, the average amount invested is the average of the initial book value for each period, i.e.,

$$\frac{1}{n}\left[\left(1 + \frac{n}{n}k\right) + \left(1 + \frac{n-1}{n}k\right) + \cdots + \left(1 + \frac{2}{n}k\right) + \left(1 + \frac{1}{n}k\right)\right]$$
$$= 1 + \frac{n+1}{2n}k.$$

In summary, formula (6.13) can be interpreted roughly as the average interest return divided by the average amount invested.

Formula (6.13) forms the basis of a very simple method for calculating yield rates called the *bond salesman's method*. As usually applied, the bond salesman's method replaces $\dfrac{n+1}{2n}$ by $\frac{1}{2}$ in formula (6.13) obtaining

$$i = \frac{g - \dfrac{k}{n}}{1 + \frac{1}{2}k}. \qquad (6.14)$$

In general, formula (6.14) produces poorer results than formula (6.13).

Formulas (6.13) and (6.14) are very simple to apply, since no values from the bond tables or interest tables are used. They yield reasonable results as long as the term of the bond is not too long and the coupon rate and yield rate do not differ drastically.

More accurate formulas can be developed using formula (3.25) to higher powers of i. However, then the solution of the equation by hand becomes more difficult.

The third main approach to finding yield rates is to use the method of successive approximation or iteration. This method was described in Section 3.8. To find an expression for $f(i)$ we can use formula (6.3) obtaining

$$i = \frac{Cg[1 - (1 + i)^{-n}]}{P - C(1 + i)^{-n}},$$

i.e.,

$$f(i) = \frac{Cg[1 - (1 + i)^{-n}]}{P - C(1 + i)^{-n}}.$$

It should be noted that the amount of the coupon, Cg, the redemption value, C, and the price, P, will all be given. Since each step in the successive approximation will involve a rate of interest not usually tabulated, there will be a problem in evaluating $(1 + i)^{-n}$. In practice, either logarithms or direct calculation by a computer will be necessary.

As with annuities, the number of successive approximations necessary will be greatly reduced if the starting value is close to the true yield rate. Good starting values can be obtained by interpolation, i.e., by the first method described above.

Example 6.4. A $100 par value 10-year bond with 4% semiannual coupons is selling for $90. Find the yield rate convertible semiannually (1) by interpolation in the bond tables, (2) by interpolation in the interest tables, (3) by the bond salesman's method, and (4) by successive approximation.

1. From Table 6.4 using linear interpolation

$$i^{(2)} = .0500 + .0050 \frac{92.21 - 90.00}{92.21 - 88.58} = .0530, \text{ or } 5.30\%.$$

2. From formula (6.2) we have

$$90 = 100 + (2 - 100j)a_{\overline{20}|j}.$$

Define $f(j) = 10 + (2 - 100j)a_{\overline{20}|j}$. We seek to find j such that $f(j) = 0$. By inspection of the interest tables

$$f(.0250) = 10 + (2 - 2.50)(15.5892) = 2.2054$$
$$f(.0275) = 10 + (2 - 2.75)(15.2273) = -1.4205$$

and performing a linear interpolation

$$j = .0250 + .0025 \, \frac{2.2054 + 0}{2.2054 + 1.4205} = .0265$$

and

$$i^{(2)} = 2j = .0530, \text{ or } 5.30\%.$$

3. Using the bond salesman's method, i.e., formula (6.14), the average interest return is

$$100(.02) + \frac{100 - 90}{20} = 2.5.$$

The average principal invested is

$$\tfrac{1}{2}(90) + \tfrac{1}{2}(100) = 95.$$

Thus, the yield rate per half year is

$$\frac{2.5}{95} = .0263, \text{ or } 5.26\% \text{ per annum}.$$

If the more refined version of the bond salesman's method, i.e., formula (6.13), is used, then the average principal invested is

$$\frac{21}{40}\,(90) + \frac{19}{40}\,(100) = 94.75$$

and the yield rate is

$$\frac{2.5}{94.75} = .0264, \text{ or } 5.28\% \text{ per annum, which is closer to the true yield.}$$

4. Use successive approximation starting with $j_0 = .0250$.

$$j_1 = \frac{2[1 - (1.0250)^{-20}]}{90 - 100(1.0250)^{-20}} = \frac{2[1 - .61027]}{90 - 61.027} = .0269$$

$$j_2 = \frac{2[1 - (1.0269)^{-20}]}{90 - 100(1.0269)^{-20}} = \frac{2[1 - .58808]}{90 - 58.808} = .0264$$

$$j_3 = \frac{2[1 - (1.0264)^{-20}]}{90 - 100(1.0264)^{-20}} = \frac{2[1 - .59384]}{90 - 59.384} = .0265$$

$$j_4 = \frac{2[1 - (1.0265)^{-20}]}{90 - 100(1.0265)^{-20}} = \frac{2[1 - .59268]}{90 - 59.268} = .0265$$

Thus $j = .0265$ or $i^{(2)} = .0530$, or 5.30%.

It should be noted that successive approximation can be carried to any desired degree of accuracy by carrying more decimal places. It should also be noted that any error made in a calculation will be corrected automatically in succeeding iterations if the work thereafter is done correctly.

6.7. CALLABLE BONDS

A *callable bond* is a bond in which the borrower has an option to redeem the bond prior to the maturity date. The earliest such *call date* will generally be several years after the issue date.

Callable bonds present a problem in calculating prices and yield rates, since the term of the bond is uncertain. Since the borrower has an option whether or not to call the bond, the investor should assume that the borrower will exercise his option to the disadvantage of the investor and should calculate his price or yield rate accordingly.

This principle is relatively easy to apply if the redemption values on all the redemption dates, including the maturity date, are equal. The following general rules will hold if this is the case:

1. If the yield rate is less than the modified coupon rate, i.e., if the bond sells at a premium, then assume that the redemption date will be the earliest possible date.
2. If the yield rate is greater than the modified coupon rate, i.e., if the bond sells at a discount, then assume that the redemption date will be the latest possible date.

The rationale for the above rules is clear. In case 1 there will be a loss at redemption, since the bond was bought at a premium. The most unfavorable situation occurs when the loss is as early as possible. In case 2 there will be a gain at redemption, since the bond was bought at a discount. The most unfavorable situation occurs when the gain is as late as possible.

If the redemption values on all the redemption dates, including the maturity date, are not equal, then the above principle is more difficult to apply. In general, it may be necessary to make some trial calculations at the various possible redemption dates to see which is the most unfavorable to the investor. The most unfavorable date will not necessarily be either the earliest or latest possible redemption date. Example 6.5 will illustrate this situation.

It should be noted that if a callable bond is redeemed at a date other than that assumed initially, then the yield rate, after the fact, is higher than originally assumed. However, in this situation the original purchase price and the term are both fixed so that the methods of Section 6.6 may be used directly.

Example 6.5. Consider a $100 par value 4% bond with semiannual coupons callable at $109 on any coupon date from the 5th through the 9th years, at $104.50 from the 10th through the 14th years and maturing at $100 at the end of 15 years. What is the highest price which an investor can pay and still be certain of a yield of (1) 5% convertible semiannually and (2) 3% convertible semiannually?

1. If the yield rate is to be 5%, then it is immediately clear that the latest possible redemption date will be least favorable to an investor, since the bond will be selling at a discount. Thus, the price is

$$P = 100 + (2 - 2.50)a_{\overline{30}|.025}$$
$$= 100 - (.50)(20.9303) = \$89.53 .$$

2. If the yield rate is to be 3%, then it is not immediately clear which redemption date is least favorable, since the bond will be selling at a premium. The price would be

$$109.00 + (2 - 1.6350)a_{\overline{n}|.015} \quad \text{for } n = 10, 11, \ldots, 19$$
$$104.50 + (2 - 1.5675)a_{\overline{n}|.015} \quad \text{for } n = 20, 21, \ldots, 29$$
$$100.00 + (2 - 1.5000)a_{\overline{n}|.015} \quad \text{for } n = 30 .$$

It is evident that the lowest price in each category will result when the lowest value of n is used, i.e., $n = 10$, 20, and 30. Thus, the prices to compare are

$$109.00 + (.3650)a_{\overline{10}|.015} = 109.00 + (.3650)(9.2222) \quad = \$112.37 ,$$
$$104.50 + (.4325)a_{\overline{20}|.015} = 104.50 + (.4325)(17.1686) = \$111.93 ,$$
$$100.00 + (.5000)a_{\overline{30}|.015} = 100.00 + (.5000)(24.0158) = \$112.01 .$$

The lowest price \$111.93 occurs for $n = 20$, i.e., for redemption 10 years after issue. This example illustrates that the least favorable redemption date can occur between the earliest and latest possible redemption dates when the redemption values are not equal at all the possible redemption dates. It is fairly common in practice for a callable bond to have redemption values which decrease as the term of the bond increases, as in this example. The excess of the redemption value over the par value, i.e., \$9 and \$4.50 in this example, is often termed the *call premium*.

6.8. SERIAL BONDS

As mentioned in Section 6.2 a borrower in need of a large amount of funds may choose to have a series of bonds issued with staggered redemption dates instead of with a common maturity date. These types of bonds are called *serial bonds* and are considered further in this section.

If the redemption date of each individual bond is known, then the valuation of any one bond can be performed by methods already described. The value of the entire issue of bonds is merely the sum of the values of the individual bonds. It will be shown that the value of the entire issue of bonds can be found more efficiently than by summing the individual bond values, however.

In some cases, the bonds to be redeemed on each successive redemption date are not known in advance but are chosen by lot. The value of any one bond is impossible to determine with certainty, since its redemption date depends upon chance. However, the value of the entire issue of bonds can be determined with certainty. Often a large investor will purchase an entire issue of serial bonds under these conditions.

The valuation of an issue of serial bonds can most efficiently be performed using Makeham's formula:

$$P = K + \frac{g}{i}(C - K). \tag{6.3}$$

Let the purchase price, redemption value, and present value of the redemption value for the first redemption date be denoted by P_1, C_1, and K_1, for the second redemption date by P_2, C_2, and K_2, and so forth until the last redemption date when we have P_n, C_n, and K_n. Thus we have

$$P_1 = K_1 + \frac{g}{i}(C_1 - K_1)$$

$$P_2 = K_2 + \frac{g}{i}(C_2 - K_2)$$

$$\cdot \qquad \cdot$$
$$\cdot \qquad \cdot$$
$$\cdot \qquad \cdot$$

$$P_n = K_n + \frac{g}{i}(C_n - K_n),$$

and summing, we obtain

$$P' = K' + \frac{g}{i}(C' - K') \tag{6.15}$$

where

$$P' = \sum_{t=1}^{n} P_t$$

$$C' = \sum_{t=1}^{n} C_t$$

and

$$K' = \sum_{t=1}^{n} K_t.$$

Thus, the price of an entire issue of serial bonds is denoted by P' and is given by formula (6.15). This formula is more efficient than a laborious summation of the prices of each individual bond, since C' and K' are usually quite simple to obtain. The sum C' is merely the sum of the redemption values for the entire issue of bonds, a figure readily obtainable. The sum K' is of simple form if the bonds are redeemed according to some systematic pattern at regular intervals. In this case, K' is some form of annuity for which a simple expression is possible. The following example illustrates this, as well as the rest of this section.

Example 6.6. Find the price of a $1000 issue of 5¼% bonds with annual coupons which will be redeemed in 10 annual installments at the end of the 11th through the 20th years from the issue date at 105. The bonds are bought to yield 4% effective.

In this example we have

$$F = 100$$
$$C = 105$$
$$r = .0525$$
$$g = \frac{100}{105}(.0525) = .05$$
$$i = .04$$
$$C' = 1050$$
$$K' = 105(v^{11} + v^{12} + \cdots + v^{20})$$
$$= 105(a_{\overline{20}|.04} - a_{\overline{10}|.04})$$
$$= 105(13.5903 - 8.1109)$$
$$= 575.337,$$

so that the price is

$$P' = 575.337 + \frac{.05}{.04}(1050 - 575.337)$$
$$= \$1168.67.$$

6.9. SOME GENERALIZATIONS

Several generalizations of bond formulas already discussed are possible. This section will describe two of these. It should be noted that a more general type of bond can always be handled by generalizing formula (6.1), i.e., by finding the present value of coupons and the present value of the redemption value separately and summing the two.

The two generalizations considered in this section are (1) yield rate and coupon rate at different frequencies and (2) yield rate and/or coupon rate not constant.

Yield rate and coupon rate at different frequencies

First, consider the case in which each coupon period contains k yield rate conversion periods. Let the term of the bond be n yield rate conversion periods. There is a coupon of Fr paid at the end of each k conversion periods. Thus, there are $\frac{n}{k}$ coupons paid in total.

From first principles, the general formula is

$$P = Fr\frac{a_{\overline{n}|}}{s_{\overline{k}|}} + Cv^n. \tag{6.16}$$

By simple algebra, it can be shown that the alternate formula is

$$P = C + \left(\frac{Fr}{s_{\overline{k}|}} - Ci\right)a_{\overline{n}|} . \tag{6.17}$$

Likewise, it is possible to show that the Makeham formula is

$$P = K + \frac{g}{is_{\overline{k}|}} (C - K) . \tag{6.18}$$

Formulas (6.16), (6.17), and (6.18) are generalized versions of formulas (6.1), (6.2), and (6.3) respectively.

Second, consider the case in which each yield rate conversion period contains m coupon periods. Let the term of the bond be n yield rate conversion periods. There is a coupon of $\frac{Fr}{m}$ paid at the end of each mth of a conversion period. Thus, there are mn coupons in total.

From first principles, the general formula is

$$P = Fr\, a_{\overline{n}|}^{(m)} + Cv^n . \tag{6.19}$$

By simple algebra, it can be shown that the alternate formula is

$$P = C + (Fr - Ci^{(m)})\, a_{\overline{n}|}^{(m)} . \tag{6.20}$$

Likewise, it is possible to show that the Makeham formula is

$$P = K + \frac{g}{i^{(m)}} (C - K) . \tag{6.21}$$

Formulas (6.19), (6.20), and (6.21) are generalized versions of formulas (6.1), (6.2), and (6.3) respectively.

Yield rate and/or coupon rate not constant

Preceding sections have assumed that the yield rate and the coupon rate are constant throughout the term of the bond. Cases in which one or the other or both rates are not constant can best be handled by generalizing formula (6.1). Example 6.7 is an illustration of this type.

Example 6.7. *Find the price of a $100 par value 20-year bond with annual coupons of 1 the first year, 2 the second year, . . . , 20 the last year, bought to yield 5% effective over the first 10 years and 4% effective over the second 10 years.*

From the general formula the price is

$$P = 100 v_{.05}^{10} v_{.04}^{10} + (Ia)_{\overline{10}|.05} + v_{.05}^{10}[10a_{\overline{10}|.04} + (Ia)_{\overline{10}|.04}] .$$

Now

$$(Ia)_{\overline{10}|.05} = \frac{\ddot{a}_{\overline{10}|.05} - 10v^{10}_{.05}}{.05} = \frac{8.1078 - 10(.61391)}{.05} = 39.3740$$

and

$$(Ia)_{\overline{10}|.04} = \frac{\ddot{a}_{\overline{10}|.04} - 10v^{10}_{.04}}{.04} = \frac{8.4353 - 10(.67556)}{.04} = 41.9925,$$

and the price is

$$P = 100(.61391)(.67556) + 39.3740 + (.61391)[10(8.1109) + 41.9925] = \$156.42.$$

6.10. OTHER SECURITIES

The preceding sections have been limited to a discussion of redeemable bonds. This section is concerned with two other types of securities: (1) preferred stock and irredeemable bonds and (2) common stock.

Preferred stock and irredeemable bonds

Preferred stock and irredeemable bonds are similar in that they both are types of fixed-income securities without redemption dates. Thus, the price must be equal to the present value of dividends or coupons forever, i.e., the dividends or coupons form a perpetuity. A version of formula (6.1) for this case would be

$$P = \frac{Fr}{i}. \tag{6.22}$$

Common stock

Common stock presents a different problem, since it is not a fixed-income security, i.e., the dividends are not level. In practice, common stock prices fluctuate widely in the stock market, often for little apparent reason. In theory, common stock prices should represent the present value of dividends. Of course, this calculation should take into account projected increases in the dividend scale. A theoretical calculation of this type is illustrated in Example 6.8.

Example 6.8.   A common stock is currently earning $2 per share and paying $1 per share in dividends. Assuming that the earnings of the corporation increase 5% per year indefinitely and that the corporation plans to continue to pay 50% of its earnings as divi-

dends, find the theoretical price to earn an investor a yield rate of
(1) 10%, (2) 8%, and (3) 6%.

1. The present value of dividends is

$$\frac{1}{1.10} + \frac{1.05}{(1.10)^2} + \frac{(1.05)^2}{(1.10)^3} + \cdots = \frac{\dfrac{1}{1.10}}{1 - \dfrac{1.05}{1.10}} = \$20 \; .$$

Thus, the theoretical price is 10 times current earnings.

2. The present value of dividends is

$$\frac{1}{1.08} + \frac{1.05}{(1.08)^2} + \frac{(1.05)^2}{(1.08)^3} + \cdots = \frac{\dfrac{1}{1.08}}{1 - \dfrac{1.05}{1.08}} = \$33\tfrac{1}{3} \; .$$

Thus, the theoretical price is $16\tfrac{2}{3}$ times current earnings.

3. The present value of dividends is

$$\frac{1}{1.06} + \frac{1.05}{(1.06)^2} + \frac{(1.05)^2}{(1.06)^3} + \cdots = \frac{\dfrac{1}{1.06}}{1 - \dfrac{1.05}{1.06}} = \$100 \; .$$

Thus, the theoretical price is 50 times current earnings.

EXERCISES

6.1. Introduction;   6.2. Types of securities

1. A 10-year accumulation bond with an initial par value of $1000 earns interest of 4% compounded semiannually. Find the price to yield an investor 5% effective.

6.3. Price of a bond

2. A $1000 par value 6% bond has coupons maturing January 1 and July 1 and will be redeemed July 1, 1971. The bond is bought January 1, 1969, to yield 4% compounded semiannually. Find the price.

3. A 20-year bond bearing 5% annual coupons and redeemable at $105 is bought to yield 4% effective. Find the price.

4. One bond with 4% semiannual coupons costs $112. Another with $4\tfrac{1}{2}$% semiannual coupons costs $118. Both are redeemable in n years and have the same yield rate convertible semiannually.
   a) Find the yield rate without the use of interest tables.
   b) Find n to the nearest integer.

5. Two $1000 bonds redeemable at par at the end of the same period are bought to yield 4% convertible semiannually. One bond costs $1136.78 and pays coupons

at 5% semiannually. The other bond pays coupons at $2\frac{1}{2}$% semiannually. Find the price of the second bond.

6. A \$1000 bond with coupons at $4\frac{1}{2}$% payable semiannually is redeemable after an unspecified number of years at \$1125. The bond is bought to yield 5% convertible semiannually. If the present value of the redemption value is \$225 at this yield rate, find the purchase price.

6.4. Premium and discount

7. Show that formula (6.6) reduces to formula (6.1) if $i' = i$.

8. Show algebraically that the sum of the interest paid column in Table 6.1 is equal to $ng - p$.

9. In Table 6.1 the amount of principal adjustment during the first period is $(g - i)v^n$. From the sinking fund point of view, show verbally and algebraically that

$$[(g - i)v^n]s_{\overline{n}|} = p .$$

10. For a \$1 bond the coupon rate is 150% of the yield rate and the premium is p. For another \$1 bond with the same number of coupons and the same yield rate, the coupon rate is 75% of the yield rate. Find the price of the second bond.

11. For a certain period a bond amortization schedule shows that the amount for amortization of premium is \$5 and that the required interest is 75% of the coupon. Find the amount of the coupon.

12. A \$1000 par value 5% bond with semiannual coupons has a book value of \$1100 on March 1, 1970, at a yield rate of 3% compounded semiannually. Find the amount for amortization of premium on September 1, 1970, and the new book value on that date.

13. A 20-year bond with annual coupons is bought at a discount to yield 5% effective. If the amount for accumulation of discount in the last year is \$5, find the total amount of discount in the original purchase price.

14. A \$1000 par value 10-year bond with 5% semiannual coupons is bought to yield 6% compounded semiannually. Find the total of the interest paid column in the bond amortization schedule.

15. A 20-year bond with annual coupons is bought at a premium to yield 5% effective. If the amount for amortization of premium in the 3rd payment is \$10, find the amount for amortization of premium in the 17th payment.

6.5. Valuation between interest payment dates

16. Derive formula (6.7).

17. Show that formula (6.8) can be written as

$$Fr \cdot {}_{1-k}|\ddot{a}_{\overline{n}|} + Cv^{n-k}$$

where n is the remaining number of coupons.

18. Show that formulas (6.10) and (6.11) are equivalent.

19. Find the market price and the flat price for the bond in Table 6.2 bought three months after its issue date.

6.6. Determination of yield rates

20. It is desired to find the price of a \$100 par value n-year bond with redemption value $C(C \neq 100)$, coupon rate r, and yield rate i. The instructions to a set of bond tables specify the following procedure:
    a) Find the price of a \$100 n-year 6% bond bought to yield i.
    b) Find the price of a \$100 n-year 3% bond bought to yield i.
    c) Subtract (b) from (a), and then subtract the result from (b).
    d) Multiply (c) by .01 $(C - 100)$.
    e) The price of the n-year bond with redemption value C, coupon rate r, and yield rate i is equal to the price of an n-year bond with redemption value 100, coupon rate r, and yield rate i, plus the result from (d).
    Verify the validity of this procedure. All rates are convertible semiannually.

21. A \$100 par value 10-year bond with $4\frac{1}{2}\%$ semiannual coupons is selling for \$95. Find the yield rate:
    a) By interpolating in Table 6.4.
    b) By using formula (6.13).
    c) By using formula (6.12), together with formula (3.25) carried to the second power in i.

22. A \$100 bond with annual coupons is redeemable at par at the end of 15 years. At a purchase price of \$112 the yield rate is exactly 1% less than the coupon rate. Find the yield rate by interpolation in the interest tables.

6.7. Callable bonds

23. A \$1000 par value bond has 4% semiannual coupons and is callable at the end of the 10th through the 15th years at par.
    a) Find the price to yield 3% compounded semiannually.
    b) Find the price to yield 5% compounded semiannually.

24. If the bond in Exercise 23(b) were actually called at the end of 10 years, calculate the yield rate to the owner of the bond by interpolation in Table 6.4.

6.8. Serial bonds

25. A \$100 serial bond is to be redeemed in \$10 installments of principal per year over the next 10 years. Interest at the rate of 6% is paid annually on the balance outstanding. How much should an investor pay for this bond if he desires a yield rate of 4% effective? Express your answer as a function of $a_{\overline{10}|.04}$.

26. A \$1000 serial bond is redeemed in \$50 installments of principal at the end of the 6th through the 25th years from the date of issue. Interest at the rate of 6% is paid annually on the balance outstanding. What is the price to yield an investor 4% effective?

27. A \$100,000 issue of 4% serial bonds dated July 1, 1968, with interest payable semiannually on the balance outstanding, are to be redeemed in installments of \$25,000 each on the first of July in 1971, 1973, 1975, and 1977. The price to yield 3% convertible semiannually is $100,000(1 + k)$. Prove that

$$k = \frac{1}{3}\left(1 - \frac{a_{\overline{22}|} - a_{\overline{6}|}}{4a_{\overline{4}|}}\right)$$

where all interest functions are evaluated at $1\frac{1}{2}\%$.

28. A \$78,000 issue of serial bonds with annual coupons of 4% on the balance outstanding is to be redeemed in 12 annual installments beginning at the end of the 5th year. The amount redeemed at the end of the 5th year is \$12,000, at the end of the 6th year \$11,000, and so forth, until all the bonds are redeemed. Find an expression for the price to yield an investor 5% effective.

6.9. Some generalizations

29. *a*) Derive formula (6.17).
    b) Derive formula (6.18).
30. *a*) Derive formula (6.20).
    b) Derive formula (6.21).
31. Find the price of a \$1000 par value 10-year bond which has coupons at 8% per annum payable quarterly and is bought to yield 6% per annum compounded semiannually.
32. The price of a \$100 bond, which matures in n years for \$105, has semiannual coupons of \$2, and is bought to yield an effective rate i, can be expressed as

$$\frac{Av^n + B}{i^{(2)}}.$$

Find A and B.

33. A \$1000 par value 20-year bond has annual coupons of 5% for the first 10 years and 4% for the second 10 years. Find an expression for the price of the bond bought to yield a rate of interest convertible quarterly.
34. A 10-year bond has annual coupons which vary $10, 9, 8, \ldots, 1$, and it matures for \$100. If the bond is bought to yield i effective, find expressions for
    a) The amount of the fifth coupon which is required interest.
    b) The amount of the fifth coupon used to amortize the book value.

6.10. Other securities

35. Find the price of a preferred stock paying \$5 dividends at the end of each quarter, which is bought to yield 5% effective.
36. What would be the answer to Example (6.8) for a yield rate of 5% or less?
37. Find an expression for the theoretical price of a common stock paying annual dividends at the end of each year. The earnings in the year just ending were E. It is assumed that the percentage growth in earnings for the tth year is k_t, the

yield rate for the tth year is i_t, and the percentage of earnings which the corporation plans to pay out as dividends in the tth year is $p_t (0 \le p_t \le 1)$.

Miscellaneous problems

38. If P is the price of a bond given by formula (6.1), show that

a) $\dfrac{dP}{di} = -Cv[g(Ia)_{\overline{n}|} + nv^n]$.

b) $\dfrac{dP}{dg} = C \cdot a_{\overline{n}|}$.

39. A \$1 bond has annual coupons of g at the end of the 11th through the 25th years from the date of issue. The bond matures at the end of 25 years for \$1 and is bought to yield i effective. Find an expression for the price in a modified Makeham form

$$K' + \frac{g}{i}(C' - K').$$

Define K' and C'.

40. A \$100 par value 12-year bond has coupons at the annual rate of 5% payable continuously. If the bond is bought to yield δ, find the price of the bond expressed strictly as a function of δ.

41. A bond of amount 1 sells for $1 + p$ at a certain fixed yield rate. If the bond's coupon rate were halved, the price would be $1 + q$. If the bond's coupon rate were doubled, the price can be expressed as $1 + Ap + Bq$. Find A and B.

42. A corporation has an issue of bonds with annual 6% coupons maturing in five years, which are quoted at a price that yields 4% effective. It is proposed to replace this issue of bonds with an issue of 5% bonds with annual coupons. How long must the new issue run so that the bondholders will still realize 4% effective? Express your answer to the nearest year.

43. An investor buys a \$100 par value 3% bond with semiannual coupons of which \$50 matures in 9 years at \$51 and the other \$50 matures in 10 years at \$50. Show that the price to yield an effective rate of interest i is

$$3a_{\overline{10}|}^{(2)} + (101 + 51i - 1.5s_{\overline{1}|}^{(2)})v^{10}.$$

44. Unsophisticated investors often use the "straight-line" method of writing up or writing down the book values of bonds. By this method the book values are linear. It is interesting to note that the "straight-line" method is equivalent to the assumptions underlying formula (6.13).

a) Find the book values for the bond in Table 6.2 by this method.

b) Find the book values for the bond in Table 6.3 by this method.

c) What can you conclude from a comparison of the answers in (a) and (b) with the true values from Table 6.2 and Table 6.3?

45. A 6% bond with annual coupons redeemable at the end of n years at \$105, sells at \$93 to yield $7\frac{1}{2}\%$ compounded annually. Find the price of a 5% bond with

annual coupons redeemable at the end of $2n$ years at \$104 to yield $7\frac{1}{2}\%$ compounded annually. Express the answer to four decimal places.

46. Find the price of a \$1000 par value 10-year bond with 5% annual coupons bought to yield 4% effective. It is assumed a certainty that the coupons will be paid when due, but it is assumed that the probability the borrower will repay the principal is only .98, i.e., there is a 2% chance of complete default at maturity. Assume that an appropriate price is given by the expected present value of payments by the borrower. (The expected present value of a payment is equal to the present value of the payment multiplied by the probability that it will be paid.)

CHAPTER 7. Miscellaneous topics

7.1. INTRODUCTION

Chapter 7 includes several miscellaneous topics in the theory of interest not previously discussed directly. Each section is largely independent of the other sections in the chapter.

7.2. VALUATION OF SECURITIES

Financial institutions, such as insurance companies and banks, which invest in securities must assign values to the securities which they hold for financial statements. The determination of appropriate asset values for these securities is an issue on which universal agreement does not exist.

The determination of asset values often reflects accepted accounting principles, legal restrictions, and tradition, as well as theoretical considerations. Valuation methods will often vary depending upon the situation at hand. For example, identical securities may have widely different reported asset values for a private pension fund as compared with a life insurance company. Also valuation methods will often tend to vary widely depending upon the type of security being valued. For example, an appropriate method for bonds may differ substantially from an appropriate method for common stocks.

In practice, three main approaches to the determination of asset values have developed. Each approach is subject to various refinements and modifications. All three methods are in current use for the valuation of securities in various situations.

It is not the intent of this section to give a complete description of all the modifications of the various methods, nor is it within the scope of this section to try to determine which method should be used in any given situation. Rather, the purpose of this section is to briefly acquaint the student with these three main approaches which are being used in practice.

The first approach is to use *market value* as the measure of asset value. There is a school of thought which believes that market value is the only true measure of the current worth of a security. Also it is maintained that market value is objective and is easily understood.

The big disadvantage of market value is that it often exhibits rather marked fluctuations. This lack of stability in asset value often creates serious problems. For this reason modified market value methods have been developed. These methods attempt to smooth out part of the peaks and valleys in the pure market value approach. Of course, any such modified market value method introduces an element of arbitrariness and results in a loss of simplicity.

The second approach is to use original *cost* as a measure of asset value. For redeemable bonds an adjusted cost method is often used. This adjusted cost method is equivalent to the amortized value resulting from the amortization of premium or the accumulation of discount as described in Chapter 6.

The actual cost or adjusted cost of an asset is often called the *book value* of the asset, since this is the value assigned to the asset in the books of the investor. Any excess of market value over book value is termed an *unrealized capital gain*, while any excess of book value over market value is termed an *unrealized capital loss*. If an asset is sold for a price in excess of book value, the profit is termed a *realized capital gain*, while if the price is less than the book value, the loss is termed a *realized capital loss*.

Unrealized capital gains and losses on amortized bonds are frequently ignored on the books of the investor on the theory that bonds are usually held to maturity. In periods of high interest rates, book values for bonds are substantially in excess of market values; whereas the opposite is true in periods of low interest rates.

The distinction between unrealized and realized capital gains and losses is important, since in the United States realized capital gains and losses are reflected in the income tax return of the investor whereas unrealized capital gains and losses are not. Also, for income tax purposes, a distinction is made between *long-term* capital gains and losses (currently applicable to assets held over periods longer than six months) and *short-term* capital gains and losses (currently applicable to assets held over periods shorter than or equal to six months).

Book value produces asset values which are quite stable, objective, and easily understood. Also book value produces an element of conservatism if market value is greater than book value. However, book value does tend to become an increasingly unrealistic measure of asset value if market value and book value diverge, and it is nonconservative if book value is greater than market value.

The third approach can be described as a *present value method*. According to this method the asset value is equal to the present value of all future payments under the security, where the present value is taken at some appropriate rate of interest. Calculations of this type are illustrated in Chapter 6 for bonds, preferred stock, and common stock.

The present value method has the advantage that a whole portfolio can be valued on a consistent basis, since the same interest rate can be used in taking all the present values. This is especially significant if an interest rate is assumed in calculating values for the liabilities which offset the assets. Examples of this type would be life insurance companies and pension funds, which assume interest rates in calculating most of their liability values.

The present value method is very sensitive to the choice of interest rate used in taking the present values. This can be both an advantage and a disadvantage of the method. The present value method can produce asset values which are significantly different from either market value or book value. Also the method is less easily understood and less easily applied in practice than either market value or book value.

In summary, there is no valuation method for securities which is used in all situations. The student should be careful when encountering asset values in practical situations to ascertain the method of valuation.

7.3. INTEREST MEASUREMENT OF A FUND

A significant problem in practical work is the determination of the effective rate of interest earned by a fund of money. Recall that the basic definition of an effective rate of interest given in Section 1.3 assumed that the principal remains constant throughout the year and that all the interest earned is paid at the end of the year. In practice these assumptions are often not satisfied. It is common for a fund to be incremented with new principal additions, decremented with principal withdrawals, and incremented with interest earnings many times throughout a year, often at irregular intervals. Some method must be devised for these situations to determine reasonable effective rates of interest.

Consider finding the effective rate of interest earned by a fund over a period of one year. We make the following definitions:

A = the amount in the fund at the beginning of the year.

B = the amount in the fund at the end of the year.

I = the amount of interest earned during the year.

n_t = the amount of new principal added at time t where $0 \le t \le 1$.

n = the total amount of new principal added during the year, i.e.,

$$n = \sum_t n_t.$$

w_t = the amount of principal withdrawn at time t where $0 \le t \le 1$.

w = the total amount of principal withdrawn during the year, i.e.,

$$w = \sum_t w_t.$$

$_a i_b$ = the amount of interest earned by 1 invested at time b over the following a years where $a \ge 0$, $b \ge 0$, and $a + b \le 1$.

The fund at the end of the year must equal the fund at the beginning of the year plus new principal added minus principal withdrawn plus interest earned, i.e.,

$$B = A + n - w + I. \tag{7.1}$$

To be consistent with the definition of the effective rate of interest given in Chapter 1 we will assume that all the interest earned, I, is received at the end of the year. Then an exact equation of value for the interest earned over the year $(0 \le t \le 1)$ is:

$$I = iA + \sum_t n_t \cdot {}_{1-t}i_t - \sum_t w_t \cdot {}_{1-t}i_t. \tag{7.2}$$

Unfortunately, formula (7.2) is not in a form which can be directly solved for i. It is necessary to find a value for $_{1-t}i_t$. Assuming compound interest throughout the year, we have

$$_{1-t}i_t = (1 + i)^{1-t} - 1. \tag{7.3}$$

We can substitute formula (7.3) into formula (7.2) obtaining an exact equation for i. Unfortunately, the equation is still not readily solvable for i. However, it can be solved by successive approximation or iteration. Since the summations may involve many terms each involving a fractional exponent, a digital computer will usually be necessary. Section 5.7 guarantees that the rate found by iteration will be unique as long as the fund balance never becomes negative.

If a computer is not available or if only approximate answers are required, it is possible to produce a simplified formula by making the assumption that

$$_{1-t}i_t = (1 - t)i. \tag{7.4}$$

Formula (7.4) is a version of simple interest for this situation. We can substitute formula (7.4) into formula (7.2) and solve for i, obtaining

$$i = \frac{I}{A + \sum_t n_t(1 - t) - \sum_t w_t(1 - t)} . \tag{7.5}$$

The numerator of formula (7.5) is the amount of interest earned on the fund. The denominator can be interpreted as the effective amount of principal invested and is often called the *exposure associated with i*. Although formula (7.5) does not produce a true effective rate of interest because of the simple interest assumption, it will generally produce results quite close to a true effective rate of interest as long as n and w are small in relation to A, which is often the case in practice.

Formula (7.5) is in a form which can be directly calculated. However, the two summation terms in the denominator are often rather laborious. Therefore, a further simplifying assumption is often made; namely, that principal additions and principal withdrawals occur uniformly throughout the year. Thus, on the average, we can assume that all principal additions and withdrawals occur at $t = \frac{1}{2}$. If this assumption is made, then formula (7.5) becomes

$$\begin{aligned} i &= \frac{I}{A + \frac{1}{2}n - \frac{1}{2}w} \\ &= \frac{I}{A + \frac{1}{2}(B - A - I)} \qquad \text{from formula (7.1)} \\ &= \frac{2I}{A + B - I} . \end{aligned} \tag{7.6}$$

Figure (7.1) is an illustrative time diagram for this formula.

FIGURE 7.1

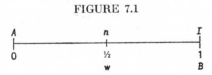

Formula (7.6) is a very important formula which is widely used in practice to calculate effective rates of interest, e.g., it is used by all life insurance companies in the United States for their annual statements. It is a very convenient formula, since it involves only A, B, and I, which are readily available. However, it should be remembered that it does assume a uniform distribution of principal additions and withdrawals throughout the year. If this assumption is not warranted, then the more exact formula (7.5) should be used.

Formula (7.4) looks very similar to simple interest as defined in Section 1.4. However, it can be shown that the two are not equivalent by considering the form of δ_t under each assumption.

As defined in Chapter 1, the accumulation function for simple interest is given by

$$a(t) = 1 + ti. \tag{1.5}$$

This is equivalent to the assumption that

$$_t i_0 = ti. \tag{7.7}$$

We can find δ_t as follows:

$$\delta_t = \frac{Da(t)}{a(t)}$$
$$= \frac{D[1 + ti]}{1 + ti}$$
$$= \frac{i}{1 + ti}. \tag{7.8}$$

Alternatively, we have

$$e^{\int_0^t \delta_r dr} = 1 + {}_t i_0 = 1 + ti$$

or

$$\int_0^t \delta_r dr = \log_e [1 + ti],$$

and differentiating with respect to t

$$\delta_t = \frac{i}{1 + ti}. \tag{7.8}$$

For the version of simple interest defined by formula (7.4) we have

$$e^{\int_t^1 \delta_r dr} = 1 + {}_{1-t} i_t = 1 + (1 - t)i$$

or

$$\int_t^1 \delta_r dr = \log_e [1 + (1 - t)i],$$

and differentiating with respect to t

$$\delta_t = \frac{i}{1 + (1 - t)i} \qquad 0 \leq t \leq 1. \tag{7.9}$$

Clearly formulas (7.8) and (7.9) are not equivalent; in fact, they are equal only for $t = \frac{1}{2}$. It should be noted that formula (7.8) is a decreasing function of t, while formula (7.9) is an increasing function of t.

It is instructive to derive formula (7.6) by an alternate argument. As before, we assume that the interest earned, I, is paid at the end of the year. Also we assume that the excess of principal additions over withdrawals ignoring interest, $B - A - I$, is received uniformly throughout the year. Thus we have

$$A(1 + i) + (B - A - I)\overline{s}_{\overline{1}|} = B.$$

Now

$$\overline{s}_{\overline{1}|} = \frac{i}{\delta} = \frac{i}{i - \dfrac{i^2}{2} + \dfrac{i^3}{3} - \cdots} = \frac{1}{1 - \dfrac{i}{2} + \dfrac{i^2}{3} - \cdots},$$

which is approximately equal to $1 + \frac{1}{2}i$, ignoring terms of higher than the first degree in i. Therefore

$$A(1 + i) + (B - A - I)(1 + \tfrac{1}{2}i) = B$$

or

$$i = \frac{2I}{A + B - I}. \tag{7.6}$$

There are several relevant points in connection with the use of formula (7.6) in practice. First, it should be noted that the values of A and B are dependent upon the method of valuation of the assets of the fund as discussed in Section 7.2. Thus the effective rate of interest can vary significantly depending upon whether assets are valued on a market value, book value, or present value basis. Second, the value of I may vary substantially depending upon whether or not capital gains are included in I. Capital gains may or may not be included depending upon the purpose of the calculation. Third, the value of I will usually be the net investment income after investment expenses.

Example 7.1. At the beginning of the year an investment fund was established with an initial deposit of $1000. A new deposit of $500 was made at the end of four months. Withdrawals of $200 and $100 were made at the end of six months and eight months, respectively. The amount in the fund at the end of the year is $1272. Find the effective rate of interest earned by the fund during the year, using formula (7.5).

The interest earned, I, is

$$1272 - (1000 + 500 - 200 - 100) = 72 \, .$$

Applying formula (7.5) we have

$$i = \frac{72}{1000 + \frac{2}{3} \cdot 500 - (\frac{1}{2} \cdot 200 + \frac{1}{3} \cdot 100)} = \frac{72}{1200} = .06, \text{ or } 6\% \, .$$

Example 7.2.   Find the effective rate of interest earned during 1969 by a life insurance company with the following data:

Assets, December 31, 1968............	***10,000,000***
Premium income....................	***1,000,000***
Gross investment income..........	***530,000***
Policy benefits.....................	***420,000***
Investment expenses..............	***20,000***
Other expenses....................	***180,000***

We have

$$A = 10,000,000$$
$$B = 10,000,000 + 1,000,000 + 530,000 - 420,000 - 20,000 - 180,000$$
$$\quad = 10,910,000$$
$$I = 530,000 - 20,000$$
$$\quad = 510,000 \, .$$

Therefore, using formula (7.6)

$$i = \frac{2(510,000)}{10,000,000 + 10,910,000 - 510,000}$$
$$\quad = .05, \text{ or } 5\% \, .$$

7.4. CONSTRUCTION OF TABLES

It is important in practical work to have tabulated values of interest functions available for the great majority of situations which arise. Many such tables are readily available in published form. These tables are frequently much more extensive than the tables in the Appendices. However, even with extensive tables available, situations will arise in which a large number of nontabulated values are required. In these cases, tables of the required values will have to be constructed.

There are several decisions which must be made before any tables can be constructed.

1. The first decision involves the functions to be tabulated. General purpose interest tables will usually include values of v^n, $(1 + i)^n$, $a_{\overline{n}|}$, $s_{\overline{n}|}$, and $\frac{1}{s_{\overline{n}|}} \left(\text{or } \frac{1}{a_{\overline{n}|}} \right)$. Also values of the various constants such as $i^{(m)}$, $d^{(m)}$, and δ

will generally be included. For special situations tables of other functions may be required. For example, tables similar to Appendix II are useful for annuity values payable $m$thly. Another example is a table which divides installment payments into principal and interest. Still another example is a table of bond values as described in Chapter 6.

2. The second decision is the number of interest rates to include in the tables. In many cases this will largely be determined by whatever interest rates are desired which are not included in published tables. It should be remembered that tables must include values for nominal as well as effective rates of interest. This can significantly increase the number of very low interest rates which must be tabulated. For example, if the lowest annual rate of interest is 1% but frequencies of conversion as great as monthly are required, then rates of interest as low as $\frac{1}{12}\%$ must be tabulated.

3. The third decision is the range of the functional values. This decision is dependent upon the terms of various common financial transactions for which the tables will be used. The range will also depend upon the frequency of conversion. For example, values up to $n = 120$ would cover more than a century at an effective rate of interest but would cover only 10 years at a nominal rate of interest convertible monthly.

4. The fourth decision is the number of significant digits to which the functional values are carried. This decision is dependent upon the purpose for which the tables are to be used.

5. The fifth decision is the arrangement of the functional values in the tables. It is possible to arrange the functional values either by function or by rate of interest. Most tables are arranged by rate of interest, as is the case in Appendix I. This is the most convenient arrangement in any problem requiring several functions at one rate of interest.

After the above decisions have been made, the actual construction of the tables remains. If the number of tables to be constructed is large, then it will be efficient to use a digital computer if one is available. With a computer direct calculation of interest functions is both straightforward and efficient. The checking of results from a computer is relatively simple, since checking a few sample values of each function is generally sufficient to establish the accuracy of the entire table.

Often a computer will not be used to construct interest tables, either because one is not available or because the volume of calculations is not sufficient to warrant the use of a computer. In these cases, the tables will be constructed by hand with the aid of a desk calculator.

When tables are being constructed by hand, it is important to adopt methods which will involve the minimum amount of computation, the minimum chance of error, and the minimum amount of checking. Direct calculation of each functional value is very probably not the most efficient method for construction of interest tables by hand.

A method frequently used which is more efficient than direct calculation is the *continuous method*. By this method functional values are generated successively, i.e., each one is obtained from the immediately preceding one. The continuous method involves three steps:

1. A *starting value* by which to start the process.
2. A *recursive formula* by which successive values are calculated.
3. *Check values* calculated independently of the recursive process.

A starting value is usually obtained by direct calculation using a standard formula for the function in question. For example, if it is desired to construct a table of values of $s_{\overline{n}|}$ for $n = 1$ to 50, then the starting value would be $s_{\overline{1}|} = 1$.

A recursive formula is a formula which connects successive values of the function, i.e., if $f(n - 1)$ is given, the recursive formula gives an expression for $f(n)$. In the above example, the recursive formula would be $s_{\overline{n}|} = s_{\overline{n-1}|} + (1 + i)^{n-1}$ or, alternatively, $s_{\overline{n}|} = (1 + i)s_{\overline{n-1}|} + 1$. Using the starting value and the recursive formula, values of $s_{\overline{n}|}$ would be generated for each successive n up to and including $n = 50$.

Check values are functional values calculated independently of the recursive process. The most complete check would be to perform the calculations twice independently and compare the results. However, there are several checks possible short of a complete check.

The first of these would be to calculate the last functional value independently. Ideally if the ending value is correct, then all the values are probably correct, since each value was obtained from the preceding value. The only possible errors left would be two compensating errors which offset each other or an error in copying answers from a desk calculator. In practice, several check values could be calculated to lessen the chance of the above errors and to avoid carrying one error forward too far. In the above example, check values for $n = 10, 20, 30, 40, 50,$ and 60 could be calculated.

A second check would be a summation check, i.e., an independent check of the total of a series of functional values. For example, the sum of values of v^n for $n = 1$ to 50 would have to add up to $a_{\overline{50}|}$ calculated independently. As another example, the sum of the principal repaid column in an amortization schedule must equal the original amount of principal.

A third check would be to examine differences of the functional values to see that they progress smoothly. This method is often useful in providing a quick check for any significant errors.

The continuous method does have disadvantages. First, it may be difficult to apply if no simple recursive formula exists. For example, the continuous method would not work well for values of $\dfrac{1}{s_{\overline{n}|}}$. Second, it is subject to accumulated rounding errors. For example, values of $(1 + i)^n$ generated by a recursive formula would be subject to rounding error unless several decimal places past the required degree of accuracy are carried.

7.5. LIFE INSURANCE SETTLEMENT OPTIONS

One application of the theory of interest is in the settlement of life insurance policies. A life insurance settlement occurs (1) upon the death of the insured, (2) upon surrender for the net cash value, or (3) upon maturity as an endowment. The settlement may take the form of a lump sum. However, almost all policies allow the election of one of several possible *settlement options* in lieu of the lump sum. These options allow the recipient of the proceeds of a policy to spread them out over a period of time.

For all types of settlement options the insurance company normally credits interest from the date at which the net proceeds could have been taken as a lump sum. In all cases the fundamental principle is that the present value of payments under the settlement option must be equal to the net proceeds on a lump-sum basis.

Almost all policies have a minimum guaranteed interest rate specified in the policy for the calculation of settlement options. This rate is often relatively low, since it is guaranteed indefinitely into the future. However, many companies in periods of higher rates of interest will credit *excess interest*, so that the recipient of the proceeds will be credited with total interest at the prevailing market rate of interest.

Most standard policies will have the following five options:

1. *Proceeds left on deposit at interest.* This option is essentially identical to depositing a lump sum in a bank or other financial institution. The insurance company will credit interest, usually at an effective rate. The interest can either be left to accumulate or can be taken in cash as it is earned. Under this option the recipient usually can at some future date take the accumulated value as a lump sum or can apply it under some other settlement option. No new principles are involved in settlements under this option.

2. *A specified number of equal installments.* This option involves using the lump-sum amount to buy an annuity-certain for a fixed period of time. The annuity-certain can be an annuity-immediate or an annuity-due, with the latter being by far the most common. Also the payments may

be made at varying frequencies. Annual, semiannual, quarterly, and monthly modes are the most common. Factors for this settlement option usually are printed in the policy. Table 7.1 is an example of this type of table for an interest rate of 3%. The factors are tabulated per $1000 of net proceeds, so that the formula is

$$\frac{1000}{m\ddot{a}_{\overline{n}|}^{(m)}} \tag{7.10}$$

for values of $m = 1$, 2, 4, and 12 and values of $n = 1 - 30$. The denominator of formula (7.10) can be evaluated from the functions in Appendix I. If nonintegral values of n are allowed, tables such as Appendix II will have to be used.

TABLE 7.1

Number of Years Payable	Annual Installments	Semiannual Installments	Quarterly Installments	Monthly Installments
1	$1000.00	$503.69	$252.78	$84.47
2	507.38	255.56	128.25	42.86
3	343.23	172.88	86.76	28.99
4	261.19	131.56	66.02	22.06
5	211.99	106.78	53.59	17.91
6	179.22	90.27	45.30	15.14
7	155.83	78.49	39.39	13.16
8	138.31	69.67	34.96	11.68
9	124.69	62.81	31.52	10.53
10	113.82	57.33	28.77	9.61
11	104.93	52.85	26.52	8.86
12	97.54	49.13	24.66	8.24
13	91.29	45.98	23.08	7.71
14	85.95	43.29	21.73	7.26
15	81.33	40.97	20.56	6.87
16	77.29	38.93	19.54	6.53
17	73.74	37.14	18.64	6.23
18	70.59	35.56	17.84	5.96
19	67.78	34.14	17.13	5.73
20	65.26	32.87	16.50	5.51
21	62.98	31.72	15.92	5.32
22	60.92	30.69	15.40	5.15
23	59.04	29.74	14.92	4.99
24	57.33	28.88	14.49	4.84
25	55.76	28.09	14.09	4.71
26	54.31	27.36	13.73	4.59
27	52.98	26.69	13.39	4.47
28	51.74	26.06	13.08	4.37
29	50.60	25.49	12.79	4.27
30	49.53	24.95	12.52	4.18

3. *Installments of a certain level amount.* This option involves using the lump-sum amount to buy an annuity-certain for a fixed amount of installment payments for as long as the proceeds will last. In general there will be an irregular final payment necessary. The annuity-certain can be an annuity-immediate or an annuity-due, with the latter being by far the most common. Annual, semiannual, quarterly, and monthly modes are most common. Factors are not printed in the policy form, since the number of combinations is essentially limitless. Therefore, each case will require a special calculation. Since the term of the annuity will in general be a fractional number of years, tables such as Appendix II will have to be used. The type of calculation that is necessary for these cases is illustrated by Example 4.5.

4. *Installments for life with a period certain.* This option the lump-sum amount to buy a life annuity with a period certain. The annuity can be an annuity-immediate or an annuity-due, with the latter being by far the most common. Also the payments may be made at varying frequencies, with a monthly mode being most common. Factors for this settlement option usually are printed in the policy. Table 7.2 is an example of this type of table. The factors are tabulated per $1000 of proceeds similarly to Table 7.1 for the annuity-certain. The values for a life annuity with a period certain depend upon probabilities of living and dying and therefore are beyond the scope of this book. For a complete discussion of life annuities the reader is referred to a textbook on life contingencies.

The formula for the settlement option factor is

$$\frac{1000}{m\left(\ddot{a}_{\overline{n}|}^{(m)} + {}_{n|}\ddot{a}_x^{(m)}\right)} \tag{7.11}$$

where ${}_{n|}\ddot{a}_x^{(m)}$ is the present value of an n-year deferred life annuity-due payable $m$thly to the recipient aged x at the date of settlement. This term continues payments for life after the expiration of the certain period.

Table 7.2 includes values for $m = 12$ and for $n = 5, 10, 15,$ and 20. In practice other values of n are often allowed; e.g., if $n = 0$, then the annuity becomes a straight life annuity. Table 7.2 is based upon the Annuity Table for 1949 projected 30 years with Projection Scale B at 3% interest. It should be noted that a separate table is necessary for males and females. This differential by sex is necessary to reflect the greater life expectancy of females.

TABLE 7.2

MONTHLY INSTALLMENTS

Male Age	Certain Period				Female Age	Certain Period			
	5 Yrs.	10 Yrs.	15 Yrs.	20 Yrs.		5 Yrs.	10 Yrs.	15 Yrs.	20 Yrs.
51	4.57	4.52	4.43	4.31	51	4.16	4.14	4.11	4.05
52	4.66	4.61	4.51	4.37	52	4.24	4.22	4.18	4.11
53	4.76	4.70	4.59	4.44	53	4.32	4.30	4.25	4.18
54	4.87	4.80	4.68	4.50	54	4.41	4.38	4.33	4.25
55	4.98	4.90	4.76	4.57	55	4.50	4.47	4.41	4.31
56	5.10	5.01	4.85	4.64	56	4.60	4.57	4.50	4.39
57	5.22	5.12	4.95	4.71	57	4.71	4.67	4.59	4.46
58	5.36	5.24	5.04	4.77	58	4.82	4.77	4.68	4.53
59	5.50	5.36	5.14	4.84	59	4.94	4.88	4.77	4.61
60	5.65	5.50	5.24	4.91	60	5.07	5.00	4.88	4.68
61	5.81	5.63	5.35	4.97	61	5.21	5.13	4.98	4.76
62	5.98	5.78	5.45	5.03	62	5.35	5.26	5.09	4.83
63	6.17	5.93	5.56	5.09	63	5.51	5.40	5.20	4.90
64	6.36	6.09	5.67	5.15	64	5.68	5.55	5.31	4.97
65	6.57	6.25	5.77	5.21	65	5.86	5.70	5.43	5.04
66	6.79	6.43	5.88	5.25	66	6.05	5.87	5.55	5.11
67	7.03	6.60	5.98	5.30	67	6.26	6.04	5.67	5.17
68	7.28	6.79	6.09	5.34	68	6.48	6.22	5.78	5.23
69	7.55	6.98	6.18	5.37	69	6.72	6.41	5.90	5.28
70	7.84	7.17	6.28	5.40	70	6.98	6.60	6.02	5.33
71	8.15	7.36	6.37	5.43	71	7.25	6.81	6.13	5.37
72	8.48	7.56	6.45	5.45	72	7.55	7.01	6.23	5.40
73	8.82	7.76	6.52	5.47	73	7.86	7.23	6.33	5.43
74	9.19	7.95	6.59	5.48	74	8.20	7.44	6.42	5.45
75	9.58	8.14	6.64	5.49	75	8.56	7.66	6.51	5.47

5. *Any other option mutually agreed upon.* Many companies will allow a variety of other options, some of which involve probabilities of living and dying as well as interest, and some of which involve interest only. Also many companies allow the proceeds to be divided and placed into more than one option.

Example 7.3.   A man dies leaving a life insurance policy with net proceeds of $10,000. Determine the distribution of proceeds under the following settlement options assuming 3% interest and that any payments to be made commence immediately: (1) leave the proceeds on deposit for 10 years; (2) monthly installments for 10 years; (3) monthly installments of $100; (4) monthly installments to his wife aged 55 for 10 years certain and as long thereafter as she lives; and (5) monthly installments to his son who is just entering *college as a freshman, installments to be paid at the beginning of each month for nine months for each of the next four years.*

1. At the end of 10 years the proceeds will amount to

$$10,000(1.03)^{10} = \$13,439.20 \,.$$

Alternatively, the \$10,000 can be left intact and the interest can be taken in cash as it is earned.

2. From Table 7.1 the amount of the monthly installment is

$$10(9.61) = \$96.10 \,.$$

3. From Example 4.5 the proceeds will provide for 114 regular monthly payments plus a smaller final payment of \$64.22.

4. From Table 7.2 the amount of the monthly installment is

$$10(4.47) = \$44.70 \,.$$

5. The equation of value is

$$10,000 = 12R\ddot{a}^{(12)}_{\frac{9}{12}}(1 + v + v^2 + v^3)$$

$$= 12R\ddot{a}^{(12)}_{\frac{9}{12}}\ddot{a}_{\overline{4}|}$$

or

$$R = \frac{10,000}{12\ddot{a}^{(12)}_{\frac{9}{12}}\ddot{a}_{\overline{4}|}}$$

$$= \frac{10,000}{(8.91194)(3.8286)}$$

$$= \$293.08 \text{ per month.}$$

7.6. INSTALLMENT LOANS

In recent years it has become common for sales of expensive items, such as cars and household appliances, to be made on the *installment loan* basis. In such transactions a down payment is often required and the balance is paid off in installments including principal and interest.

There are a variety of methods used in practice to determine the amount of each installment payment, given the amount of the down payment and the term of the loan. The most common method is to add a *carrying charge* to the balance after the down payment and to divide this total by the number of payments to obtain the installment payment. We make the following definitions, which will serve throughout the rest of this section:

A = initial loan balance after the down payment.

K = carrying charge.

m = number of payments per year.

n = total number of payments in the term of the loan.

i = annual rate of interest.

The amount of each installment payment made m times per year is $\dfrac{A + K}{n}$. For example, if a \$650 color television set is sold with a down payment of \$50 and the balance is to be paid in 12 monthly installments with a carrying charge of \$60, then the monthly installment would be

$$\frac{600 + 60}{12} = \$55.$$

In general, the rate of interest in an installment loan is not stated directly but is implied by the original amount of the loan, the amount of the carrying charge, and the term of the loan. Various methods of calculating the rate of interest on an installment loan are in common use, and the remainder of this section will describe several of these.

The theoretically correct method of calculating the rate of interest on an installment loan would be to assume compound interest and to find that rate of interest at which the present value of the installment payments is equal to the amount of the loan. In terms of the symbols previously defined, the fundamental equation of value would be

$$\frac{A + K}{n} a_{\overline{n}|j} = A , \qquad (7.12)$$

which can be solved for j by the methods of Section 3.8. The rate j is a rate per mth of a year so that in practice the annual rate, i, would generally be quoted as

$$i = mj . \qquad (7.13)$$

Of course, the true effective rate of interest is not mj but rather is

$$i = (1 + j)^m - 1 . \qquad (7.14)$$

The use of compound interest implies that each installment payment is divided into principal and interest as in the amortization schedule discussed in Chapter 5. This method of calculating principal and interest was given legal sanction by the United States Supreme Court and is often called the *United States Rule* or the *actuarial method*. According to the United States Rule, each installment payment must first be used to pay for the entire amount of the accrued interest with any excess being used for principal repayment.

A strict application of the United States Rule will result in a compounding of interest whenever an installment payment is made. If installment payments are made at a regular frequency, then interest will be convertible at the same regular frequency as payments are made. However, if installment payments are made at an irregular frequency, then the United States Rule produces the rather odd result that the rate of interest quoted is convertible at the same irregular frequency as payments are made. This result is illustrated in Example 7.5.

The calculation of the rate of interest by the above method is relatively sophisticated and requires the use of interest tables. As a result, several simplified methods of calculating the rate of interest which do not require values from the interest tables have been developed. We will examine four of these methods.

All of these methods are similar in that they replace the true division of the installment payments into principal and interest with an arbitrary division into principal and interest. It is assumed that the amount of principal invested during each mth of a year is invested at rate $\dfrac{i}{m}$ for that mth of a year. Thus, if we denote the amount of principal during the tth mth of a year by P_t, we have

$$\frac{i}{m} \sum_{t=1}^{n} P_t = K,$$

or

$$i = \frac{mK}{\displaystyle\sum_{t=1}^{n} P_t}. \qquad (7.15)$$

The various methods differ only the arbitrary division of installment payments into principal and interest, which will be reflected in the denominator of formula (7.15).

The first method is often called the *maximum yield method,* since it produces larger answers than any of the other methods. This method assumes that all installment payments are applied entirely to principal until it is paid off and thereafter are applied entirely to interest. We also assume that the carrying charge is less than one installment payment, i.e.,

$$K < \frac{A + K}{n}.$$

This leads to the result that all installment payments except part of the last one are used for principal repayment. This will generally be the case, since installment loans cover relatively short periods of time. With these assumptions Table 7.3 is a modified amortization schedule for this method. The student should verify the entries in Table 7.3 and note the various relationships in the table.

TABLE 7.3

MAXIMUM YIELD METHOD

Duration	Payment Amount	Interest Paid	Principal Repaid	Outstanding Principal
0				A
$\dfrac{1}{m}$	$\dfrac{A+K}{n}$	0	$\dfrac{A+K}{n}$	$A - \dfrac{A+K}{n}$
$\dfrac{2}{m}$	$\dfrac{A+K}{n}$	0	$\dfrac{A+K}{n}$	$A - 2\dfrac{A+K}{n}$
$\cdot$	$\cdot$	$\cdot$	$\cdot$	$\cdot$
$\cdot$	$\cdot$	$\cdot$	$\cdot$	$\cdot$
$\dfrac{n-1}{m}$	$\dfrac{A+K}{n}$	0	$\dfrac{A+K}{n}$	$A - (n-1)\dfrac{A+K}{n}$
$\dfrac{n}{m}$	$\dfrac{A+K}{n}$	K	$\dfrac{A+K}{n} - K$	0
Total	$A+K$	K	A	

We now need to sum the outstanding principal column to evaluate formula (7.15).

$$\sum_{t=1}^{n} P_t = An - \frac{A+K}{n} \cdot \frac{(n-1)(n)}{2},$$

so that

$$i = \frac{mK}{An - (A+K)\dfrac{n-1}{2}}$$

$$= \frac{2mK}{A(n+1) - K(n-1)}. \tag{7.16}$$

It is interesting to note that formula (7.16) can be derived by an alternative argument which assumes simple interest throughout the life of the loan. This alternative derivation is left as an exercise.

The assumption of simple interest throughout the life of a loan is fairly common and is often termed the *Merchant's Rule*. This term is often used in contrast with the United States Rule which assumes compound interest. It has not always been recognized in the literature that the maximum yield method and the Merchant's Rule are equivalent.

The second method is often called the *minimum yield method,* since it produces smaller answers than any of the other methods. This method assumes that all installment payments are applied entirely to interest until it is paid and thereafter are applied entirely to principal. Again we assume that the carrying charge is less than one installment payment, so that the first payment is at least enough to pay the entire amount of interest. Table 7.4 is a modified amortization schedule for this method. The student should

TABLE 7.4

MINIMUM YIELD METHOD

Duration	Payment Amount	Interest Paid	Principal Repaid	Outstanding Principal
0				$(n)\dfrac{A+K}{n} - K = A$
$\dfrac{1}{m}$	$\dfrac{A+K}{n}$	K	$\dfrac{A+K}{n} - K$	$(n-1)\dfrac{A+K}{n}$
$\dfrac{2}{m}$	$\dfrac{A+K}{n}$	0	$\dfrac{A+K}{n}$	$(n-2)\dfrac{A+K}{n}$
$\cdot$	$\cdot$	$\cdot$	$\cdot$	$\cdot$
$\cdot$	$\cdot$	$\cdot$	$\cdot$	$\cdot$
$\cdot$	$\cdot$	$\cdot$	$\cdot$	$\cdot$
$\dfrac{n-1}{m}$	$\dfrac{A+K}{n}$	0	$\dfrac{A+K}{n}$	$\dfrac{A+K}{n}$
$\dfrac{n}{m}$	$\dfrac{A+K}{n}$	0	$\dfrac{A+K}{n}$	0
Total	$A+K$	K	A	

verify the entries in Table 7.4 and note the various relationships in the table.

We now need to sum the outstanding principal column to evaluate formula (7.15).

$$\sum_{t=1}^{n} P_t = \frac{A+K}{n} \cdot \frac{(n)(n+1)}{2} - K,$$

so that

$$\iota = \frac{mK}{(A+K)\dfrac{n+1}{2} - K}$$

$$= \frac{2mK}{A(n+1) + K(n-1)}. \tag{7.17}$$

The maximum yield method and minimum yield method have been justifiably criticized, since they do not reflect the fact that each installment payment is partially principal and partially interest. The other two methods do reflect this fact.

The third, and simplest, method is the *constant ratio method*. This method assumes that a constant percentage of each installment is principal and that a constant percentage is interest. Table 7.5 is a modified amortization sched-

TABLE 7.5

CONSTANT RATIO METHOD

Duration	Payment Amount	Interest Paid	Principal Repaid	Outstanding Principal
0				$\dfrac{n}{n}A = A$
$\dfrac{1}{m}$	$\dfrac{A+K}{n}$	$\dfrac{K}{n}$	$\dfrac{A}{n}$	$\dfrac{n-1}{n}A$
$\dfrac{2}{m}$	$\dfrac{A+K}{n}$	$\dfrac{K}{n}$	$\dfrac{A}{n}$	$\dfrac{n-2}{n}A$
$\cdot$	$\cdot$	$\cdot$	$\cdot$	$\cdot$
$\cdot$	$\cdot$	$\cdot$	$\cdot$	$\cdot$
$\cdot$	$\cdot$	$\cdot$	$\cdot$	$\cdot$
$\dfrac{n-1}{m}$	$\dfrac{A+K}{n}$	$\dfrac{K}{n}$	$\dfrac{A}{n}$	$\dfrac{1}{n}A$
$\dfrac{n}{m}$	$\dfrac{A+K}{n}$	$\dfrac{K}{n}$	$\dfrac{A}{n}$	0
Total	$A+K$	K	A	

ule for this method. The student should verify the entries in Table 7.5 and note the various relationships in the table.

We now need to sum the outstanding principal column to evaluate formula (7.15).

$$\sum_{t=1}^{n} P_t = A \cdot \frac{(n)(n+1)}{2n},$$

so that

$$i = \frac{mK}{A \cdot \dfrac{n+1}{2}}$$

$$= \frac{2mK}{A(n+1)}. \qquad (7.18)$$

It is interesting to note that formula (7.18) can be derived by an alternative argument. The amount of interest per year is $m \cdot \dfrac{K}{n}$. The average amount of principal can be found by averaging the amount of principal during the first period and the last period, i.e.,

$$\frac{1}{2} \cdot A \cdot \frac{n}{n} + \frac{1}{2} \cdot A \cdot \frac{1}{n} = A \frac{n+1}{2n}.$$

The rate of interest must be the annual amount of interest divided by the average amount of principal, i.e.,

$$i = \frac{m \cdot \dfrac{K}{n}}{A \dfrac{n+1}{2n}}$$

$$= \frac{2mK}{A(n+1)}. \tag{7.18}$$

The two methods are equivalent, since the outstanding principal is linear under these assumptions.

On occasion an even simpler version of the constant ratio method is encountered in which the average amount of principal is taken to be the average of the beginning balance and the ending balance, i.e.,

$$\frac{1}{2} A + \frac{1}{2} \cdot 0 = \frac{1}{2} A.$$

With this assumption the rate of interest is

$$i = \frac{2mK}{An}. \tag{7.19}$$

Formula (7.19) essentially replaces the term $\dfrac{n+1}{2n}$ with $\dfrac{1}{2}$. The student should note that the relationship between formulas (7.18) and (7.19) is quite analogous to the relationship between formulas (6.13) and (6.14), the two versions of the bond salesman's formula. In general, formula (7.19) produces poorer results than formula (7.18).

The fourth method is the *direct ratio method*. This method uses an approximate division into principal and interest which is closest to the exact division by the actuarial method. In the true amortization schedule the interest paid column decreases with duration while the principal repaid column increases. The direct ratio method reflects this pattern whereas none of the other approximate methods do. In general, the direct ratio method will produce better results than the other approximate methods.

The direct ratio method can best be illustrated by example. Consider a one-year loan repaid with 12 monthly installments. The sum of the positive integers from 1 to 12 is 78. The direct ratio method assumes that the interest paid is $\frac{12}{78}$ of the carrying charge in the first month, $\frac{11}{78}$ in the second month, $\ldots$, $\frac{1}{78}$ in the last month. This decreasing pattern of interest payments will produce a corresponding increasing pattern of principal repayments. The direct ratio method is often called the *rule of 78*, although the number 78 is valid only for a term of 12 months.

Table 7.6 is a modified amortization schedule for this method. We define S_r to be the sum of the first r positive integers, i.e.,

$$S_r = 1 + 2 + \cdots + r = \frac{r(r + 1)}{2}.$$

TABLE 7.6

DIRECT RATIO METHOD

Dura-tion	Payment Amount	Interest Paid	Principal Repaid	Outstanding Principal
0				$(n)\dfrac{A + K}{n} - K \cdot \dfrac{S_n}{S_n} = A$
$\dfrac{1}{m}$	$\dfrac{A + K}{n}$	$K \cdot \dfrac{n}{S_n}$	$\dfrac{A + K}{n} - K \cdot \dfrac{n}{S_n}$	$(n - 1)\dfrac{A + K}{n} - K \cdot \dfrac{S_{n-1}}{S_n}$
$\dfrac{2}{m}$	$\dfrac{A + K}{n}$	$K \cdot \dfrac{n - 1}{S_n}$	$\dfrac{A + K}{n} - K \cdot \dfrac{n - 1}{S_n}$	$(n - 2)\dfrac{A + K}{n} - K \cdot \dfrac{S_{n-2}}{S_n}$
.	.	.	.	.
.	.	.	.	.
.	.	.	.	.
$\dfrac{n - 1}{m}$	$\dfrac{A + K}{n}$	$K \cdot \dfrac{2}{S_n}$	$\dfrac{A + K}{n} - K \cdot \dfrac{2}{S_n}$	$\dfrac{A + K}{n} - K \cdot \dfrac{S_1}{S_n}$
$\dfrac{n}{m}$	$\dfrac{A + K}{n}$	$K \cdot \dfrac{1}{S_n}$	$\dfrac{A + K}{n} - K \cdot \dfrac{1}{S_n}$	0
Total	$A + K$	K	A	

The student should verify the entries in Table 7.6 and note the various relationships in the table.

We now need to sum the outstanding principal column to evaluate formula (7.15). Before we can do this it is necessary to find the sum of S_r as r ranges from 1 to n. There are several methods of doing this. The theory of finite differences provides one of the simplest methods. Recall that

$$x^{(m)} = x(x - 1)(x - 2) \ldots (x - m + 1).$$

Then we have

$$\sum_{r=1}^{n} S_r = \frac{1}{2} \sum_{r=1}^{n} (r + 1)(r) = \frac{1}{2} \sum_{r=1}^{n} (r + 1)^{(2)}$$

$$= \frac{1}{6} (r + 1)^{(3)} \Big]_{1}^{n+1} = \frac{1}{6} n(n + 1)(n + 2).$$

Alternatively this result can be derived by algebraic or inductive techniques. Using this result we have

$$\sum_{t=1}^{n} P_t = \frac{A + K}{n} \cdot \frac{(n)(n + 1)}{2} - K \frac{\frac{1}{6} n(n + 1)(n + 2)}{\frac{1}{2} n(n + 1)},$$

so that

$$i = \frac{mK}{(A + K) \dfrac{n + 1}{2} - K \dfrac{n + 2}{3}}$$

$$= \frac{mK}{\frac{1}{6} [3(A + K)(n + 1) - 2K(n + 2)]}$$

$$= \frac{mK}{\frac{1}{6} [3A(n + 1) + K(n - 1)]}$$

$$= \frac{2mK}{A(n + 1) + \frac{1}{3} K(n - 1)}. \tag{7.20}$$

In recent years there has been growing criticism of the lack of disclosure of the true cost of installment loans by the lenders to the borrowers. As a result, in 1968 the United States Congress passed the Consumer Credit Protection Act, widely referred to as the "truth-in-lending" act. This law requires the uniform reporting of the costs of installment loans. The disclosure must include both the total carrying charge, including all extra charges and fees, and the annual rate of interest implicit in the carrying charge and the term of the loan. The basis specified for the rate of interest is the United States Rule.

It should be noted that this method will not report effective rates of interest but will report nominal rates in which interest is compounded on each installment payment date. Thus the costs of various installment loans cannot be compared directly unless they all involve payments according to the same pattern which are made at the same frequency.

More information concerning the "truth-in-lending" act can be obtained from the Federal Reserve Board's Regulation Z.

Example 7.4. Find the rate of interest on the installment loan for the color television set given as an example in this section: (1) by the actuarial method (United States Rule), (2) as an effective rate of interest, (3) by the maximum yield method (Merchant's Rule), (4) by the minimum yield method, (5) by the constant ratio method, and (6) by the direct ratio method (rule of 78).

1. The equation of value is

$$55a_{\overline{12}|j} = 600$$

or

$$a_{\overline{12}|j} = 10.9091 .$$

Now

$$a_{\overline{12}|.0125} = 11.0793 ,$$
$$a_{\overline{12}|.0150} = 10.9075 ,$$

and performing a linear interpolation

$$j = .0125 + .0025 \frac{11.0793 - 10.9091}{11.0793 - 10.9075} = .01498 .$$

Thus, the nominal annual rate is

$$12(.01498) = .180, \text{ or } 18.0\% .$$

2. The effective rate of interest is

$$i = (1.01498)^{12} - 1 = .195, \text{ or } 19.5\% .$$

3. Using formula (7.16),

$$i = \frac{(2)(12)(60)}{(600)(13) - (60)(11)} = .202, \text{ or } 20.2\% .$$

4. Using formula (7.17),

$$i = \frac{(2)(12)(60)}{(600)(13) + (60)(11)} = .170, \text{ or } 17.0\% .$$

5. *a)* Using formula (7.18),

$$i = \frac{(2)(12)(60)}{(600)(13)} = .185, \text{ or } 18.5\% .$$

b) Using formula (7.19),

$$i = \frac{(2)(12)(60)}{(600)(12)} = .200, \text{ or } 20.0\% .$$

6. Using formula (7.20),

$$i = \frac{(2)(12)(60)}{(600)(13) + (\frac{1}{3})(60)(11)} = .180, \text{ or } 18.0\%.$$

It should be noted that the direct ratio method produces an answer closer to that obtained by the actuarial method than do any of the other approximate methods.

Example 7.5. *A man borrows $1000 at 5% interest for 12 months. If he repays $200 at the end of 3 months and $300 at the end of 8 months, find how much he must repay at the end of 12 months: (1) using a true effective rate of interest, (2) using the Merchant's Rule (simple interest), and (3) using the United States Rule.*

1. The equation of value is

$$R = 1000(1.05) - 200(1.05)^{\frac{3}{4}} - 300(1.05)^{\frac{1}{3}} = \$537.63.$$

2. The equation of value is

$$R = 1000(1.05) - 200(1.0375) - 300(1.016\tfrac{2}{3}) = \$537.50.$$

3. At the end of three months, the accumulated interest is

$$1000(.05)(\tfrac{1}{4}) = \$12.50.$$

Thus, $12.50 is applied to interest and $187.50 is applied to principal, reducing the outstanding balance to $812.50. At the end of eight months, the accumulated interest is

$$812.50(.05)(\tfrac{5}{12}) = \$16.93.$$

Thus $16.93 is applied to interest and $283.07 is applied to principal, reducing the outstanding balance to $529.43. At the end of 12 months, the outstanding balance is

$$529.43[1 + (.05)(\tfrac{1}{3})] = \$538.25.$$

It should be noted that the United States Rule does not assume either 5% effective or 5% nominal convertible with any regular frequency but rather assumes 5% with conversions at the end of three and eight months. This example illustrates one undesirable feature of the United States Rule, which has been sanctioned by the United States Supreme Court and is the basis for the "truth-in-lending" act.

7.7. DEPRECIATION, DEPLETION, AND CAPITALIZED COST

One final application of the theory of interest is the analysis of costs and yield rates of investments in fixed assets. These are questions of considerable importance to businessmen who are investing in fixed assets. The concepts of depreciation, depletion, and capitalized cost are important in the analysis of these costs and yield rates.

We make the following definitions:

n = number of interest conversion periods in the period under consideration.
A = value of the asset at the beginning of the n periods.
S = value of the asset at the end of the n periods (S may be zero or negative).
R = level periodic return after expenses from the asset.
i' = yield rate on the investment per interest conversion period.
i = sinking fund rate of interest per interest conversion period.

If $A = S$, i.e., if the asset neither increases nor decreases in value through time, then the yield rate each period is the periodic net return divided by the value of the asset, i.e.,

$$i' = \frac{R}{A}. \tag{7.21}$$

In general $A \neq S$, since the asset value will change through time. If $A < S$, the asset is known as an *appreciating asset;* while if $A > S$, the asset is known as a *depreciating asset.* An example of the former may be real estate, and an example of the latter is a factory machine. We will generally be concerned with depreciating assets, although many of our results can be used for either.

If $A \neq S$, then formula (7.21) is invalid, since it fails to recognize that the asset value is changing. In this case it is necessary to replace the capital by means of a sinking fund, so that the fundamental equation of value from the principles of Chapter 5 is

$$R = Ai' + \frac{A - S}{s_{\overline{n}|i}}. \tag{7.22}$$

If $A = S$, then formula (7.22) reduces to formula (7.21). In practice it is often assumed that $i = i'$ especially if no sinking fund is actually established. Formula (7.22) is not restricted to $A > S$ but is also valid for $A < S$.

The student should note the similarity between the above discussion and the analysis of bonds in Chapter 6. A bond bought at a discount is analogous to an appreciating asset, while a bond bought at a premium is analogous to a depreciating asset. In fact, formula (7.22) is valid for bonds, noting that A plays the role of the price, S the redemption value, and R the coupon. The proof of this result is left as an exercise.

The decline in the value over time of a depreciating asset is termed *depreciation.* This depreciation is largely due to physical deterioration and obsolescence. Sound accounting practice dictates that the value of the asset must be written down over time in the books of the investor. The value of the asset in the books of the investor at any point in time is called the *book value* at that time, and the amount by which the book value is decreased over each period is called the *depreciation charge* for that period. In practice there are several methods of calculating book values and depreciation charges. We will examine four of these.

Let B_t be the book value of the asset at the end of the tth period, $0 \leq t \leq n$. Clearly, $B_0 = A$ and $B_n = S$. Let D_t be the depreciation charge for the tth period, $1 \leq t \leq n$. Then we have

$$D_t = B_{t-1} - B_t . \tag{7.23}$$

The first method is the *sinking-fund method* or the *compound-interest method*. This method is consistent with formula (7.22). The book value at any time must be the initial value of the asset less the amount in the sinking fund, i.e.,

$$B_t = A - \left(\frac{A - S}{s_{\overline{n}|i}} \right) s_{\overline{t}|i} . \tag{7.24}$$

Note that formula (7.24) produces the proper values for B_0 and B_n. Then the depreciation charge is

$$
\begin{aligned}
D_t &= B_{t-1} - B_t \\
&= \left[A - \left(\frac{A - S}{s_{\overline{n}|i}} \right) s_{\overline{t-1}|i} \right] - \left[A - \left(\frac{A - S}{s_{\overline{n}|i}} \right) s_{\overline{t}|i} \right] \\
&= \left(\frac{A - S}{s_{\overline{n}|i}} \right) \left(s_{\overline{t}|i} - s_{\overline{t-1}|i} \right) \\
&= \left(\frac{A - S}{s_{\overline{n}|i}} \right) (1 + i)^{t-1} .
\end{aligned}
\tag{7.25}
$$

It is evident from formula (7.25) that the sinking-fund method produces depreciation charges which increase over the life of the asset. This may or may not be a reasonable pattern of depreciation charges, depending upon the nature of the asset. For example, it may produce a reasonable pattern of depreciation charges for an office building which depreciates slowly at first and then more rapidly later on. However, it probably would not produce a reasonable pattern of depreciation charges for an automobile.

It should not be thought that the sinking-fund method actually requires the use of a sinking fund. It is merely a method of calculating book values and charges. A sinking fund may or may not actually be accumulated to replace the loss of capital.

The second, and simplest, method is the *straight-line method*. This method is the most widely used method in practice because of its simplicity. In this method the depreciation charge is constant, so that

$$D_t = \frac{A - S}{n} . \tag{7.26}$$

As a result the book values are linear,

$$B_t = \left(1 - \frac{t}{n}\right) A + \frac{t}{n} S. \qquad (7.27)$$

Note that formula (7.27) produces the proper values for B_0 and B_n.

It is interesting to note that the straight-line method is a special case of the sinking-fund method in which $i = 0$. One of the criticisms of the method is that it ignores interest. Another criticism is that few assets actually depreciate on a linear basis.

The third method is the *constant-percentage method*, the *declining-balance method*, or the *compound-discount method*. This method produces depreciation charges which decrease throughout the life of the asset, as opposed to the sinking-fund method in which they increase and the straight-line method in which they are constant.

The constant-percentage method is characterized by the fact that the depreciation charge is a constant percentage of the book value at the beginning of the period, i.e.,

$$D_t = d \cdot B_{t-1}. \qquad (7.28)$$

Now $D_t = B_{t-1} - B_t$, so that

$$B_t = B_{t-1}(1 - d),$$

and since this is true for all t we have

$$
\begin{aligned}
B_0 &= & A \\
B_1 &= B_0(1 - d) &= A(1 - d) \\
B_2 &= B_1(1 - d) &= A(1 - d)^2 \\
B_3 &= B_2(1 - d) &= A(1 - d)^3 \\
&\ \ \vdots & \vdots \\
B_t &= B_{t-1}(1 - d) &= A(1 - d)^t \\
&\ \ \vdots & \vdots \\
B_n &= B_{n-1}(1 - d) &= A(1 - d)^n = S. \qquad (7.29)
\end{aligned}
$$

Since A and S are given, d can be found by

$$A(1 - d)^n = S$$
$$(1 - d)^n = \frac{S}{A}$$

$$1 - d = \left(\frac{S}{A}\right)^{\frac{1}{n}}$$

$$d = 1 - \left(\frac{S}{A}\right)^{\frac{1}{n}}. \tag{7.30}$$

The name "compound-discount method" is evident from formula (7.29), in which d can be interpreted as a rate of discount. It should be noted that this method assumes that S is positive. If S is zero or negative, the method breaks down.

The fourth method is the *sum-of-the-digits method*. This method also produces depreciation charges which decrease throughout the life of the asset.

The reasoning involved in this method is similar to the reasoning involved in the direct ratio method of calculating yields on installment loans as described in Section 7.6. Let S_n be the sum of the first n positive integers

$$S_n = 1 + 2 + \cdots + n = \frac{n(n+1)}{2}.$$

The depreciation charges progress as follows:

$$D_1 = \frac{n}{S_n}(A - S)$$

$$D_2 = \frac{n-1}{S_n}(A - S)$$

$$D_t = \frac{n-t+1}{S_n}(A - S)$$

$$D_n = \frac{1}{S_n}(A - S). \tag{7.31}$$

The sum of the depreciation charges equals $A - S$, as it must. The book value is given by

$$B_t = A - \sum_{r=1}^{t} D_r$$

$$= S + \sum_{r=t+1}^{n} D_r, \quad \text{since} \quad \sum_{r=1}^{n} D_r = A - S$$

$$= S + \frac{S_{n-t}}{S_n}(A - S). \tag{7.32}$$

Depletion refers to the exhaustion of a supply of natural resources, such as coal and oil. Mathematically it is similar to depreciation in the sense that a coal mine or an oil field is a depreciating asset as the supplies of coal or oil are extracted. The above methods of calculating depreciation charges could also be used in calculating *depletion charges*.

A problem of considerable importance in practice is the comparison of the costs of alternate possible assets to produce a certain item. There are three costs involved in owning a fixed asset:

1. The loss of interest on the original purchase price, since that money could have been invested elsewhere at interest.
2. The cost of depreciation.
3. The cost of maintenance.

The *periodic charge* of an asset is defined to be the cost per period of owning the asset. If we let H be the periodic charge and M be the periodic maintenance cost, then the fundamental equation of value is

$$H = Ai' + \frac{A - S}{s_{\overline{n}|i'}} + M. \tag{7.33}$$

Formula (7.33) is quite analogous to formula (7.22). The term Ai' is the loss of interest on the original purchase price. The term $\dfrac{A - S}{s_{\overline{n}|i'}}$ is the periodic cost of depreciation assuming $i = i'$. The term M is the periodic maintenance cost. Recall that in formula (7.22) the term M is not needed, since R is net of expenses.

The *capitalized cost* of an asset is defined to be the present value of the periodic charges forever, i.e., the present value of a perpetuity for the amount of the periodic charge. The capitalized cost can be looked upon as the present value of maintaining an identical asset in operation indefinitely. Denoting the capitalized cost by K, we have

$$K = \frac{H}{i'} = A + \frac{A - S}{i' s_{\overline{n}|i'}} + \frac{M}{i'}. \tag{7.34}$$

In making comparisons of alternate possible assets either the periodic charge or the capitalized cost may be used. One complication is that differing assets may produce items at a varying rate per unit of time. In these cases it is necessary to divide by the number of items produced per unit of time. For example, if U is the number of items produced per unit of time, then machine 1 and machine 2 would be equivalent if

$$\frac{A_1 i' + \dfrac{A_1 - S_1}{s_{\overline{n_1}|i'}} + M_1}{U_1} = \frac{A_2 i' + \dfrac{A_2 - S_2}{s_{\overline{n_2}|i'}} + M_2}{U_2}$$

or

$$\frac{\dfrac{A_1}{a_{\overline{n_1}|\,i'}} - \dfrac{S_1}{s_{\overline{n_1}|\,i'}} + M_1}{U_1} = \frac{\dfrac{A_2}{a_{\overline{n_2}|\,i'}} - \dfrac{S_2}{s_{\overline{n_2}|\,i'}} + M_2}{U_2}. \tag{7.35}$$

Another problem of considerable importance in practice is the allocation of a limited amount of capital into various alternative investments. The process of allocating such capital is often called *capital budgeting.*

In practice, two major approaches of capital budgeting are most commonly encountered. The first of these is to find the yield rate for each alternative investment. The yield rate is that rate of interest at which the present value of flows into the investment is equal to the present value of flows from the investment. The various investment alternatives are ranked and those with the highest yield rates are selected in descending order until the amount of capital available for investment is exhausted. Although this approach will usually produce reasonable results, serious problems exist in those situations for which no yield rate or multiple yield rates exist.

The second approach is to calculate the excess of the present value of returns from an investment over the present value of inputs into the investment for each alternative. The discounting is normally done at a rate of interest commensurate with the firm's cost of borrowing capital. Capital is then allocated in such a manner that the total present value of returns over inputs is maximized.

Example 7.6. A machine costs $10,000, will last for five years and will have a salvage value of $1000 at the end of the five years. Calculate the book values and depreciation charges (1) using the sinking-fund method where $i = i' = .05$, (2) using the straight-line method, (3) using the constant-percentage method, and (4) using the sum-of-the-digits method.

1. Using formulas (7.24) and (7.25) we have

$$\frac{A - S}{s_{\overline{n}|}} = \frac{9000}{s_{\overline{5}|}} = 1628.775$$

and

t	D_t	B_t
0.............		10,000
1..............	1,629	8,371
2..............	1,710	6,661
3..............	1,796	4,865
4..............	1,886	2,979
5..............	1,979	1,000

2. Using formulas (7.26) and (7.27) we have

t	D_t	B_t
0.............		10,000
1.............1,800	1,800	8,200
2.............1,800	1,800	6,400
3.............1,800	1,800	4,600
4.............1,800	1,800	2,800
5.............1,800	1,800	1,000

3. Using formula (7.30) we obtain

$$d = 1 - (.1)^{.2} = 1 - .631 = .369,$$

and using formulas (7.28) and (7.29) we have

t	D_t	B_t
0.............		10,000
1.............3,690	3,690	6,310
2.............2,328	2,328	3,982
3.............1,470	1,470	2,512
4............. 927	927	1,585
5............. 585	585	1,000

4. Using formulas (7.31) and (7.32) we have

t	D_t	B_t
0.............		10,000
1.............3,000	3,000	7,000
2.............2,400	2,400	4,600
3.............1,800	1,800	2,800
4.............1,200	1,200	1,600
5............. 600	600	1,000

Example 7.7. Machine 1 sells for $100,000, has an annual maintenance expense of $2,500, and has a life of 25 years with a salvage value of $2,000. Machine 2 has an annual maintenance expense of $5,000 and a life of 20 years with no salvage value. Assuming an effective rate of interest of 5%, find the price of Machine 2 so that a buyer is indifferent between the two machines if Machine 2 produces output three times as fast as Machine 1.

Using formula (7.35), we have

$$\frac{100,000}{a_{\overline{25}|}} - \frac{2000}{s_{\overline{25}|}} + 2500 = \frac{1}{3}\left(\frac{A_2}{a_{\overline{20}|}} + 5000\right)$$

$A_2 = \{3[100,000(.070952) - 2000(.020952) + 2500] - 5000\}12.4622$

    $= \$294,854$, or $295,000 to the nearest $1000.

Example 7.8. A telephone company uses telephone poles costing $10 apiece. These poles last 14 years. How much per pole would the company be justified in spending on a preservative to lengthen the life of the poles to 22 years? Assume that the poles do not have salvage value, that the annual maintenance expense of either type of pole is equivalent, and that interest is 4% effective.

Using formula (7.35) we have

$$\frac{10}{a_{\overline{14}|}} = \frac{10 + x}{a_{\overline{22}|}}$$

$$x = 10 \left(\frac{a_{\overline{22}|}}{a_{\overline{14}|}} - 1 \right)$$

$$= 10 \left(\frac{14.4511}{10.5631} - 1 \right)$$

$$= \$3.68 .$$

EXERCISES

7.1. Introduction;   7.2. Valuation of securities

1. On January 1, 1965, a pension fund invested $1,000,000 in corporate bonds and $1,000,000 in preferred stock. The investment in bonds was a purchase of 1000 bonds maturing January 1, 1985, each with a par value of $1000 and bearing annual 4% coupons. The investment in preferred stock was a purchase of 10,000 shares, each with a par value of $100 and bearing annual 6% dividends. On January 1, 1970, the bonds are selling for $900 per bond and the preferred stock is selling for $115 per share. Find the asset value for the pension fund on January 1, 1970, if—

    a) All assets are assigned market value.

    b) All assets are assigned book value.

    c) Bonds are assigned book value and stocks are assigned market value.

    d) All assets are valued using the present value method at a yield rate of 5%.

7.3. Interest measurement of a fund

2. The funds of a firm at the beginning of the year were $500,000 and at the end of the year $520,000. Gross interest earned was $30,000, against which there were investment expenses of $5000. Find the net effective rate of interest yielded by the funds.

3. Find an expression analogous to formula (7.2) if principal additions and withdrawals are occurring continuously throughout the year.

4. A fund earning 4% effective has a balance of $1000 at the beginning of the year. If $200 is added to the fund at the end of three months and if $300 is withdrawn from the fund at the end of nine months, find the ending balance under the assumption

$$_{1-t}i_t = (1 - t)i.$$

5. *a*) Under the assumption that $_{1-t}i_t = (1 - t)i$, find an expression for $_ti_0$.

   b) Under the assumption that $_ti_0 = ti$, find an expression for $_{1-t}i_t$.

6. Let the exposure associated with i (i.e., the denominator of formula (7.5)) be denoted by E. By using formula (7.9) show that the force of interest at any point is given by

$$\delta_t = \frac{I}{E + (1 - t)I}.$$

It should be noted that in terms of the time diagram, this is equivalent to bringing the entire amount of interest, I, onto the time diagram at time t instead of time 1. The expression, $E + (1 - t)I$, is often called the "exposure associated with δ_t."

7.4. Construction of tables

7. Find recursive formulas for the following functions:

   a) $a_{\overline{n}}$.

   b) $s_{\overline{n}}$.

   c) $(Ia)_{\overline{n}}$.

   d) $(Da)_{\overline{n}}$.

8. Find summation check formulas over the range $t = 1$ to n for the following functions:

   a) $a_{\overline{t}}$.

   b) $s_{\overline{t}}$.

   c) $(Ia)_{\overline{t}}$.

   d) $(Da)_{\overline{t}}$.

7.5. Life insurance settlement options

9. Verify the results for $n = 10$ in Table 7.1, using the tables in Appendix I.

10. Find to the nearest dollar, the lump-sum amount that the recipient could obtain at the end of five years on each of the five settlement options in Example 7.3, assuming that the insurance company would allow the recipient to take the remaining proceeds as a lump sum.

11. An insured dies leaving net proceeds of $10,000 on a policy. The beneficiary is to receive an annuity-due payable monthly for 10 years. The insurance company agrees to calculate the installments assuming 5 % effective. To the nearest dollar, what initial liability must the company set up on this policy if the company must use $3\frac{1}{2}$ % in the calculation of its liabilities?

12. A beneficiary of a $1000 policy takes a 10-year annuity-immediate payable annually. At the end of 5 years the beneficiary changes the basis so that the payments will continue for another 10 years. Find the payment for years 1–5 and the revised payment for years 6–15, assuming $i = 3\%$.

13. A beneficiary of a $1000 policy leaves the proceeds on deposit for 10 years at a

guaranteed interest rate of 3%. If each year the company pays excess interest of 2%, find the total accumulated value at the end of 10 years:

a) Assuming each year the 2% is taken on the balance at the beginning of the year.

b) Assuming each year the 2% is taken on the balance at the end of the year after the guaranteed interest has been credited.

7.6. Installment loans

14. Show that if the carrying charge is larger than one installment payment but smaller than two installment payments, then—

   a) The maximum yield formula (7.16) becomes

$$\frac{2mnK}{4A(n - 1) + (A - K)(n - 2)(n - 1)}.$$

   b) The minimum yield formula (7.17) becomes

$$\frac{2mnK}{4An + (A + K)(n - 2)(n - 1)}.$$

15. Derive formula (7.16) by assuming simple interest.

16. An installment loan over a nine-month period is being repaid by the direct ratio method. If the amount of interest in the second payment is $20, find the amount of interest in the eighth payment.

17. An installment loan of $690 is being repaid with six monthly payments of $50 each followed by six monthly payments of $75 each. Use the constant ratio method to approximate the rate of interest on the loan.

18. For a loan of $100 a finance company requires monthly repayments of $7.66 at the end of each month for 16 months. Use only the compound interest tables in Appendix I to find the effective rate of interest which the company earns on the loan.

19. A finance company uses a carrying charge of 6% on the loan for 12-month loans. Use interpolation in the interest tables to find the nominal rate of interest convertible monthly which is earned.

7.7. Depreciation, depletion, and capitalized cost

20. Verify that formula (7.22) is valid for bonds; where A is the price, S the redemption value, and R the coupon. Do this by showing that formula (7.22) reduces to formula (6.6).

21. Show algebraically that $\sum_{t=1}^{n} D_t = A - S$.

22. a) An asset is being depreciated over a 10-year period. It has no salvage value at the end of the 10 years, i.e., $S = 0$. If the depreciation charge in the third year is $1000, find the depreciation charge in the ninth year:

   (1) By the sinking-fund method, assuming $i = .05$.

(2) By the straight-line method.

(3) By the sum-of-the-digits method.

Why can the declining-balance method not be used?

b) Find the original value of the asset in each of the above three cases.

23. The United States Internal Revenue Code defines a method of depreciation called the 200% declining-balance method. This method is equivalent to the declining-balance method in which

$$d = \frac{2}{n},$$

i.e., 200% of the straight-line rate for the first year. The Internal Revenue Code also defines a 150% declining-balance method similarly. Set up a depreciation schedule for Example 7.6 using the 200% method. Do not depreciate the machine below $1000.

24. A machine sells for $10,000 and has a salvage value of $1000 at the end of 10 years. The annual maintenance expense of the machine is $500. Assuming 5% interest:

a) Calculate the periodic charge of the asset.

b) Calculate the capitalized cost of the asset.

25. Machine 1 sells for $1000 with a salvage value of $50 at the end of nine years. Machine 2 sells for $1100 with a salvage value of $200 at the end of nine years. At what rate of interest would a purchaser be indifferent between the two machines? Assume equal maintenance expenses for the two machines.

APPENDIX I

COMPOUND INTEREST FUNCTIONS
$$i = \tfrac{1}{2}\%$$

Constants		n	v^n	$(1+i)^n$	$a_{\overline{n}|}$	$s_{\overline{n}|}$	$1/s_{\overline{n}|}$
Function	**Value**	1	.99502	1.00500	.9950	1.0000	1.000000
		2	.99007	1.01003	1.9851	2.0050	.498753
i	.005000	3	.98515	1.01508	2.9702	3.0150	.331672
$i^{(2)}$	.004994	4	.98025	1.02015	3.9505	4.0301	.248133
$i^{(4)}$	.004991	5	.97537	1.02525	4.9259	5.0503	.198010
$i^{(12)}$	.004989	6	.97052	1.03038	5.8964	6.0755	.164595
δ	.004988	7	.96569	1.03553	6.8621	7.1059	.140729
		8	.96089	1.04071	7.8230	8.1414	.122829
d	.004975	9	.95610	1.04591	8.7791	9.1821	.108907
$d^{(2)}$	.004981	10	.95135	1.05114	9.7304	10.2280	.097771
$d^{(4)}$	.004984	11	.94661	1.05640	10.6770	11.2792	.088659
$d^{(12)}$	.004987	12	.94191	1.06168	11.6189	12.3356	.081066
δ	.004988	13	.93722	1.06699	12.5562	13.3972	.074642
		14	.93256	1.07232	13.4887	14.4642	.069136
v	.995025	15	.92792	1.07768	14.4166	15.5365	.064364
$v^{\frac{1}{2}}$	.997509	16	.92330	1.08307	15.3399	16.6142	.060189
$v^{\frac{1}{4}}$	.998754	17	.91871	1.08849	16.2586	17.6973	.056506
$v^{\frac{1}{12}}$	.999584	18	.91414	1.09393	17.1728	18.7858	.053232
		19	.90959	1.09940	18.0824	19.8797	.050303
$1+i$	1.005000	20	.90506	1.10490	18.9874	20.9791	.047666
$(1+i)^{\frac{1}{2}}$	1.002497	21	.90056	1.11042	19.8880	22.0840	.045282
$(1+i)^{\frac{1}{4}}$	1.001248	22	.89608	1.11597	20.7841	23.1944	.043114
$(1+i)^{\frac{1}{12}}$	1.000416	23	.89162	1.12155	21.6757	24.3104	.041135
		24	.88719	1.12716	22.5629	25.4320	.039321
$i/i^{(2)}$	1.001248	25	.88277	1.13280	23.4456	26.5591	.037652
$i/i^{(4)}$	1.001873	26	.87838	1.13846	24.3240	27.6919	.036112
$i/i^{(12)}$	1.002290	27	.87401	1.14415	25.1980	28.8304	.034686
i/δ	1.002498	28	.86966	1.14987	26.0677	29.9745	.033362
		29	.86533	1.15562	26.9330	31.1244	.032129
$i/d^{(2)}$	1.003748	30	.86103	1.16140	27.7941	32.2800	.030979
$i/d^{(4)}$	1.003123	31	.85675	1.16721	28.6508	33.4414	.029903
$i/d^{(12)}$	1.002706	32	.85248	1.17304	29.5033	34.6086	.028895
i/δ	1.002498	33	.84824	1.17891	30.3515	35.7817	.027947
		34	.84402	1.18480	31.1955	36.9606	.027056
		35	.83982	1.19073	32.0354	38.1454	.026215
		36	.83564	1.19668	32.8710	39.3361	.025422
		37	.83149	1.20266	33.7025	40.5328	.024671
		38	.82735	1.20868	34.5299	41.7354	.023960
		39	.82323	1.21472	35.3531	42.9441	.023286
		40	.81914	1.22079	36.1722	44.1588	.022646
		41	.81506	1.22690	36.9873	45.3796	.022036
		42	.81101	1.23303	37.7983	46.6065	.021456
		43	.80697	1.23920	38.6053	47.8396	.020903
		44	.80296	1.24539	39.4082	49.0788	.020375
		45	.79896	1.25162	40.2072	50.3242	.019871
		46	.79499	1.25788	41.0022	51.5758	.019389
		47	.79103	1.26417	41.7932	52.8337	.018927
		48	.78710	1.27049	42.5803	54.0978	.018485
		49	.78318	1.27684	43.3635	55.3683	.018061
		50	.77929	1.28323	44.1428	56.6452	.017654

COMPOUND INTEREST FUNCTIONS
$$i = \tfrac{3}{4}\%$$

	Constants	
Function		Value
i		.007500
$i^{(2)}$		.007486
$i^{(4)}$		.007479
$i^{(12)}$		.007474
δ		.007472
d		.007444
$d^{(2)}$		.007458
$d^{(4)}$		.007465
$d^{(12)}$		.007470
δ		.007472
v		.992556
$v^{\frac{1}{2}}$		.996271
$v^{\frac{1}{4}}$		.998134
$v^{\frac{1}{12}}$		.999378
$1 + i$		1.007500
$(1 + i)^{\frac{1}{2}}$		1.003743
$(1 + i)^{\frac{1}{4}}$		1.001870
$(1 + i)^{\frac{1}{12}}$		1.000623
$i/i^{(2)}$		1.001871
$i/i^{(4)}$		1.002808
$i/i^{(12)}$		1.003433
i/δ		1.003745
$i/d^{(2)}$		1.005621
$i/d^{(4)}$		1.004683
$i/d^{(12)}$		1.004058
i/δ		1.003745

n	v^n	$(1 + i)^n$	$a_{\overline{n}\rceil}$	$s_{\overline{n}\rceil}$	$1/s_{\overline{n}\rceil}$
1	.99256	1.00750	.9926	1.0000	1.000000
2	.98517	1.01506	1.9777	2.0075	.498132
3	.97783	1.02267	2.9556	3.0226	.330846
4	.97055	1.03034	3.9261	4.0452	.247205
5	.96333	1.03807	4.8894	5.0756	.197022
6	.95616	1.04585	5.8456	6.1136	.163569
7	.94904	1.05370	6.7946	7.1595	.139675
8	.94198	1.06160	7.7366	8.2132	.121756
9	.93496	1.06956	8.6716	9.2748	.107819
10	.92800	1.07758	9.5996	10.3443	.096671
11	.92109	1.08566	10.5207	11.4219	.087551
12	.91424	1.09381	11.4349	12.5076	.079951
13	.90743	1.10201	12.3423	13.6014	.073522
14	.90068	1.11028	13.2430	14.7034	.068012
15	.89397	1.11860	14.1370	15.8137	.063236
16	.88732	1.12699	15.0243	16.9323	.059059
17	.88071	1.13544	15.9050	18.0593	.055373
18	.87416	1.14396	16.7792	19.1947	.052098
19	.86765	1.15254	17.6468	20.3387	.049167
20	.86119	1.16118	18.5080	21.4912	.046531
21	.85478	1.16989	19.3628	22.6528	.044145
22	.84842	1.17867	20.2112	23.8223	.041977
23	.84210	1.18751	21.0533	25.0010	.039998
24	.83583	1.19641	21.8891	26.1885	.038185
25	.82961	1.20539	22.7188	27.3849	.036516
26	.82343	1.21443	23.5422	28.5903	.034977
27	.81730	1.22354	24.3595	29.8047	.033552
28	.81122	1.23271	25.1707	31.0282	.032229
29	.80518	1.24196	25.9759	32.2609	.030997
30	.79919	1.25127	26.7751	33.5029	.029848
31	.79324	1.26066	27.5683	34.7542	.028774
32	.78733	1.27011	28.3557	36.0148	.027766
33	.78147	1.27964	29.1371	37.2849	.026820
34	.77565	1.28923	29.9128	38.5646	.025931
35	.76988	1.29890	30.6827	39.8538	.025092
36	.76415	1.30865	31.4468	41.1527	.024300
37	.75846	1.31846	32.2053	42.4614	.023551
38	.75281	1.32835	32.9581	43.7798	.022842
39	.74721	1.33831	33.7053	45.1082	.022169
40	.74165	1.34835	34.4469	46.4465	.021530
41	.73613	1.35846	35.1831	47.7948	.020923
42	.73065	1.36865	35.9137	49.1533	.020345
43	.72521	1.37891	36.6389	50.5219	.019793
44	.71981	1.38926	37.3587	51.9009	.019268
45	.71445	1.39968	38.0732	53.2901	.018765
46	.70913	1.41017	38.7823	54.6898	.018285
47	.70385	1.42075	39.4862	56.1000	.017825
48	.69861	1.43141	40.1848	57.5207	.017385
49	.69341	1.44214	40.8782	58.9521	.016963
50	.68825	1.45296	41.5664	60.3943	.016558

COMPOUND INTEREST FUNCTIONS
$$i = 1\%$$

	Constants		n	v^n	$(1 + i)^n$	$a_{\overline{n}|}$	$s_{\overline{n}|}$	$1/s_{\overline{n}|}$
Function		*Value*	1	.99010	1.01000	.9901	1.0000	1.000000
			2	.98030	1.02010	1.9704	2.0100	.497512
i		.010000	3	.97059	1.03030	2.9410	3.0301	.330022
$i^{(2)}$		.009975	4	.96098	1.04060	3.9020	4.0604	.246281
$i^{(4)}$		.009963	5	.95147	1.05101	4.8534	5.1010	.196040
$i^{(12)}$		.009954	6	.94205	1.06152	5.7955	6.1520	.162548
δ		.009950	7	.93272	1.07214	6.7282	7.2135	.138628
			8	.92348	1.08286	7.6517	8.2857	.120690
d		.009901	9	.91434	1.09369	8.5660	9.3685	.106740
$d^{(2)}$		.009926	10	.90529	1.10462	9.4713	10.4622	.095582
$d^{(4)}$		.009938	11	.89632	1.11567	10.3676	11.5668	.086454
$d^{(12)}$		.009946	12	.88745	1.12683	11.2551	12.6825	.078849
δ		.009950	13	.87866	1.13809	12.1337	13.8093	.072415
			14	.86996	1.14947	13.0037	14.9474	.066901
v		.990099	15	.86135	1.16097	13.8651	16.0969	.062124
$v^{\frac{1}{2}}$		.995037	16	.85282	1.17258	14.7179	17.2579	.057945
$v^{\frac{1}{4}}$		.997516	17	.84438	1.18430	15.5623	18.4304	.054258
$v^{\frac{1}{12}}$		.999171	18	.83602	1.19615	16.3983	19.6147	.050982
			19	.82774	1.20811	17.2260	20.8109	.048052
$1 + i$		1.010000	20	.81954	1.22019	18.0456	22.0190	.045415
$(1 + i)^{\frac{1}{2}}$		1.004988	21	.81143	1.23239	18.8570	23.2392	.043031
$(1 + i)^{\frac{1}{4}}$		1.002491	22	.80340	1.24472	19.6604	24.4716	.040864
$(1 + i)^{\frac{1}{12}}$		1.000830	23	.79544	1.25716	20.4558	25.7163	.038886
			24	.78757	1.26973	21.2434	26.9735	.037073
$i/i^{(2)}$		1.002494	25	.77977	1.28243	22.0232	28.2432	.035407
$i/i^{(4)}$		1.003742	26	.77205	1.29526	22.7952	29.5256	.033869
$i/i^{(12)}$		1.004575	27	.76440	1.30821	23.5596	30.8209	.032446
i/δ		1.004992	28	.75684	1.32129	24.3164	32.1291	.031124
			29	.74934	1.33450	25.0658	33.4504	.029895
$i/d^{(2)}$		1.007494	30	.74192	1.34785	25.8077	34.7849	.028748
$i/d^{(4)}$		1.006242	31	.73458	1.36133	26.5423	36.1327	.027676
$i/d^{(12)}$		1.005408	32	.72730	1.37494	27.2696	37.4941	.026671
i/δ		1.004992	33	.72010	1.38869	27.9897	38.8690	.025727
			34	.71297	1.40258	28.7027	40.2577	.024840
			35	.70591	1.41660	29.4086	41.6603	.024004
			36	.69892	1.43077	30.1075	43.0769	.023214
			37	.69200	1.44508	30.7995	44.5076	.022468
			38	.68515	1.45953	31.4847	45.9527	.021761
			39	.67837	1.47412	32.1630	47.4123	.021092
			40	.67165	1.48886	32.8347	48.8864	.020456
			41	.66500	1.50375	33.4997	50.3752	.019851
			42	.65842	1.51879	34.1581	51.8790	.019276
			43	.65190	1.53398	34.8100	53.3978	.018727
			44	.64545	1.54932	35.4555	54.9318	.018204
			45	.63906	1.56481	36.0945	56.4811	.017705
			46	.63273	1.58046	36.7272	58.0459	.017228
			47	.62646	1.59626	37.3537	59.6263	.016771
			48	.62026	1.61223	37.9740	61.2226	.016334
			49	.61412	1.62835	38.5881	62.8348	.015915
			50	.60804	1.64463	39.1961	64.4632	.015513

COMPOUND INTEREST FUNCTIONS
$$i = 1\tfrac{1}{4}\%$$

Constants	
Function	Value
i	.012500
$i^{(2)}$	.012461
$i^{(4)}$	.012442
$i^{(12)}$	.012429
δ	.012423
d	.012346
$d^{(2)}$	.012384
$d^{(4)}$	.012403
$d^{(12)}$	.012416
δ	.012423
v	.987654
$v^{\frac{1}{2}}$	.993808
$v^{\frac{1}{4}}$	.996899
$v^{\frac{1}{12}}$	.998965
$1+i$	1.012500
$(1+i)^{\frac{1}{2}}$	1.006231
$(1+i)^{\frac{1}{4}}$	1.003110
$(1+i)^{\frac{1}{12}}$	1.001036
$i/i^{(2)}$	1.003115
$i/i^{(4)}$	1.004675
$i/i^{(12)}$	1.005716
i/δ	1.006237
$i/d^{(2)}$	1.009365
$i/d^{(4)}$	1.007800
$i/d^{(12)}$	1.006758
i/δ	1.006237

n	v^n	$(1+i)^n$	$a_{\overline{n}|}$	$s_{\overline{n}|}$	$1/s_{\overline{n}|}$
1	.98765	1.01250	.9877	1.0000	1.000000
2	.97546	1.02516	1.9631	2.0125	.496894
3	.96342	1.03797	2.9265	3.0377	.329201
4	.95152	1.05095	3.8781	4.0756	.245361
5	.93978	1.06408	4.8178	5.1266	.195062
6	.92817	1.07738	5.7460	6.1907	.161534
7	.91672	1.09085	6.6627	7.2680	.137589
8	.90540	1.10449	7.5681	8.3589	.119633
9	.89422	1.11829	8.4623	9.4634	.105671
10	.88318	1.13227	9.3455	10.5817	.094503
11	.87228	1.14642	10.2178	11.7139	.085368
12	.86151	1.16075	11.0793	12.8604	.077758
13	.85087	1.17526	11.9302	14.0211	.071321
14	.84037	1.18995	12.7706	15.1964	.065805
15	.82999	1.20483	13.6005	16.3863	.061026
16	.81975	1.21989	14.4203	17.5912	.056847
17	.80963	1.23514	15.2299	18.8111	.053160
18	.79963	1.25058	16.0295	20.0462	.049885
19	.78976	1.26621	16.8193	21.2968	.046955
20	.78001	1.28204	17.5993	22.5630	.044320
21	.77038	1.29806	18.3697	23.8450	.041938
22	.76087	1.31429	19.1306	25.1431	.039772
23	.75147	1.33072	19.8820	26.4574	.037797
24	.74220	1.34735	20.6242	27.7881	.035987
25	.73303	1.36419	21.3573	29.1354	.034322
26	.72398	1.38125	22.0813	30.4996	.032787
27	.71505	1.39851	22.7963	31.8809	.031367
28	.70622	1.41599	23.5025	33.2794	.030049
29	.69750	1.43369	24.2000	34.6954	.028822
30	.68889	1.45161	24.8889	36.1291	.027679
31	.68038	1.46976	25.5693	37.5807	.026609
32	.67198	1.48813	26.2413	39.0504	.025608
33	.66369	1.50673	26.9050	40.5386	.024668
34	.65549	1.52557	27.5605	42.0453	.023784
35	.64740	1.54464	28.2079	43.5709	.022951
36	.63941	1.56394	28.8473	45.1155	.022165
37	.63152	1.58349	29.4788	46.6794	.021423
38	.62372	1.60329	30.1025	48.2629	.020720
39	.61602	1.62333	30.7185	49.8662	.020054
40	.60841	1.64362	31.3269	51.4896	.019421
41	.60090	1.66416	31.9278	53.1332	.018821
42	.59348	1.68497	32.5213	54.7973	.018249
43	.58616	1.70603	33.1075	56.4823	.017705
44	.57892	1.72735	33.6864	58.1883	.017186
45	.57177	1.74895	34.2582	59.9157	.016690
46	.56471	1.77081	34.8229	61.6646	.016217
47	.55774	1.79294	35.3806	63.4354	.015764
48	.55086	1.81535	35.9315	65.2284	.015331
49	.54406	1.83805	36.4755	67.0437	.014916
50	.53734	1.86102	37.0129	68.8818	.014518

COMPOUND INTEREST FUNCTIONS
$$i = 1\tfrac{1}{2}\%$$

Constants			n	v^n	$(1+i)^n$	$a_{\overline{n}|}$	$s_{\overline{n}|}$	$1/s_{\overline{n}|}$
Function	Value		1	.98522	1.01500	.9852	1.0000	1.000000
			2	.97066	1.03023	1.9559	2.0150	.496278
i	.015000		3	.95632	1.04568	2.9122	3.0452	.328383
$i^{(2)}$	.014944		4	.94218	1.06136	3.8544	4.0909	.244445
$i^{(4)}$	.014916		5	.92826	1.07728	4.7826	5.1523	.194089
$i^{(12)}$	.014898		6	.91454	1.09344	5.6972	6.2296	.160525
δ	.014889		7	.90103	1.10984	6.5982	7.3230	.136556
			8	.88771	1.12649	7.4859	8.4328	.118584
d	.014778		9	.87459	1.14339	8.3605	9.5593	.104610
$d^{(2)}$	.014833		10	.86167	1.16054	9.2222	10.7027	.093434
$d^{(4)}$	.014861		11	.84893	1.17795	10.0711	11.8633	.084294
$d^{(12)}$	.014879		12	.83639	1.19562	10.9076	13.0412	.076680
δ	.014889		13	.82403	1.21355	11.7315	14.2368	.070240
			14	.81185	1.23176	12.5434	15.4504	.064723
v	.985222		15	.79985	1.25023	13.3432	16.6821	.059944
$v^{\frac{1}{2}}$	.992583		16	.78803	1.26899	14.1313	17.9324	.055765
$v^{\frac{1}{4}}$	.996285		17	.77639	1.28802	14.9076	19.2014	.052080
$v^{\frac{1}{12}}$	.998760		18	.76491	1.30734	15.6726	20.4894	.048806
			19	.75361	1.32695	16.4262	21.7967	.045878
$1+i$	1.015000		20	.74247	1.34686	17.1686	23.1237	.043246
$(1+i)^{\frac{1}{2}}$	1.007472		21	.73150	1.36706	17.9001	24.4705	.040865
$(1+i)^{\frac{1}{4}}$	1.003729		22	.72069	1.38756	18.6208	25.8376	.038703
$(1+i)^{\frac{1}{12}}$	1.001241		23	.71004	1.40838	19.3309	27.2251	.036731
			24	.69954	1.42950	20.0304	28.6335	.034924
$i/i^{(2)}$	1.003736		25	.68921	1.45095	20.7196	30.0630	.033263
$i/i^{(4)}$	1.005608		26	.67902	1.47271	21.3986	31.5140	.031732
$i/i^{(12)}$	1.006857		27	.66899	1.49480	22.0676	32.9867	.030315
i/δ	1.007481		28	.65910	1.51722	22.7267	34.4815	.029001
			29	.64936	1.53998	23.3761	35.9987	.027779
$i/d^{(2)}$	1.011236		30	.63976	1.56308	24.0158	37.5387	.026639
$i/d^{(4)}$	1.009358		31	.63031	1.58653	24.6461	39.1018	.025574
$i/d^{(12)}$	1.008107		32	.62099	1.61032	25.2671	40.6883	.024577
i/δ	1.007481		33	.61182	1.63448	25.8790	42.2986	.023641
			34	.60277	1.65900	26.4817	43.9331	.022762
			35	.59387	1.68388	27.0756	45.5921	.021934
			36	.58509	1.70914	27.6607	47.2760	.021152
			37	.57644	1.73478	28.2371	48.9851	.020414
			38	.56792	1.76080	28.8051	50.7199	.019716
			39	.55953	1.78721	29.3646	52.4807	.019055
			40	.55126	1.81402	29.9158	54.2679	.018427
			41	.54312	1.84123	30.4590	56.0819	.017831
			42	.53509	1.86885	30.9941	57.9231	.017264
			43	.52718	1.89688	31.5212	59.7920	.016725
			44	.51939	1.92533	32.0406	61.6889	.016210
			45	.51171	1.95421	32.5523	63.6142	.015720
			46	.50415	1.98353	33.0565	65.5684	.015251
			47	.49670	2.01328	33.5532	67.5519	.014803
			48	.48936	2.04348	34.0426	69.5652	.014375
			49	.48213	2.07413	34.5247	71.6087	.013965
			50	.47500	2.10524	34.9997	73.6828	.013572

COMPOUND INTEREST FUNCTIONS
$$i = 1\tfrac{3}{4}\%$$

Constants			n	v^n	$(1+i)^n$	$a_{\overline{n}\rvert}$	$s_{\overline{n}\rvert}$	$1/s_{\overline{n}\rvert}$
Function	**Value**		1	.98280	1.01750	.9828	1.0000	1.000000
			2	.96590	1.03531	1.9487	2.0175	.495663
i	.017500		3	.94929	1.05342	2.8980	3.0528	.327567
$i^{(2)}$	.017424		4	.93296	1.07186	3.8309	4.1062	.243532
$i^{(4)}$	.017386		5	.91691	1.09062	4.7479	5.1781	.193121
$i^{(12)}$	.017361		6	.90114	1.10970	5.6490	6.2687	.159523
δ	.017349		7	.88564	1.12912	6.5346	7.3784	.135531
			8	.87041	1.14888	7.4051	8.5075	.117543
d	.017199		9	.85544	1.16899	8.2605	9.6564	.103558
$d^{(2)}$	.017274		10	.84073	1.18944	9.1012	10.8254	.092375
$d^{(4)}$	.017311		11	.82627	1.21026	9.9275	12.0148	.083230
$d^{(12)}$	.017336		12	.81206	1.23144	10.7395	13.2251	.075614
δ	.017349		13	.79809	1.25299	11.5376	14.4505	.069173
			14	.78436	1.27492	12.3220	15.7095	.063656
v	.982801		15	.77087	1.29723	13.0929	16.9844	.058877
$v^{\frac{1}{2}}$	.991363		16	.75762	1.31993	13.8505	18.2817	.054700
$v^{\frac{1}{4}}$	.995672		17	.74459	1.34303	14.5951	19.6016	.051016
$v^{\frac{1}{12}}$	.998555		18	.73178	1.36653	15.3269	20.9446	.047745
			19	.71919	1.39045	16.0461	22.3112	.044821
$1+i$	1.017500		20	.70682	1.41478	16.7529	23.7016	.042191
$(1+i)^{\frac{1}{2}}$	1.008712		21	.69467	1.43954	17.4475	25.1164	.039815
$(1+i)^{\frac{1}{4}}$	1.004347		22	.68272	1.46473	18.1303	26.5559	.037656
$(1+i)^{\frac{1}{12}}$	1.001447		23	.67098	1.49036	18.8012	28.0207	.035688
			24	.65944	1.51644	19.4607	29.5110	.033886
$i/i^{(2)}$	1.004356		25	.64810	1.54298	20.1088	31.0275	.032230
$i/i^{(4)}$	1.006539		26	.63695	1.56998	20.7457	32.5704	.030703
$i/i^{(12)}$	1.007996		27	.62599	1.59746	21.3717	34.1404	.029291
i/δ	1.008725		28	.61523	1.62541	21.9870	35.7379	.027982
			29	.60465	1.65386	22.5916	37.3633	.026764
$i/d^{(2)}$	1.013106		30	.59425	1.68280	23.1858	39.0172	.025630
$i/d^{(4)}$	1.010914		31	.58403	1.71225	23.7699	40.7000	.024570
$i/d^{(12)}$	1.009454		32	.57398	1.74221	24.3439	42.4122	.023578
i/δ	1.008725		33	.56411	1.77270	24.9080	44.1544	.022648
			34	.55441	1.80372	25.4624	45.9271	.021774
			35	.54487	1.83529	26.0073	47.7308	.020951
			36	.53550	1.86741	26.5428	49.5661	.020175
			37	.52629	1.90009	27.0690	51.4335	.019443
			38	.51724	1.93334	27.5863	53.3336	.018750
			39	.50834	1.96717	28.0946	55.2670	.018094
			40	.49960	2.00160	28.5942	57.2341	.017472
			41	.49101	2.03663	29.0852	59.2357	.016882
			42	.48256	2.07227	29.5678	61.2724	.016321
			43	.47426	2.10853	30.0421	63.3446	.015787
			44	.46611	2.14543	30.5082	65.4532	.015278
			45	.45809	2.18298	30.9663	67.5986	.014793
			46	.45021	2.22118	31.4165	69.7816	.014330
			47	.44247	2.26005	31.8589	72.0027	.013888
			48	.43486	2.29960	32.2938	74.2628	.013466
			49	.42738	2.33984	32.7212	76.5624	.013061
			50	.42003	2.38079	33.1412	78.9022	.012674

COMPOUND INTEREST FUNCTIONS
$$i = 2\%$$

Constants			n	v^n	$(1+i)^n$	$a_{\overline{n}}$	$s_{\overline{n}}$	$1/s_{\overline{n}}$
Function	*Value*		1	.98039	1.02000	.9804	1.0000	1.000000
			2	.96117	1.04040	1.9416	2.0200	.495050
i	.020000		3	.94232	1.06121	2.8839	3.0604	.326755
$i^{(2)}$	.019901		4	.92385	1.08243	3.8077	4.1216	.242624
$i^{(4)}$	.019852		5	.90573	1.10408	4.7135	5.2040	.192158
$i^{(12)}$	.019819		6	.88797	1.12616	5.6014	6.3081	.158526
δ	.019803		7	.87056	1.14869	6.4720	7.4343	.134512
			8	.85349	1.17166	7.3255	8.5830	.116510
d	.019608		9	.83676	1.19509	8.1622	9.7546	.102515
$d^{(2)}$	.019705		10	.82035	1.21899	8.9826	10.9497	.091327
$d^{(4)}$	.019754		11	.80426	1.24337	9.7868	12.1687	.082178
$d^{(12)}$	.019786		12	.78849	1.26824	10.5753	13.4121	.074560
δ	.019803		13	.77303	1.29361	11.3484	14.6803	.068118
			14	.75788	1.31948	12.1062	15.9739	.062602
v	.980392		15	.74301	1.34587	12.8493	17.2934	.057825
$v^{\frac{1}{2}}$	.990148		16	.72845	1.37279	13.5777	18.6393	.053650
$v^{\frac{1}{4}}$	.995062		17	.71416	1.40024	14.2919	20.0121	.049970
$v^{\frac{1}{12}}$	.998351		18	.70016	1.42825	14.9920	21.4123	.046702
			19	.68643	1.45681	15.6785	22.8406	.043782
$1+i$	1.020000		20	.67297	1.48595	16.3514	24.2974	.041157
$(1+i)^{\frac{1}{2}}$	1.009950		21	.65978	1.51567	17.0112	25.7833	.038785
$(1+i)^{\frac{1}{4}}$	1.004963		22	.64684	1.54598	17.6580	27.2990	.036631
$(1+i)^{\frac{1}{12}}$	1.001652		23	.63416	1.57690	18.2922	28.8450	.034668
			24	.62172	1.60844	18.9139	30.4219	.032871
$i/i^{(2)}$	1.004975		25	.60953	1.64061	19.5235	32.0303	.031220
$i/i^{(4)}$	1.007469		26	.59758	1.67342	20.1210	33.6709	.029699
$i/i^{(12)}$	1.009134		27	.58586	1.70689	20.7069	35.3443	.028293
i/δ	1.009967		28	.57437	1.74102	21.2813	37.0512	.026990
			29	.56311	1.77584	21.8444	38.7922	.025778
$i/d^{(2)}$	1.014975		30	.55207	1.81136	22.3965	40.5681	.024650
$i/d^{(4)}$	1.012469		31	.54125	1.84759	22.9377	42.3794	.023596
$i/d^{(12)}$	1.010801		32	.53063	1.88454	23.4683	44.2270	.022611
i/δ	1.009967		33	.52023	1.92223	23.9886	46.1116	.021687
			34	.51003	1.96068	24.4986	48.0338	.020819
			35	.50003	1.99989	24.9986	49.9945	.020002
			36	.49022	2.03989	25.4888	51.9944	.019233
			37	.48061	2.08069	25.9695	54.0343	.018507
			38	.47119	2.12230	26.4406	56.1149	.017821
			39	.46195	2.16474	26.9026	58.2372	.017171
			40	.45289	2.20804	27.3555	60.4020	.016556
			41	.44401	2.25220	27.7995	62.6100	.015972
			42	.43530	2.29724	28.2348	64.8622	.015417
			43	.42677	2.34319	28.6616	67.1595	.014890
			44	.41840	2.39005	29.0800	69.5027	.014388
			45	.41020	2.43785	29.4902	71.8927	.013910
			46	.40215	2.48661	29.8923	74.3306	.013453
			47	.39427	2.53634	30.2866	76.8172	.013018
			48	.38654	2.58707	30.6731	79.3535	.012602
			49	.37896	2.63881	31.0521	81.9406	.012204
			50	.37153	2.69159	31.4236	84.5794	.011823

COMPOUND INTEREST FUNCTIONS
$$i = 2\tfrac{1}{4}\%$$

Constants			n	v^n	$(1+i)^n$	$a_{\overline{n}|}$	$s_{\overline{n}|}$	$1/s_{\overline{n}|}$
Function	*Value*		1	.97800	1.02250	.9780	1.0000	1.000000
			2	.95647	1.04551	1.9345	2.0225	.494438
i	.022500		3	.93543	1.06903	2.8699	3.0680	.325945
$i^{(2)}$	.022375		4	.91484	1.09308	3.7847	4.1370	.241719
$i^{(4)}$	.022313		5	.89471	1.11768	4.6795	5.2301	.191200
$i^{(12)}$	.022271		6	.87502	1.14283	5.5545	6.3478	.157535
δ	.022251		7	.85577	1.16854	6.4102	7.4906	.133500
			8	.83694	1.19483	7.2472	8.6592	.115485
d	.022005		9	.81852	1.22171	8.0657	9.8540	.101482
$d^{(2)}$	.022127		10	.80051	1.24920	8.8662	11.0757	.090288
$d^{(4)}$	.022189		11	.78290	1.27731	9.6491	12.3249	.081137
$d^{(12)}$	.022230		12	.76567	1.30605	10.4148	13.6022	.073517
δ	.022251		13	.74882	1.33544	11.1636	14.9083	.067077
			14	.73234	1.36548	11.8959	16.2437	.061562
v	.977995		15	.71623	1.39621	12.6122	17.6092	.056789
$v^{\frac{1}{2}}$	.988936		16	.70047	1.42762	13.3126	19.0054	.052617
$v^{\frac{1}{4}}$	.994453		17	.68505	1.45974	13.9977	20.4330	.048940
$v^{\frac{1}{12}}$	.998148		18	.66998	1.49259	14.6677	21.8928	.045677
			19	.65523	1.52617	15.3229	23.3853	.042762
$1+i$	1.022500		20	.64082	1.56051	15.9637	24.9115	.040142
$(1+i)^{\frac{1}{2}}$	1.011187		21	.62672	1.59562	16.5904	26.4720	.037776
$(1+i)^{\frac{1}{4}}$	1.005578		22	.61292	1.63152	17.2034	28.0676	.035628
$(1+i)^{\frac{1}{12}}$	1.001856		23	.59944	1.66823	17.8028	29.6992	.033671
			24	.58625	1.70577	18.3890	31.3674	.031880
$i/i^{(2)}$	1.005594		25	.57335	1.74415	18.9624	33.0732	.030236
$i/i^{(4)}$	1.008398		26	.56073	1.78339	19.5231	34.8173	.028721
$i/i^{(12)}$	1.010271		27	.54839	1.82352	20.0715	36,6007	.027322
i/δ	1.011208		28	.53632	1.86454	20.6078	38.4242	.026025
			29	.52452	1.90650	21.1323	40.2888	.024821
$i/d^{(2)}$	1.016844		30	.51298	1.94939	21.6453	42.1953	.023699
$i/d^{(4)}$	1.014023		31	.50169	1.99325	22.1470	44.1447	.022653
$i/d^{(12)}$	1.012146		32	.49065	2.03810	22.6377	46.1379	.021674
i/δ	1.011208		33	.47986	2.08396	23.1175	48.1760	.020757
			34	.46930	2.13085	23.5868	50.2600	.019897
			35	.45897	2.17879	24.0458	52.3908	.019087
			36	.44887	2.22782	24.4947	54.5696	.018325
			37	.43899	2.27794	24.9337	56.7974	.017606
			38	.42933	2.32920	25.3630	59.0754	.016928
			39	.41989	2.38160	25.7829	61.4046	.016285
			40	.41065	2.43519	26.1935	63.7862	.015677
			41	.40161	2.48998	26.5951	66.2214	.015101
			42	.39277	2.54601	26.9879	68.7113	.014554
			43	.38413	2.60329	27.3720	71.2574	.014034
			44	.37568	2.66186	27.7477	73.8606	.013539
			45	.36741	2.72176	28.1151	76.5225	.013068
			46	.35932	2.78300	28.4744	79.2443	.012619
			47	.35142	2.84561	28.8259	82.0273	.012191
			48	.34369	2.90964	29.1695	84.8729	.011782
			49	.33612	2.97511	29.5057	87.7825	.011392
			50	.32873	3.04205	29.8344	90.7576	.011018

COMPOUND INTEREST FUNCTIONS
$$i = 2\tfrac{1}{2}\%$$

Constants			n	v^n	$(1+i)^n$	$a_{\overline{n}\rvert}$	$s_{\overline{n}\rvert}$	$1/s_{\overline{n}\rvert}$
Function	**Value**		1	.97561	1.02500	.9756	1.0000	1.000000
			2	.95181	1.05063	1.9274	2.0250	.493827
i	.025000		3	.92860	1.07689	2.8560	3.0756	.325137
$i^{(2)}$	.024846		4	.90595	1.10381	3.7620	4.1525	.240818
$i^{(4)}$	.024769		5	.88385	1.13141	4.6458	5.2563	.190247
$i^{(12)}$	.024718		6	.86230	1.15969	5.5081	6.3877	.156550
δ	.024693		7	.84127	1.18869	6.3494	7.5474	.132495
			8	.82075	1.21840	7.1701	8.7361	.114467
d	.024390		9	.80073	1.24886	7.9709	9.9545	.100457
$d^{(2)}$	.024541		10	.78120	1.28008	8.7521	11.2034	.089259
$d^{(4)}$	.024617		11	.76214	1.31209	9.5142	12.4835	.080106
$d^{(12)}$	.024667		12	.74356	1.34489	10.2578	13.7956	.072487
δ	.024693		13	.72542	1.37851	10.9832	15.1404	.066048
			14	.70773	1.41297	11.6909	16.5190	.060537
v	.975610		15	.69047	1.44830	12.3814	17.9319	.055766
$v^{\frac{1}{2}}$	.987730		16	.67362	1.48451	13.0550	19.3802	.051599
$v^{\frac{1}{4}}$	.993846		17	.65720	1.52162	13.7122	20.8647	.047928
$v^{\frac{1}{12}}$	.997944		18	.64117	1.55966	14.3534	22.3863	.044670
			19	.62553	1.59865	14.9789	23.9460	.041761
$1+i$	1.025000		20	.61027	1.63862	15.5892	25.5447	.039147
$(1+i)^{\frac{1}{2}}$	1.012423		21	.59539	1.67958	16.1845	27.1833	.036787
$(1+i)^{\frac{1}{4}}$	1.006192		22	.58086	1.72157	16.7654	28.8629	.034647
$(1+i)^{\frac{1}{12}}$	1.002060		23	.56670	1.76461	17.3321	30.5844	.032696
			24	.55288	1.80873	17.8850	32.3490	.030913
$i/i^{(2)}$	1.006211		25	.53939	1.85394	18.4244	34.1578	.029276
$i/i^{(4)}$	1.009327		26	.52623	1.90029	18.9506	36.0117	.027769
$i/i^{(12)}$	1.011407		27	.51340	1.94780	19.4640	37.9120	.026377
i/δ	1.012449		28	.50088	1.99650	19.9649	39.8598	.025088
			29	.48866	2.04641	20.4535	41.8563	.023891
$i/d^{(2)}$	1.018711		30	.47674	2.09757	20.9303	43.9027	.022778
$i/d^{(4)}$	1.015577		31	.46511	2.15001	21.3954	46.0003	.021739
$i/d^{(12)}$	1.013491		32	.45377	2.20376	21.8492	48.1503	.020768
i/δ	1.012449		33	.44270	2.25885	22.2919	50.3540	.019859
			34	.43191	2.31532	22.7238	52.6129	.019007
			35	.42137	2.37321	23.1452	54.9282	.018206
			36	.41109	2.43254	23.5563	57.3014	.017452
			37	.40107	2.49335	23.9573	59.7339	.016741
			38	.39128	2.55568	24.3486	62.2273	.016070
			39	.38174	2.61957	24.7303	64.7830	.015436
			40	.37243	2.68506	25.1028	67.4026	.014836
			41	.36335	2.75219	25.4661	70.0876	.014268
			42	.35448	2.82100	25.8206	72.8398	.013729
			43	.34584	2.89152	26.1664	75.6608	.013217
			44	.33740	2.96381	26.5038	78.5523	.012730
			45	.32917	3.03790	26.8330	81.5161	.012268
			46	.32115	3.11385	27.1542	84.5540	.011827
			47	.31331	3.19170	27.4675	87.6679	.011407
			48	.30567	3.27149	27.7732	90.8596	.011006
			49	.29822	3.35328	28.0714	94.1311	.010623
			50	.29094	3.43711	28.3623	97.4843	.010258

COMPOUND INTEREST FUNCTIONS
$$i = 2\tfrac{3}{4}\%$$

Constants			n	v^n	$(1+i)^n$	$a_{\overline{n}\rvert}$	$s_{\overline{n}\rvert}$	$1/s_{\overline{n}\rvert}$
Function	**Value**		1	.97324	1.02750	.9732	1.0000	1.000000
			2	.94719	1.05576	1.9204	2.0275	.493218
i	.027500		3	.92184	1.08479	2.8423	3.0833	.324332
$i^{(2)}$	.027313		4	.89717	1.11462	3.7394	4.1680	.239921
$i^{(4)}$	.027221		5	.87315	1.14527	4.6126	5.2827	.189298
$i^{(12)}$	.027159		6	.84978	1.17677	5.4624	6.4279	.155571
δ	.027129		7	.82704	1.20913	6.2894	7.6047	.131497
			8	.80491	1.24238	7.0943	8.8138	.113458
d	.026764		9	.78336	1.27655	7.8777	10.0562	.099441
$d^{(2)}$	.026946		10	.76240	1.31165	8.6401	11.3328	.088240
$d^{(4)}$	.027037		11	.74199	1.34772	9.3821	12.6444	.079086
$d^{(12)}$	.027098		12	.72213	1.38478	10.1042	13.9921	.071469
δ	.027129		13	.70281	1.42287	10.8070	15.3769	.065033
			14	.68400	1.46199	11.4910	16.7998	.059525
v	.973236		15	.66569	1.50220	12.1567	18.2618	.054759
$v^{\frac{1}{2}}$	.986527		16	.64787	1.54351	12.8046	19.7640	.050597
$v^{\frac{1}{4}}$	.993241		17	.63053	1.58596	13.4351	21.3075	.046932
$v^{\frac{1}{12}}$	.997742		18	.61366	1.62957	14.0488	22.8934	.043681
			19	.59723	1.67438	14.6460	24.5230	.040778
$1+i$	1.027500		20	.58125	1.72043	15.2273	26.1974	.038172
$(1+i)^{\frac{1}{2}}$	1.013657		21	.56569	1.76774	15.7929	27.9178	.035819
$(1+i)^{\frac{1}{4}}$	1.006805		22	.55055	1.81635	16.3435	29.6856	.033686
$(1+i)^{\frac{1}{12}}$	1.002263		23	.53582	1.86630	16.8793	31.5019	.031744
			24	.52148	1.91763	17.4008	33.3682	.029969
$i/i^{(2)}$	1.006828		25	.50752	1.97036	17.9083	35.2858	.028340
$i/i^{(4)}$	1.010254		26	.49394	2.02455	18.4023	37.2562	.026841
$i/i^{(12)}$	1.012542		27	.48072	2.08022	18.8830	39.2808	.025458
i/δ	1.013688		28	.46785	2.13743	19.3508	41.3610	.024177
			29	.45533	2.19621	19.8062	43.4984	.022989
$i/d^{(2)}$	1.020578		30	.44314	2.25660	20.2493	45.6946	.021884
$i/d^{(4)}$	1.017129		31	.43128	2.31866	20.6806	47.9512	.020855
$i/d^{(12)}$	1.014834		32	.41974	2.38242	21.1003	50.2699	.019893
i/δ	1.013688		33	.40851	2.44794	21.5088	52.6523	.018993
			34	.39757	2.51526	21.9064	55.1002	.018149
			35	.38693	2.58443	22.2933	57.6155	.017356
			36	.37658	2.65550	22.6699	60.1999	.016611
			37	.36650	2.72852	23.0364	62.8554	.015910
			38	.35669	2.80356	23.3931	65.5839	.015248
			39	.34714	2.88066	23.7402	68.3875	.014623
			40	.33785	2.95987	24.0781	71.2681	.014032
			41	.32881	3.04127	24.4069	74.2280	.013472
			42	.32001	3.12491	24.7269	77.2693	.012942
			43	.31144	3.21084	25.0384	80.3942	.012439
			44	.30311	3.29914	25.3415	83.6050	.011961
			45	.29500	3.38986	25.6365	86.9042	.011507
			46	.28710	3.48309	25.9236	90.2940	.011075
			47	.27942	3.57887	26.2030	93.7771	.010664
			48	.27194	3.67729	26.4749	97.3560	.010272
			49	.26466	3.77842	26.7396	101.0333	.009898
			50	.25758	3.88232	26.9972	104.8117	.009541

COMPOUND INTEREST FUNCTIONS
$$i = 3\%$$

Constants			n	v^n	$(1 + i)^n$	$a_{\overline{n}\rvert}$	$s_{\overline{n}\rvert}$	$1/s_{\overline{n}\rvert}$
Function	*Value*		1	.97087	1.03000	.9709	1.0000	1.000000
			2	.94260	1.06090	1.9135	2.0300	.492611
i	.030000		3	.91514	1.09273	2.8286	3.0909	.323530
$i^{(2)}$	.029778		4	.88849	1.12551	3.7171	4.1836	.239027
$i^{(4)}$	.029668		5	.86261	1.15927	4.5797	5.3091	.188355
$i^{(12)}$	.029595		6	.83748	1.19405	5.4172	6.4684	.154598
δ	.029559		7	.81309	1.22987	6.2303	7.6625	.130506
			8	.78941	1.26677	7.0197	8.8923	.112456
d	.029126		9	.76642	1.30477	7.7861	10.1591	.098434
$d^{(2)}$	.029341		10	.74409	1.34392	8.5302	11.4639	.087231
$d^{(4)}$	.029450		11	.72242	1.38423	9.2526	12.8078	.078077
$d^{(12)}$	.029522		12	.70138	1.42576	9.9540	14.1920	.070462
δ	.029559		13	.68095	1.46853	10.6350	15.6178	.064030
			14	.66112	1.51259	11.2961	17.0863	.058526
v	.970874		15	.64186	1.55797	11.9379	18.5989	.053767
$v^{\frac{1}{2}}$	.985329		16	.62317	1.60471	12.5611	20.1569	.049611
$v^{\frac{1}{4}}$	.992638		17	.60502	1.65285	13.1661	21.7616	.045953
$v^{\frac{1}{12}}$	.997540		18	.58739	1.70243	13.7535	23.4144	.042709
			19	.57029	1.75351	14.3238	25.1169	.039814
$1 + i$	1.030000		20	.55368	1.80611	14.8775	26.8704	.037216
$(1 + i)^{\frac{1}{2}}$	1.014889		21	.53755	1.86029	15.4150	28.6765	.034872
$(1 + i)^{\frac{1}{4}}$	1.007417		22	.52189	1.91610	15.9369	30.5368	.032747
$(1 + i)^{\frac{1}{12}}$	1.002466		23	.50669	1.97359	16.4436	32.4529	.030814
			24	.49193	2.03279	16.9355	34.4265	.029047
$i/i^{(2)}$	1.007445		25	.47761	2.09378	17.4131	36.4593	.027428
$i/i^{(4)}$	1.011181		26	.46369	2.15659	17.8768	38.5530	.025938
$i/i^{(12)}$	1.013677		27	.45019	2.22129	18.3270	40.7096	.024564
i/δ	1.014926		28	.43708	2.28793	18.7641	42.9309	.023293
			29	.42435	2.35657	19.1885	45.2189	.022115
$i/d^{(2)}$	1.022445		30	.41199	2.42726	19.6004	47.5754	.021019
$i/d^{(4)}$	1.018681		31	.39999	2.50008	20.0004	50.0027	.019999
$i/d^{(12)}$	1.016177		32	.38834	2.57508	20.3888	52.5028	.019047
i/δ	1.014926		33	.37703	2.65234	20.7658	55.0778	.018156
			34	.36604	2.73191	21.1318	57.7302	.017322
			35	.35538	2.81386	21.4872	60.4621	.016539
			36	.34503	2.89828	21.8323	63.2759	.015804
			37	.33498	2.98523	22.1672	66.1742	.015112
			38	.32523	3.07478	22.4925	69.1594	.014459
			39	.31575	3.16703	22.8082	72.2342	.013844
			40	.30656	3.26204	23.1148	75.4013	.013262
			41	.29763	3.35990	23.4124	78.6633	.012712
			42	.28896	3.46070	23.7014	82.0232	.012192
			43	.28054	3.56452	23.9819	85.4839	.011698
			44	.27237	3.67145	24.2543	89.0484	.011230
			45	.26444	3.78160	24.5187	92.7199	.010785
			46	.25674	3.89504	24.7754	96.5015	.010363
			47	.24926	4.01190	25.0247	100.3965	.009961
			48	.24200	4.13225	25.2667	104.4084	.009578
			49	.23495	4.25622	25.5017	108.5406	.009213
			50	.22811	4.38391	25.7298	112.7969	.008865

COMPOUND INTEREST FUNCTIONS
$$i = 3\tfrac{1}{2}\%$$

Constants	
Function	Value
i	.035000
$i^{(2)}$	.034699
$i^{(4)}$	.034550
$i^{(12)}$	.034451
δ	.034401
d	.033816
$d^{(2)}$	.034107
$d^{(4)}$	.034254
$d^{(12)}$	.034352
δ	.034401
v	.966184
$v^{\frac{1}{2}}$	.982946
$v^{\frac{1}{4}}$	.991437
$v^{\frac{1}{12}}$	.997137
$1+i$	1.035000
$(1+i)^{\frac{1}{2}}$	1.017349
$(1+i)^{\frac{1}{4}}$	1.008637
$(1+i)^{\frac{1}{12}}$	1.002871
$i/i^{(2)}$	1.008675
$i/i^{(4)}$	1.013031
$i/i^{(12)}$	1.015942
i/δ	1.017400
$i/d^{(2)}$	1.026175
$i/d^{(4)}$	1.021781
$i/d^{(12)}$	1.018859
i/δ	1.017400

n	v^n	$(1+i)^n$	$a_{\overline{n}}$	$s_{\overline{n}}$	$1/s_{\overline{n}}$
1	.96618	1.03500	.9662	1.0000	1.000000
2	.93351	1.07123	1.8997	2.0350	.491400
3	.90194	1.10872	2.8016	3.1062	.321934
4	.87144	1.14752	3.6731	4.2149	.237251
5	.84197	1.18769	4.5151	5.3625	.186481
6	.81350	1.22926	5.3286	6.5502	.152668
7	.78599	1.27228	6.1145	7.7794	.128544
8	.75941	1.31681	6.8740	9.0517	.110477
9	.73373	1.36290	7.6077	10.3685	.096446
10	.70892	1.41060	8.3166	11.7314	.085241
11	.68495	1.45997	9.0016	13.1420	.076092
12	.66178	1.51107	9.6633	14.6020	.068484
13	.63940	1.56396	10.3027	16.1130	.062062
14	.61778	1.61896	10.9205	17.6770	.056571
15	.59689	1.67535	11.5174	19.2957	.051825
16	.57671	1.73399	12.0941	20.9710	.047685
17	.55720	1.79468	12.6513	22.7050	.044043
18	.53836	1.85749	13.1897	24.4997	.040817
19	.52016	1.92250	13.7098	26.3572	.037940
20	.50257	1.98979	14.2124	28.2797	.035361
21	.48557	2.05943	14.6980	30.2695	.033037
22	.46915	2.13151	15.1671	32.3289	.030932
23	.45329	2.20611	15.6204	34.4604	.029019
24	.43796	2.28333	16.0584	36.6665	.027273
25	.42315	2.36324	16.4815	38.9499	.025674
26	.40884	2.44596	16.8904	41.3131	.024205
27	.39501	2.53157	17.2854	43.7591	.022852
28	.38165	2.62017	17.6670	46.2906	.021603
29	.36875	2.71188	18.0358	48.9108	.020445
30	.35628	2.80679	18.3920	51.6227	.019371
31	.34423	2.90503	18.7363	54.4295	.018372
32	.33259	3.00671	19.0689	57.3345	.017442
33	.32134	3.11194	19.3902	60.3412	.016572
34	.31048	3.22086	19.7007	63.4532	.015760
35	.29998	3.33359	20.0007	66.6740	.014998
36	.28983	3.45027	20.2905	70.0076	.014284
37	.28003	3.57103	20.5705	73.4579	.013613
38	.27056	3.69601	20.8411	77.0289	.012982
39	.26141	3.82537	21.1025	80.7249	.012388
40	.25257	3.95926	21.3551	84.5503	.011827
41	.24403	4.09783	21.5991	88.5095	.011298
42	.23578	4.24126	21.8349	92.6074	.010798
43	.22781	4.38970	22.0627	96.8486	.010325
44	.22010	4.54334	22.2828	101.2383	.009878
45	.21266	4.70236	22.4955	105.7817	.009453
46	.20547	4.86694	22.7009	110.4840	.009051
47	.19852	5.03728	22.8994	115.3510	.008669
48	.19181	5.21359	23.0912	120.3883	.008306
49	.18532	5.39606	23.2766	125.6018	.007962
50	.17905	5.58493	23.4556	130.9979	.007634

COMPOUND INTEREST FUNCTIONS
$$i = 4\%$$

Constants			n	v^n	$(1+i)^n$	$a_{\overline{n}|}$	$s_{\overline{n}|}$	$1/s_{\overline{n}|}$
Function	*Value*		1	.96154	1.04000	.9615	1.0000	1.000000
			2	.92456	1.08160	1.8861	2.0400	.490196
i	.040000		3	.88900	1.12486	2.7751	3.1216	.320349
$i^{(2)}$	.039608		4	.85480	1.16986	3.6299	4.2465	.235490
$i^{(4)}$	.039414		5	.82193	1.21665	4.4518	5.4163	.184627
$i^{(12)}$	.039285		6	.79031	1.26532	5.2421	6.6330	.150762
δ	.039221		7	.75992	1.31593	6.0021	7.8983	.126610
			8	.73069	1.36857	6.7327	9.2142	.108528
d	.038462		9	.70259	1.42331	7.4353	10.5828	.094493
$d^{(2)}$	.038839		10	.67556	1.48024	8.1109	12.0061	.083291
$d^{(4)}$	.039029		11	.64958	1.53945	8.7605	13.4864	.074149
$d^{(12)}$	.039157		12	.62460	1.60103	9.3851	15.0258	.066552
δ	.039221		13	.60057	1.66507	9.9856	16.6268	.060144
			14	.57748	1.73168	10.5631	18.2919	.054669
v	.961538		15	.55526	1.80094	11.1184	20.0236	.049941
$v^{\frac{1}{2}}$	.980581		16	.53391	1.87298	11.6523	21.8245	.045820
$v^{\frac{1}{4}}$	.990243		17	.51337	1.94790	12.1657	23.6975	.042199
$v^{\frac{1}{12}}$	.996737		18	.49363	2.02582	12.6593	25.6454	.038993
			19	.47464	2.10685	13.1339	27.6712	.036139
$1 + i$	1.040000		20	.45639	2.19112	13.5903	29.7781	.033582
$(1+i)^{\frac{1}{2}}$	1.019804		21	.43883	2.27877	14.0292	31.9692	.031280
$(1+i)^{\frac{1}{4}}$	1.009853		22	.42196	2.36992	14.4511	34.2480	.029199
$(1+i)^{\frac{1}{12}}$	1.003274		23	.40573	2.46472	14.8568	36.6179	.027309
			24	.39012	2.56330	15.2470	39.0826	.025587
$i/i^{(2)}$	1.009902		25	.37512	2.66584	15.6221	41.6459	.024012
$i/i^{(4)}$	1.014877		26	.36069	2.77247	15.9828	44.3117	.022567
$i/i^{(12)}$	1.018204		27	.34682	2.88337	16.3296	47.0842	.021239
i/δ	1.019869		28	.33348	2.99870	16.6631	49.9676	.020013
			29	.32065	3.11865	16.9837	52.9663	.018880
$i/d^{(2)}$	1.029902		30	.30832	3.24340	17.2920	56.0849	.017830
$i/d^{(4)}$	1.024877		31	.29646	3.37313	17.5885	59.3283	.016855
$i/d^{(12)}$	1.021537		32	.28506	3.50806	17.8736	62.7015	.015949
i/δ	1.019869		33	.27409	3.64838	18.1476	66.2095	.015104
			34	.26355	3.79432	18.4112	69.8579	.014315
			35	.25342	3.94609	18.6646	73.6522	.013577
			36	.24367	4.10393	18.9083	77.5983	.012887
			37	.23430	4.26809	19.1426	81.7022	.012240
			38	.22529	4.43881	19.3679	85.9703	.011632
			39	.21662	4.61637	19.5845	90.4091	.011061
			40	.20829	4.80102	19.7928	95.0255	.010523
			41	.20028	4.99306	19.9931	99.8265	.010017
			42	.19257	5.19278	20.1856	104.8196	.009540
			43	.18517	5.40050	20.3708	110.0124	.009090
			44	.17805	5.61652	20.5488	115.4129	.008665
			45	.17120	5.84118	20.7200	121.0294	.008262
			46	.16461	6.07482	20.8847	126.8706	.007882
			47	.15828	6.31782	21.0429	132.9454	.007522
			48	.15219	6.57053	21.1951	139.2632	.007181
			49	.14634	6.83335	21.3415	145.8337	.006857
			50	.14071	7.10668	21.4822	152.6671	.006550

COMPOUND INTEREST FUNCTIONs
$$i = 4\tfrac{1}{2}\%$$

Constants			n	v^n	$(1+i)^n$	$a_{\overline{n}|}$	$s_{\overline{n}|}$	$1/s_{\overline{n}|}$
Function	Value		1	.95694	1.04500	.9569	1.0000	1.000000
			2	.91573	1.09203	1.8727	2.0450	.488998
i	.045000		3	.87630	1.14117	2.7490	3.1370	.318773
$i^{(2)}$	.044505		4	.83856	1.19252	3.5875	4.2782	.233744
$i^{(4)}$	.044260		5	.80245	1.24618	4.3900	5.4707	.182792
$i^{(12)}$	.044098		6	.76790	1.30226	5.1579	6.7169	.148878
δ	.044017		7	.73483	1.36086	5.8927	8.0192	.124701
			8	.70319	1.42210	6.5959	9.3800	.106610
d	.043062		9	.67290	1.48610	7.2688	10.8021	.092574
$d^{(2)}$	.043536		10	.64393	1.55297	7.9127	12.2882	.081379
$d^{(4)}$	.043776		11	.61620	1.62285	8.5289	13.8412	.072248
$d^{(12)}$	.043936		12	.58966	1.69588	9.1186	15.4640	.064666
δ	.044017		13	.56427	1.77220	9.6829	17.1599	.058275
			14	.53997	1.85194	10.2228	18.9321	.052820
v	.956938		15	.51672	1.93528	10.7395	20.7841	.048114
$v^{\frac{1}{2}}$	.978232		16	.49447	2.02237	11.2340	22.7193	.044015
$v^{\frac{1}{4}}$	.989056		17	.47318	2.11338	11.7072	24.7417	.040418
$v^{\frac{1}{12}}$	.996339		18	.45280	2.20848	12.1600	26.8551	.037237
			19	.43330	2.30786	12.5933	29.0636	.034407
$1+i$	1.045000		20	.41464	2.41171	13.0079	31.3714	.031876
$(1+i)^{\frac{1}{2}}$	1.022252		21	.39679	2.52024	13.4047	33.7831	.029601
$(1+i)^{\frac{1}{4}}$	1.011065		22	.37970	2.63365	13.7844	36.3034	.027546
$(1+i)^{\frac{1}{12}}$	1.003675		23	.36335	2.75217	14.1478	38.9370	.025682
			24	.34770	2.87601	14.4955	41.6892	.023987
$i/i^{(2)}$	1.011126		25	.33273	3.00543	14.8282	44.5652	.022439
$i/i^{(4)}$	1.016720		26	.31840	3.14068	15.1466	47.5706	.021021
$i/i^{(12)}$	1.020461		27	.30469	3.28201	15.4513	50.7113	.019719
i/δ	1.022335		28	.29157	3.42970	15.7429	53.9933	.018521
			29	.27902	3.58404	16.0219	57.4230	.017415
$i/d^{(2)}$	1.033626		30	.26700	3.74532	16.2889	61.0071	.016392
$i/d^{(4)}$	1.027970		31	.25550	3.91386	16.5444	64.7524	.015443
$i/d^{(12)}$	1.024211		32	.24450	4.08998	16.7889	68.6662	.014563
i/δ	1.022335		33	.23397	4.27403	17.0229	72.7562	.013745
			34	.22390	4.46636	17.2468	77.0303	.012982
			35	.21425	4.66735	17.4610	81.4966	.012270
			36	.20503	4.87738	17.6660	86.1640	.011606
			37	.19620	5.09686	17.8622	91.0413	.010984
			38	.18775	5.32622	18.0500	96.1382	.010402
			39	.17967	5.56590	18.2297	101.4644	.009856
			40	.17193	5.81636	18.4016	107.0303	.009343
			41	.16453	6.07810	18.5661	112.8467	.008862
			42	.15744	6.35162	18.7235	118.9248	.008409
			43	.15066	6.63744	18.8742	125.2764	.007982
			44	.14417	6.93612	19.0184	131.9138	.007581
			45	.13796	7.24825	19.1563	138.8500	.007202
			46	.13202	7.57442	19.2884	146.0982	.006845
			47	.12634	7.91527	19.4147	153.6726	.006507
			48	.12090	8.27146	19.5356	161.5879	.006189
			49	.11569	8.64367	19.6513	169.8594	.005887
			50	.11071	9.03264	19.7620	178.5030	.005602

COMPOUND INTEREST FUNCTIONS
$$i = 5\%$$

Constants			n	v^n	$(1+i)^n$	$a_{\overline{n}|}$	$s_{\overline{n}|}$	$1/s_{\overline{n}|}$
Function	**Value**		1	.95238	1.05000	.9524	1.0000	1.000000
			2	.90703	1.10250	1.8594	2.0500	.487805
i	.050000		3	.86384	1.15763	2.7232	3.1525	.317209
$i^{(2)}$	.049390		4	.82270	1.21551	3.5460	4.3101	.232012
$i^{(4)}$	.049089		5	.78353	1.27628	4.3295	5.5256	.180975
$i^{(12)}$	.048889		6	.74622	1.34010	5.0757	6.8019	.147017
δ	.048790		7	.71068	1.40710	5.7864	8.1420	.122820
			8	.67684	1.47746	6.4632	9.5491	.104722
d	.047619		9	.64461	1.55133	7.1078	11.0266	.090690
$d^{(2)}$	.048200		10	.61391	1.62889	7.7217	12.5779	.079505
$d^{(4)}$	.048494		11	.58468	1.71034	8.3064	14.2068	.070389
$d^{(12)}$	.048691		12	.55684	1.79586	8.8633	15.9171	.062825
δ	.048790		13	.53032	1.88565	9.3936	17.7130	.056456
			14	.50507	1.97993	9.8986	19.5986	.051024
v	.952381		15	.48102	2.07893	10.3797	21.5786	.046342
$v^{\frac{1}{2}}$	.975900		16	.45811	2.18287	10.8378	23.6575	.042270
$v^{\frac{1}{4}}$	.987877		17	.43630	2.29202	11.2741	25.8404	.038699
$v^{\frac{1}{12}}$	.995942		18	.41552	2.40662	11.6896	28.1324	.035546
			19	.39573	2.52695	12.0853	30.5390	.032745
$1+i$	1.050000		20	.37689	2.65330	12.4622	33.0660	.030243
$(1+i)^{\frac{1}{2}}$	1.024695		21	.35894	2.78596	12.8212	35.7193	.027996
$(1+i)^{\frac{1}{4}}$	1.012272		22	.34185	2.92526	13.1630	38.5052	.025971
$(1+i)^{\frac{1}{12}}$	1.004074		23	.32557	3.07152	13.4886	41.4305	.024137
			24	.31007	3.22510	13.7986	44.5020	.022471
$i/i^{(2)}$	1.012348		25	.29530	3.38635	14.0939	47.7271	.020952
$i/i^{(4)}$	1.018559		26	.28124	3.55567	14.3752	51.1135	.019564
$i/i^{(12)}$	1.022715		27	.26785	3.73346	14.6430	54.6691	.018292
i/δ	1.024797		28	.25509	3.92013	14.8981	58.4026	.017123
			29	.24295	4.11614	15.1411	62.3227	.016046
$i/d^{(2)}$	1.037348		30	.23138	4.32194	15.3725	66.4388	.015051
$i/d^{(4)}$	1.031059		31	.22036	4.53804	15.5928	70.7608	.014132
$i/d^{(12)}$	1.026881		32	.20987	4.76494	15.8027	75.2988	.013280
i/δ	1.024797		33	.19987	5.00319	16.0025	80.0638	.012490
			34	.19035	5.25335	16.1929	85.0670	.011755
			35	.18129	5.51602	16.3742	90.3203	.011072
			36	.17266	5.79182	16.5469	95.8363	.010434
			37	.16444	6.08141	16.7113	101.6281	.009840
			38	.15661	6.38548	16.8679	107.7095	.009284
			39	.14915	6.70475	17.0170	114.0950	.008765
			40	.14205	7.03999	17.1591	120.7998	.008278
			41	.13528	7.39199	17.2944	127.8398	.007822
			42	.12884	7.76159	17.4232	135.2318	.007395
			43	.12270	8.14967	17.5459	142.9933	.006993
			44	.11686	8.55715	17.6628	151.1430	.006616
			45	.11130	8.98501	17.7741	159.7002	.006262
			46	.10600	9.43426	17.8801	168.6852	.005928
			47	.10095	9.90597	17.9810	178.1194	.005614
			48	.09614	10.40127	18.0772	188.0254	.005318
			49	.09156	10.92133	18.1687	198.4267	.005040
			50	.08720	11.46740	18.2559	209.3480	.004777

n (Months)	$i = 2\frac{1}{2}\%$	$i = 3\%$	$i = 3\frac{1}{2}\%$
1	.99794	.99754	.99714
2	1.99384	1.99263	1.99142
3	2.98768	2.98526	2.98286
4	3.97949	3.97546	3.97146
5	4.96925	4.96322	4.95722
6	5.95698	5.94855	5.94017
7	6.94268	6.93145	6.92030
8	7.92635	7.91194	7.89763
9	8.90800	8.89001	8.87216
10	9.88764	9.86568	9.84390
11	10.86526	10.83895	10.81285
12	11.84087	11.80982	11.77904
13	12.81447	12.77831	12.74246
14	13.78607	13.74441	13.70312
15	14.75568	14.70814	14.66103
16	15.72329	15.66949	15.61619
17	16.68891	16.62848	16.56863
18	17.65255	17.58511	17.51833
19	18.61421	18.53939	18.46532
20	19.57389	19.49132	19.40960
21	20.53160	20.44091	20.35117
22	21.48734	21.38816	21.29005
23	22.44111	22.33308	22.22624
24	23.39293	23.27567	23.15975
25	24.34279	24.21595	24.09059
26	25.29069	25.15391	25.01876
27	26.23665	26.08957	25.94428
28	27.18066	27.02292	26.86715
29	28.12273	27.95398	27.78737
30	29.06287	28.88275	28.70496
31	30.00107	29.80923	29.61993
32	30.93735	30.73344	30.53227
33	31.87169	31.65536	31.44201
34	32.80412	32.57503	32.34913
35	33.73464	33.49242	33.25367
36	34.66324	34.40757	34.15561
37	35.58993	35.32046	35.05497
38	36.51471	36.23110	35.95176
39	37.43760	37.13950	36.84597
40	38.35858	38.04567	37.73763
41	39.27768	38.94961	38.62674
42	40.19488	39.85133	39.51330
43	41.11020	40.75083	40.39733
44	42.02364	41.64811	41.27882
45	42.93520	42.54319	42.15779
46	43.84489	43.43606	43.03424
47	44.75271	44.32674	43.90818
48	45.65866	45.21523	44.77963

ANNUITY VALUES PAYABLE MONTHLY $12a_{\frac{n}{12}}^{(12)}$

n (Months)	$i = 2\frac{1}{2}\%$	$i = 3\%$	$i = 3\frac{1}{2}\%$
49	46.56274	46.10153	45.64857
50	47.46497	46.98565	46.51503
51	48.36535	47.86760	47.37901
52	49.26387	48.74737	48.24052
53	50.16055	49.62498	49.09956
54	51.05539	50.50044	49.95614
55	51.94838	51.37373	50.81027
56	52.83954	52.24488	51.66195
57	53.72887	53.11389	52.51120
58	54.61637	53.98076	53.35801
59	55.50204	54.84550	54.20240
60	56.38590	55.70811	55.04438
61	57.26793	56.56859	55.88394
62	58.14816	57.42696	56.72110
63	59.02657	58.28322	57.55586
64	59.90318	59.13737	58.38824
65	60.77799	59.98942	59.21823
66	61.65100	60.83937	60.04584
67	62.52221	61.68724	60.87109
68	63.39164	62.53301	61.69397
69	64.25927	63.37671	62.51450
70	65.12513	64.21833	63.33267
71	65.98920	65.05788	64.14851
72	66.85149	65.85936	64.96201
73	67.71202	66.73079	65.77318
74	68.57077	67.56416	66.58203
75	69.42776	68.39547	67.38857
76	70.28299	69.22475	68.19279
77	71.13646	70.05198	68.99472
78	71.98818	70.87718	69.79434
79	72.83815	71.70035	70.59168
80	73.68636	72.52149	71.38674
81	74.53284	73.34061	72.17952
82	75.37757	74.15772	72.97003
83	76.22057	74.97281	73.75828
84	77.06184	75.78591	74.54427
85	77.90137	76.59700	75.32801
86	78.73918	77.40609	76.10950
87	79.57527	78.21320	76.88876
88	80.40964	79.01832	77.66579
89	81.24229	79.82146	78.44060
90	82.07324	80.62262	79.21319
91	82.90247	81.42181	79.98356
92	83.73000	82.21904	80.75173
93	84.55583	83.01430	81.51770
94	85.37996	83.80761	82.28148
95	86.20240	84.59896	83.04307
96	87.02314	85.38837	83.80248

ANNUITY VALUES PAYABLE MONTHLY $12a_{\frac{n}{12}}^{(12)}$

n (Months)	$i = 2\frac{1}{2}\%$	$i = 3\%$	$i = 3\frac{1}{2}\%$
97	87.84220	86.17584	84.55972
98	88.65958	86.96137	85.31479
99	89.47528	87.74497	86.06770
100	90.28929	88.52664	86.81845
101	91.10164	89.30638	87.56706
102	91.91232	90.08421	88.31352
103	92.72132	90.86013	89.05784
104	93.52867	91.63413	89.80003
105	94.33436	92.40623	90.54010
106	95.13839	93.17643	91.27805
107	95.94077	93.94474	92.01389
108	96.74149	94.71116	92.74762
109	97.54058	95.47569	93.47925
110	98.33802	96.23834	94.20879
111	99.13382	96.99911	94.93624
112	99.92798	97.75802	95.66160
113	100.72051	98.51505	96.38489
114	101.51142	99.27022	97.10611
115	102.30069	100.02354	97.82526
116	103.08835	100.77500	98.54236
117	103.87438	101.52461	99.25740
118	104.65880	102.27238	99.97039
119	105.44161	103.01831	100.68135
120	106.22281	103.76241	101.39027
121	107.00240	104.50467	102.09716
122	107.78039	105.24511	102.80202
123	108.55678	105.98372	103.50487
124	109.33158	106.72052	104.20571
125	110.10478	107.45551	104.90454
126	110.87639	108.18868	105.60136
127	111.64642	108.92006	106.29620
128	112.41486	109.64963	106.98904
129	113.18173	110.37741	107.67991
130	113.94702	111.10340	108.36879
131	114.71073	111.82760	109.05570
132	115.47288	112.55002	109.74065
133	116.23345	113.27067	110.42363
134	116.99247	113.98954	111.10466
135	117.74992	114.70664	111.78374
136	118.50582	115.42198	112.46088
137	119.26016	116.13556	113.13608
138	120.01296	116.84738	113.80934
139	120.76420	117.55745	114.48068
140	121.51390	118.26578	115.15010
141	122.26206	118.97236	115.81759
142	123.00869	119.67720	116.48318
143	123.75377	120.38031	117.14687
144	124.49733	121.08169	117.80865

ANNUITY VALUES PAYABLE MONTHLY $12a^{(12)}_{\frac{n}{12}}$

n (Months)	$i = 2\frac{1}{2}\%$	$i = 3\%$	$i = 3\frac{1}{2}\%$
145	125.23936	121.78135	118.46854
146	125.97986	122.47928	119.12654
147	126.71884	123.17550	119.78265
148	127.45630	123.87000	120.43689
149	128.19224	124.56279	121.08926
150	128.92668	125.25388	121.73975
151	129.65960	125.94327	122.38839
152	130.39102	126.63097	123.03517
153	131.12093	127.31697	123.68010
154	131.84934	128.00128	124.32318
155	132.57625	128.68392	124.96442
156	133.30167	129.36487	125.60382
157	134.02560	130.04414	126.24139
158	134.74804	130.72175	126.87714
159	135.46900	131.39769	127.51107
160	136.18848	132.07196	128.14319
161	136.90647	132.74458	128.77349
162	137.62299	133.41554	129.40199
163	138.33804	134.08485	130.02869
164	139.05161	134.75251	130.65360
165	139.76372	135.41853	131.27671
166	140.47437	136.08292	131.89805
167	141.18355	136.74566	132.51760
168	141.89128	137.40678	133.13539
169	142.59755	138.06627	133.75140
170	143.30237	138.72414	134.36565
171	144.00574	139.38039	134.97814
172	144.70767	140.03503	135.58888
173	145.40815	140.68805	136.19787
174	146.10720	141.33947	136.80511
175	146.80480	141.98929	137.41062
176	147.50097	142.63751	138.01440
177	148.19572	143.28413	138.61644
178	148.88903	143.92916	139.21677
179	149.58092	144.57261	139.81537
180	150.27138	145.21447	140.41226
181	150.96043	145.85475	141.00744
182	151.64806	146.94346	141.60092
183	152.33427	147.13059	142.19270
184	153.01908	147.76616	142.78279
185	153.70248	148.40017	143.37118
186	154.38447	149.03261	143.95789
187	155.06506	149.66350	144.54292
188	155.74426	150.29284	145.12628
189	156.42205	150.92063	145.70797
190	157.09845	151.54687	146.28799
191	157.77347	152.17158	146.86635
192	158.44709	152.79474	**147.44306**

ANNUITY VALUE PAYABLE MONTHLY $12a_{\frac{n}{12}}^{(12)}$

n (Months)	$i = 2\frac{1}{2}\%$	$i = 3\%$	$i = 3\frac{1}{2}\%$
193	159.11933	153.41638	148.01811
194	159.79019	154.03648	148.59152
195	160.45967	154.65506	149.16329
196	161.12777	155.27212	149.73342
197	161.79450	155.88766	150.30192
198	162.45986	156.50168	150.86879
199	163.12385	157.11420	151.43404
200	163.78648	157.72520	151.99767
201	164.44774	158.33471	152.55968
202	165.10765	158.94271	153.12009
203	165.76620	159.54922	153.67890
204	166.42339	160.15424	154.23610
205	167.07924	160.75777	154.79171
206	167.73373	161.35981	155.34573
207	168.38688	161.96037	155.89816
208	169.03869	162.55945	156.44901
209	169.68916	163.15707	156.99828
210	170.33829	163.75321	157.54598
211	170.98609	164.34788	158.09212
212	171.63255	164.94109	158.63669
213	172.27769	165.53284	159.17970
214	172.92150	166.12314	159.72116
215	173.56399	166.71198	160.26106
216	174.20515	167.29938	160.79942
217	174.84500	167.88532	161.33624
218	175.48353	168.46983	161.87153
219	176.12075	169.05290	162.40528
220	176.75666	169.63454	162.93750
221	177.39127	170.21474	163.46820
222	178.02456	170.79352	163.99738
223	178.65656	171.37087	164.52505
224	179.28726	171.94681	165.05120
225	179.91666	172.52132	165.57585
226	180.54477	173.09442	166.09900
227	181.17158	173.66612	166.62064
228	181.79711	174.23640	167.14080
229	182.42135	174.80529	167.65947
230	183.04431	175.37277	168.17665
231	183.66599	175.93886	168.69235
232	184.28639	176.50355	169.20658
233	184.90552	177.06686	169.71933
234	185.52337	177.62878	170.23061
235	186.13995	178.18931	170.74043
236	186.75526	178.74847	171.24880
237	187.36931	179.30625	171.75570
238	187.98210	179.86266	172.26116
239	188.59363	180.41770	172.76517
240	189.20390	180.97138	173.26773

APPENDIX III

FIVE-PLACE LOGARITHMS
(BASE 10)

N	0	1	2	3	4	5	6	7	8	9
100	00 000	043	087	130	173	217	260	303	346	389
101	432	475	518	561	604	647	689	732	775	817
102	860	903	945	988	*030	*072	*115	*157	*199	*242
103	01 284	326	368	410	452	494	536	578	620	662
104	703	745	787	828	870	912	953	995	*036	*078
105	02 119	160	202	243	284	325	366	407	449	490
106	531	572	612	653	694	735	776	816	857	898
107	938	979	*019	*060	*100	*141	*181	*222	*262	*302
108	03 342	383	423	463	503	543	583	623	663	703
109	743	782	822	862	902	941	981	*021	*060	*100
110	04 139	179	218	258	297	336	376	415	454	493
111	532	571	610	650	689	727	766	805	844	883
112	922	961	999	*038	*077	*115	*154	*192	*231	*269
113	05 308	346	385	423	461	500	538	576	614	652
114	690	729	767	805	843	881	918	956	994	*032
115	06 070	108	145	183	221	258	296	333	371	408
116	446	483	521	558	595	633	670	707	744	781
117	819	856	893	930	967	*004	*041	*078	*115	*151
118	07 188	225	262	298	335	372	408	445	482	518
119	555	591	628	664	700	737	773	809	846	882
120	918	954	990	*027	*063	*099	*135	*171	*207	*243
121	08 279	314	350	386	422	458	493	529	565	600
122	636	672	707	743	778	814	849	884	920	955
123	991	*026	*061	*096	*132	*167	*202	*237	*272	*307
124	09 342	377	412	447	482	517	552	587	621	656
125	691	726	760	795	830	864	899	934	968	*003
126	10 037	072	106	140	175	209	243	278	312	346
127	380	415	449	483	517	551	585	619	653	687
128	721	755	789	823	857	890	924	958	992	*025
129	11 059	093	126	160	193	227	261	294	327	361
130	394	428	461	494	528	561	594	628	661	694
131	727	760	793	826	860	893	926	959	992	*024
132	12 057	090	123	156	189	222	254	287	320	352
133	385	418	450	483	516	548	581	613	646	678
134	710	743	775	808	840	872	905	937	969	*001
135	13 033	066	098	130	162	194	226	258	290	322
136	354	386	418	450	481	513	545	577	609	640
137	672	704	735	767	799	830	862	893	925	956
138	988	*019	*051	*082	*114	*145	*176	*208	*239	*270
139	14 301	333	364	395	426	457	489	520	551	582
140	613	644	675	706	737	768	799	829	860	891
141	922	953	983	*014	*045	*076	*106	*137	*168	*198
142	15 229	259	290	320	351	381	412	442	473	503
143	534	564	594	625	655	685	715	746	776	806
144	836	866	897	927	957	987	*017	*047	*077	*107
145	16 137	167	197	227	256	286	316	346	376	406
146	435	465	495	524	554	584	613	643	673	702
147	732	761	791	820	850	879	909	938	967	997
148	17 026	056	085	114	143	173	202	231	260	289
149	319	348	377	406	435	464	493	522	551	580
150	609	638	667	696	725	754	782	811	840	869

$\log_{10} e = .43429$ $\log_e 10 = 2.30259$

215

FIVE-PLACE LOGARITHMS
(BASE 10)

N	0	1	2	3	4	5	6	7	8	9
150	17 609	638	667	696	725	754	782	811	840	869
151	898	926	955	984	*013	*041	*070	*099	*127	*156
152	18 184	213	241	270	298	327	355	384	412	441
153	469	498	526	554	583	611	639	667	696	724
154	752	780	808	837	865	893	921	949	977	*005
155	19 033	061	089	117	145	173	201	229	257	285
156	312	340	368	396	424	451	479	507	535	562
157	590	618	645	673	700	728	756	783	811	838
158	866	893	921	948	976	*003	*030	*058	*085	*112
159	20 140	167	194	222	249	276	303	330	358	385
160	412	439	466	493	520	548	575	602	629	656
161	683	710	737	763	790	817	844	871	898	925
162	952	978	*005	*032	*059	*085	*112	*139	*165	*192
163	21 219	245	272	299	325	352	378	405	431	458
164	484	511	537	564	590	617	643	669	696	722
165	748	775	801	827	854	880	906	932	958	985
166	22 011	037	063	089	115	141	167	194	220	246
167	272	298	324	350	376	401	427	453	479	505
168	531	557	583	608	634	660	686	712	737	763
169	789	814	840	866	891	917	943	968	994	*019
170	23 045	070	096	121	147	172	198	223	249	274
171	300	325	350	376	401	426	452	477	502	528
172	553	578	603	629	654	679	704	729	754	779
173	805	830	855	880	905	930	955	980	*005	*030
174	24 055	080	105	130	155	180	204	229	254	279
175	304	329	353	378	403	428	452	477	502	527
176	551	576	601	625	650	674	699	724	748	773
177	797	822	846	871	895	920	944	969	993	*018
178	25 042	066	091	115	139	164	188	212	237	261
179	285	310	334	358	382	406	431	455	479	503
180	527	551	575	600	624	648	672	696	720	744
181	768	792	816	840	864	888	912	935	959	983
182	26 007	031	055	079	102	126	150	174	198	221
183	245	269	293	316	340	364	387	411	435	458
184	482	505	529	553	576	600	623	647	670	694
185	717	741	764	788	811	834	858	881	905	928
186	951	975	998	*021	*045	*068	*091	*114	*138	*161
187	27 184	207	231	254	277	300	323	346	370	393
188	416	439	462	485	508	531	554	577	600	623
189	646	669	692	715	738	761	784	807	830	852
190	875	898	921	944	967	989	*012	*035	*058	*081
191	28 103	126	149	171	194	217	240	262	285	307
192	330	353	375	398	421	443	466	488	511	533
193	556	578	601	623	646	668	691	713	735	758
194	780	803	825	847	870	892	914	937	959	981
195	29 003	026	048	070	092	115	137	159	181	203
196	226	248	270	292	314	336	358	380	403	425
197	447	469	491	513	535	557	579	601	623	645
198	667	688	710	732	754	776	798	820	842	863
199	885	907	929	951	973	994	*016	*038	*060	*081
200	30 103	125	146	168	190	211	233	255	276	298

$$\log_{10} e = .43429 \qquad\qquad \log_e 10 = 2.30259$$

FIVE-PLACE LOGARITHMS
(BASE 10)

N	0	1	2	3	4	5	6	7	8	9
200	30 103	125	146	168	190	211	233	255	276	298
201	320	341	363	384	406	428	449	471	492	514
202	535	557	578	600	621	643	664	685	707	728
203	750	771	792	814	835	856	878	899	920	942
204	963	984	*006	*027	*048	*069	*091	*112	*133	*154
205	31 175	197	218	239	260	281	302	323	345	366
206	387	408	429	450	471	492	513	534	555	576
207	597	618	639	660	681	702	723	744	765	785
208	806	827	848	869	890	911	931	952	973	994
209	32 015	035	056	077	098	118	139	160	181	201
210	222	243	263	284	305	325	346	366	387	408
211	428	449	469	490	510	531	552	572	593	613
212	634	654	675	695	715	736	756	777	797	818
213	838	858	879	899	919	940	960	980	*001	*021
214	33 041	062	082	102	122	143	163	183	203	224
215	244	264	284	304	325	345	365	385	405	425
216	445	465	486	506	526	546	566	586	606	626
217	646	666	686	706	726	746	766	786	806	826
218	846	866	885	905	925	945	965	985	*005	*025
219	34 044	064	084	104	124	143	163	183	203	223
220	242	262	282	301	321	341	361	380	400	420
221	439	459	479	498	518	537	557	577	596	616
222	635	655	674	694	713	733	753	772	792	811
223	830	850	869	889	908	928	947	967	986	*005
224	35 025	044	064	083	102	122	141	160	180	199
225	218	238	257	276	295	315	334	353	372	392
226	411	430	449	468	488	507	526	545	564	583
227	603	622	641	660	679	698	717	736	755	774
228	793	813	832	851	870	889	908	927	946	965
229	984	*003	*021	*040	*059	*078	*097	*116	*135	*154
230	36 173	192	211	229	248	267	286	305	324	342
231	361	380	399	418	436	455	474	493	511	530
232	549	568	586	605	624	642	661	680	698	717
233	736	754	773	791	810	829	847	866	884	903
234	922	940	959	977	996	*014	*033	*051	*070	*088
235	37 107	125	144	162	181	199	218	236	254	273
236	291	310	328	346	365	383	401	420	438	457
237	475	493	511	530	548	566	585	603	621	639
238	658	676	694	712	731	749	767	785	803	822
239	840	858	876	894	912	931	949	967	985	*003
240	38 021	039	057	075	093	112	130	148	166	184
241	202	220	238	256	274	292	310	328	346	364
242	382	399	417	435	453	471	489	507	525	543
243	561	578	596	614	632	650	668	686	703	721
244	739	757	775	792	810	828	846	863	881	899
245	917	934	952	970	987	*005	*023	*041	*058	*076
246	39 094	111	129	146	164	182	199	217	235	252
247	270	287	305	322	340	358	375	393	410	428
248	445	463	480	498	515	533	550	568	585	602
249	620	637	655	672	690	707	724	742	759	777
250	794	811	829	846	863	881	898	915	933	950

$$\log_{10} e = .43429 \qquad\qquad \log_e 10 = 2.30259$$

FIVE-PLACE LOGARITHMS
(BASE 10)

N	0	1	2	3	4	5	6	7	8	9
250	39 794	811	829	846	863	881	898	915	933	950
251	967	985	*002	*019	*037	*054	*071	*088	*106	*123
252	40 140	157	175	192	209	226	243	261	278	295
253	312	329	346	364	381	398	415	432	449	466
254	483	500	518	535	552	569	586	603	620	637
255	654	671	688	705	722	739	756	773	790	807
256	824	841	858	875	892	909	926	943	960	976
257	993	*010	*027	*044	*061	*078	*095	*111	*128	*145
258	41 162	179	196	212	229	246	263	280	296	313
259	330	347	363	380	397	414	430	447	464	481
260	497	514	531	547	564	581	597	614	631	647
261	664	681	697	714	731	747	764	780	797	814
262	830	847	863	880	896	913	929	946	963	979
263	996	*012	*029	*045	*062	*078	*095	*111	*127	*144
264	42 160	177	193	210	226	243	259	275	292	308
265	325	341	357	374	390	406	423	439	455	472
266	488	504	521	537	553	570	586	602	619	635
267	651	667	684	700	716	732	749	765	781	797
268	813	830	846	862	878	894	911	927	943	959
269	975	991	*008	*024	*040	*056	*072	*088	*104	*120
270	43 136	152	169	185	201	217	233	249	265	281
271	297	313	329	345	361	377	393	409	425	441
272	457	473	489	505	521	537	553	569	584	600
273	616	632	648	664	680	696	712	727	743	759
274	775	791	807	823	838	854	870	886	902	917
275	933	949	965	981	996	*012	*028	*044	*059	*075
276	44 091	107	122	138	154	170	185	201	217	232
277	248	264	279	295	311	326	342	358	373	389
278	404	420	436	451	467	483	498	514	529	545
279	560	576	592	607	623	638	654	669	685	700
280	716	731	747	762	778	793	809	824	840	855
281	871	886	902	917	932	948	963	979	994	*010
282	45 025	040	056	071	086	102	117	133	148	163
283	179	194	209	225	240	255	271	286	301	317
284	332	347	362	378	393	408	423	439	454	469
285	484	500	515	530	545	561	576	591	606	621
286	637	652	667	682	697	712	728	743	758	773
287	788	803	818	834	849	864	879	894	909	924
288	939	954	969	984	*000	*015	*030	*045	*060	*075
289	46 090	105	120	135	150	165	180	195	210	225
290	240	255	270	285	300	315	330	345	359	374
291	389	404	419	434	449	464	479	494	509	523
292	538	553	568	583	598	613	627	642	657	672
293	687	702	716	731	746	761	776	790	805	820
294	835	850	864	879	894	909	923	938	953	967
295	982	997	*012	*026	*041	*056	*070	*085	*100	*114
296	47 129	144	159	173	188	202	217	232	246	261
297	276	290	305	319	334	349	363	378	392	407
298	422	436	451	465	480	494	509	524	538	553
299	567	582	596	611	625	640	654	669	683	698
300	712	727	741	756	770	784	799	813	828	842

$\log_{10} e = .43429$ $\log_e 10 = 2.30259$

FIVE-PLACE LOGARITHMS
(BASE 10)

N	0	1	2	3	4	5	6	7	8	9
300	47 712	727	741	756	770	784	799	813	828	842
301	857	871	885	900	914	929	943	958	972	986
302	48 001	015	029	044	058	073	087	101	116	130
303	144	159	173	187	202	216	230	244	259	273
304	287	302	316	330	344	359	373	387	401	416
305	430	444	458	473	487	501	515	530	544	558
306	572	586	601	615	629	643	657	671	686	700
307	714	728	742	756	770	785	799	813	827	841
308	855	869	883	897	911	926	940	954	968	982
309	996	*010	*024	*038	*052	*066	*080	*094	*108	*122
310	49 136	150	164	178	192	206	220	234	248	262
311	276	290	304	318	332	346	360	374	388	402
312	415	429	443	457	471	485	499	513	527	541
313	554	568	582	596	610	624	638	651	665	679
314	693	707	721	734	748	762	776	790	803	817
315	831	845	859	872	886	900	914	927	941	955
316	969	982	996	*010	*024	*037	*051	*065	*079	*092
317	50 106	120	133	147	161	174	188	202	215	229
318	243	256	270	284	297	311	325	338	352	365
319	379	393	406	420	433	447	461	474	488	501
320	515	529	542	556	569	583	596	610	623	637
321	651	664	678	691	705	718	732	745	759	772
322	786	799	813	826	840	853	866	880	893	907
323	920	934	947	961	974	987	*001	*014	*028	*041
324	51 055	068	081	095	108	121	135	148	162	175
325	188	202	215	228	242	255	268	282	295	308
326	322	335	348	362	375	388	402	415	428	441
327	455	468	481	495	508	521	534	548	561	574
328	587	601	614	627	640	654	667	680	693	706
329	720	733	746	759	772	786	799	812	825	838
330	851	865	878	891	904	917	930	943	957	970
331	983	996	*009	*022	*035	*048	*061	*075	*088	*101
332	52 114	127	140	153	166	179	192	205	218	231
333	244	257	270	284	297	310	323	336	349	362
334	375	388	401	414	427	440	453	466	479	492
335	504	517	530	543	556	569	582	595	608	621
336	634	647	660	673	686	699	711	724	737	750
337	763	776	789	802	815	827	840	853	866	879
338	892	905	917	930	943	956	969	982	994	*007
339	53 020	033	046	058	071	084	097	110	122	135
340	148	161	173	186	199	212	224	237	250	263
341	275	288	301	314	326	339	352	364	377	390
342	403	415	428	441	453	466	479	491	504	517
343	529	542	555	567	580	593	605	618	631	643
344	656	668	681	694	706	719	732	744	757	769
345	782	794	807	820	832	845	857	870	882	895
346	908	920	933	945	958	970	983	995	*008	*020
347	54 033	045	058	070	083	095	108	120	133	145
348	158	170	183	195	208	220	233	245	258	270
349	283	295	307	320	332	345	357	370	382	394
350	407	419	432	444	456	469	481	494	506	518

$\log_{10} e = .43429$ $\log_e 10 = 2.30259$

FIVE-PLACE LOGARITHMS
(BASE 10)

N	0	1	2	3	4	5	6	7	8	9
350	54 407	419	432	444	456	469	481	494	506	518
351	531	543	555	568	580	593	605	617	630	642
352	654	667	679	691	704	716	728	741	753	765
353	777	790	802	814	827	839	851	864	876	888
354	900	913	925	937	949	962	974	986	998	*011
355	55 023	035	047	060	072	084	096	108	121	133
356	145	157	169	182	194	206	218	230	242	255
357	267	279	291	303	315	328	340	352	364	376
358	388	400	413	425	437	449	461	473	485	497
359	509	522	534	546	558	570	582	594	606	618
360	630	642	654	666	678	691	703	715	727	739
361	751	763	775	787	799	811	823	835	847	859
362	871	883	895	907	919	931	943	955	967	979
363	991	*003	*015	*027	*038	*050	*062	*074	*086	*098
364	56 110	122	134	146	158	170	182	194	205	217
365	229	241	253	265	277	289	301	312	324	336
366	348	360	372	384	396	407	419	431	443	455
367	467	478	490	502	514	526	538	549	561	573
368	585	597	608	620	632	644	656	667	679	691
369	703	714	726	738	750	761	773	785	797	808
370	820	832	844	855	867	879	891	902	914	926
371	937	949	961	972	984	996	*008	*019	*031	*043
372	57 054	066	078	089	101	113	124	136	148	159
373	171	183	194	206	217	229	241	252	264	276
374	287	299	310	322	334	345	357	368	380	392
375	403	415	426	438	449	461	473	484	496	507
376	519	530	542	553	565	576	588	600	611	623
377	634	646	657	669	680	692	703	715	726	738
378	749	761	772	784	795	807	818	830	841	852
379	864	875	887	898	910	921	933	944	955	967
380	978	990	*001	*013	*024	*035	*047	*058	*070	*081
381	58 092	104	115	127	138	149	161	172	184	195
382	206	218	229	240	252	263	274	286	297	309
383	320	331	343	354	365	377	388	399	410	422
384	433	444	456	467	478	490	501	512	524	535
385	546	557	569	580	591	602	614	625	636	647
386	659	670	681	692	704	715	726	737	749	760
387	771	782	794	805	816	827	838	850	861	872
388	883	894	906	917	928	939	950	961	973	984
389	995	*006	*017	*028	*040	*051	*062	*073	*084	*095
390	59 106	118	129	140	151	162	173	184	195	207
391	218	229	240	251	262	273	284	295	306	318
392	329	340	351	362	373	384	395	406	417	428
393	439	450	461	472	483	494	506	517	528	539
394	550	561	572	583	594	605	616	627	638	649
395	660	671	682	693	704	715	726	737	748	759
396	770	780	791	802	813	824	835	846	857	868
397	879	890	901	912	923	934	945	956	966	977
398	988	999	*010	*021	*032	*043	*054	*065	*076	*086
399	60 097	108	119	130	141	152	163	173	184	195
400	206	217	228	239	249	260	271	282	293	304

$$\log_{10} e = .43429 \qquad \log_e 10 = 2.30259$$

FIVE-PLACE LOGARITHMS
(BASE 10)

N	0	1	2	3	4	5	6	7	8	9
400	60 206	217	228	239	249	260	271	282	293	304
401	314	325	336	347	358	369	379	390	401	412
402	423	433	444	455	466	477	487	498	509	520
403	531	541	552	563	574	584	595	606	617	627
404	638	649	660	670	681	692	703	713	724	735
405	746	756	767	778	788	799	810	821	831	842
406	853	863	874	885	895	906	917	927	938	949
407	959	970	981	991	*002	*013	*023	*034	*045	*055
408	61 066	077	087	098	109	119	130	140	151	162
409	172	183	194	204	215	225	236	247	257	268
410	278	289	300	310	321	331	342	352	363	374
411	384	395	405	416	426	437	448	458	469	479
412	490	500	511	521	532	542	553	563	574	584
413	595	606	616	627	637	648	658	669	679	690
414	700	711	721	731	742	752	763	773	784	794
415	805	815	826	836	847	857	868	878	888	899
416	909	920	930	941	951	962	972	982	993	*003
417	62 014	024	034	045	055	066	076	086	097	107
418	118	128	138	149	159	170	180	190	201	211
419	221	232	242	252	263	273	284	294	304	315
420	325	335	346	356	366	377	387	397	408	418
421	428	439	449	459	469	480	490	500	511	521
422	531	542	552	562	572	583	593	603	613	624
423	634	644	655	665	675	685	696	706	716	726
424	737	747	757	767	778	788	798	808	818	829
425	839	849	859	870	880	890	900	910	921	931
426	941	951	961	972	982	992	*002	*012	*022	*033
427	63 043	053	063	073	083	094	104	114	124	134
428	144	155	165	175	185	195	205	215	225	236
429	246	256	266	276	286	296	306	317	327	337
430	347	357	367	377	387	397	407	417	428	438
431	448	458	468	478	488	498	508	518	528	538
432	548	558	568	579	589	599	609	619	629	639
433	649	659	669	679	689	699	709	719	729	739
434	749	759	769	779	789	799	809	819	829	839
435	849	859	869	879	889	899	909	919	929	939
436	949	959	969	979	988	998	*008	*018	*028	*038
437	64 048	058	068	078	083	098	108	118	128	137
438	147	157	167	177	187	197	207	217	227	237
439	246	256	266	276	286	296	306	316	326	335
440	345	355	365	375	385	395	404	414	424	434
441	444	454	464	473	483	493	503	513	523	532
442	542	552	562	572	582	591	601	611	621	631
443	640	650	660	670	680	689	699	709	719	729
444	738	748	758	768	777	787	797	807	816	826
445	836	846	856	865	875	885	895	904	914	924
446	933	943	953	963	972	982	992	*002	*011	*021
447	65 031	040	050	060	070	079	089	099	108	118
448	128	137	147	157	167	176	186	196	205	215
449	225	234	244	254	263	273	283	292	302	312
450	321	331	341	350	360	369	379	389	398	408

$\log_{10} e = .43429$ $\qquad\qquad$ $\log_e 10 = 2.30259$

FIVE-PLACE LOGARITHMS
(BASE 10)

N	0	1	2	3	4	5	6	7	8	9
450	65 321	331	341	350	360	369	379	389	398	408
451	418	427	437	447	456	466	475	485	495	504
452	514	523	533	543	552	562	571	581	591	600
453	610	619	629	639	648	658	667	677	686	696
454	706	715	725	734	744	753	763	772	782	792
455	801	811	820	830	839	849	858	868	877	887
456	896	906	916	925	935	944	954	963	973	982
457	992	*001	*011	*020	*030	*039	*049	*058	*068	*077
458	66 087	096	106	115	124	134	143	153	162	172
459	181	191	200	210	219	229	238	247	257	266
460	276	285	295	304	314	323	332	342	351	361
461	370	380	389	398	408	417	427	436	445	455
462	464	474	483	492	502	511	521	530	539	549
463	558	567	577	586	596	605	614	624	633	642
464	652	661	671	680	689	699	708	717	727	736
465	745	755	764	773	783	792	801	811	820	829
466	839	848	857	867	876	885	894	904	913	922
467	932	941	950	960	969	978	987	997	*006	*015
468	67 025	034	043	052	062	071	080	089	099	108
469	117	127	136	145	154	164	173	182	191	201
470	210	219	228	237	247	256	265	274	284	293
471	302	311	321	330	339	348	357	367	376	385
472	394	403	413	422	431	440	449	459	468	477
473	486	495	504	514	523	532	541	550	560	569
474	578	587	596	605	614	624	633	642	651	660
475	669	679	688	697	706	715	724	733	742	752
476	761	770	779	788	797	806	815	825	834	843
477	852	861	870	879	888	897	906	916	925	934
478	943	952	961	970	979	988	997	*006	*015	*024
479	68 034	043	052	061	070	079	088	097	106	115
480	124	133	142	151	160	169	178	187	196	205
481	215	224	233	242	251	260	269	278	287	296
482	305	314	323	332	341	350	359	368	377	386
483	395	404	413	422	431	440	449	458	467	476
484	485	494	502	511	520	529	538	547	556	565
485	574	583	592	601	610	619	628	637	646	655
486	664	673	681	690	699	708	717	726	735	744
487	753	762	771	780	789	797	806	815	824	833
488	842	851	860	869	878	886	895	904	913	922
489	931	940	949	958	966	975	984	993	*002	*011
490	69 020	028	037	046	055	064	073	082	090	099
491	108	117	126	135	144	152	161	170	179	188
492	197	205	214	223	232	241	249	258	267	276
493	285	294	302	311	320	329	338	346	355	364
494	373	381	390	399	408	417	425	434	443	452
495	461	469	478	487	496	504	513	522	531	539
496	548	557	566	574	583	592	601	609	618	627
497	636	644	653	662	671	679	688	697	705	714
498	723	732	740	749	758	767	775	784	793	801
499	810	819	827	836	845	854	862	871	880	888
500	897	906	914	923	932	940	949	958	966	975

$\log_{10} e = .43429$ $\log_e 10 = 2.30259$

FIVE-PLACE LOGARITHMS
(BASE 10)

N	0	1	2	3	4	5	6	7	8	9
500	69 897	906	914	923	932	940	949	958	966	975
501	984	992	*001	*010	*018	*027	*036	*044	*053	*062
502	70 070	079	088	096	105	114	122	131	140	148
503	157	165	174	183	191	200	209	217	226	234
504	243	252	260	269	278	286	295	303	312	321
505	329	338	346	355	364	372	381	389	398	406
506	415	424	432	441	449	458	467	475	484	492
507	501	509	518	526	535	544	552	561	569	578
508	586	595	603	612	621	629	638	646	655	663
509	672	680	689	697	706	714	723	731	740	749
510	757	766	774	783	791	800	808	817	825	834
511	842	851	859	868	876	885	893	902	910	919
512	927	935	944	952	961	969	978	986	995	*003
513	71 012	020	029	037	046	054	063	071	079	088
514	096	105	113	122	130	139	147	155	164	172
515	181	189	198	206	214	223	231	240	248	257
516	265	273	282	290	299	307	315	324	332	341
517	349	357	366	374	383	391	399	408	416	425
518	433	441	450	458	466	475	483	492	500	508
519	517	525	533	542	550	559	567	575	584	592
520	600	609	617	625	634	642	650	659	667	675
521	684	692	700	709	717	725	734	742	750	759
522	767	775	784	792	800	809	817	825	834	842
523	850	858	867	875	883	892	900	908	917	925
524	933	941	950	958	966	975	983	991	999	*008
525	72 016	024	032	041	049	057	066	074	082	090
526	099	107	115	123	132	140	148	156	165	173
527	181	189	198	206	214	222	230	239	247	255
528	263	272	280	288	296	304	313	321	329	337
529	346	354	362	370	378	387	395	403	411	419
530	428	436	444	452	460	469	477	485	493	501
531	509	518	526	534	542	550	558	567	575	583
532	591	599	607	616	624	632	640	648	656	665
533	673	681	689	697	705	713	722	730	738	746
534	754	762	770	779	787	795	803	811	819	827
535	835	843	852	860	868	876	884	892	900	908
536	916	925	933	941	949	957	965	973	981	989
537	997	*006	*014	*022	*030	*038	*046	*054	*062	*070
538	73 078	086	094	102	111	119	127	135	143	151
539	159	167	175	183	191	199	207	215	223	231
540	239	247	255	263	272	280	288	296	304	312
541	320	328	336	344	352	360	368	376	384	392
542	400	408	416	424	432	440	448	456	464	472
543	480	488	496	504	512	520	528	536	544	552
544	560	568	576	584	592	600	608	616	624	632
545	640	648	656	664	672	679	687	695	703	711
546	719	727	735	743	751	759	767	775	783	791
547	799	807	815	823	830	838	846	854	862	870
548	878	886	894	902	910	918	926	933	941	949
549	957	965	973	981	989	997	*005	*013	*020	*028
550	74 036	044	052	060	068	076	084	092	099	107

$$\log_{10} e = .43429 \qquad \log_e 10 = 2.30259$$

FIVE-PLACE LOGARITHMS
(BASE 10)

N	0	1	2	3	4	5	6	7	8	9
550	74 036	044	052	060	068	076	084	092	099	107
551	115	123	131	139	147	155	162	170	178	186
552	194	202	210	218	225	233	241	249	257	265
553	273	280	288	296	304	312	320	327	335	343
554	351	359	367	374	382	390	398	406	414	421
555	429	437	445	453	461	468	476	484	492	500
556	507	515	523	531	539	547	554	562	570	578
557	586	593	601	609	617	624	632	640	648	656
558	663	671	679	687	695	702	710	718	726	733
559	741	749	757	764	772	780	788	796	803	811
560	819	827	834	842	850	858	865	873	881	889
561	896	904	912	920	927	935	943	950	958	966
562	974	981	989	997	*005	*012	*020	*028	*035	*043
563	75 051	059	066	074	082	089	097	105	113	120
564	128	136	143	151	159	166	174	182	189	197
565	205	213	220	228	236	243	251	259	266	274
566	282	289	297	305	312	320	328	335	343	351
567	358	366	374	381	389	397	404	412	420	427
568	435	442	450	458	465	473	481	488	496	504
569	511	519	526	534	542	549	557	565	572	580
570	587	595	603	610	618	626	633	641	648	656
571	664	671	679	686	694	702	709	717	724	732
572	740	747	755	762	770	778	785	793	800	808
573	815	823	831	838	846	853	861	868	876	884
574	891	899	906	914	921	929	937	944	952	959
575	967	974	982	989	997	*005	*012	*020	*027	*035
576	76 042	050	057	065	072	080	087	095	103	110
577	118	125	133	140	148	155	163	170	178	185
578	193	200	208	215	223	230	238	245	253	260
579	268	275	283	290	298	305	313	320	328	335
580	343	350	358	365	373	380	388	395	403	410
581	418	425	433	440	448	455	462	470	477	485
582	492	500	507	515	522	530	537	545	552	559
583	567	574	582	589	597	604	612	619	626	634
584	641	649	656	664	671	678	686	693	701	708
585	716	723	730	738	745	753	760	768	775	782
586	790	797	805	812	819	827	834	842	849	856
587	864	871	879	886	893	901	908	916	923	930
588	938	945	953	960	967	975	982	989	997	*004
589	77 012	019	026	034	041	048	056	063	070	078
590	085	093	100	107	115	122	129	137	144	151
591	159	166	173	181	188	195	203	210	217	225
592	232	240	247	254	262	269	276	283	291	298
593	305	313	320	327	335	342	349	357	364	371
594	379	386	393	401	408	415	422	430	437	444
595	452	459	466	474	481	488	495	503	510	517
596	525	532	539	546	554	561	568	576	583	590
597	597	605	612	619	627	634	641	648	656	663
598	670	677	685	692	699	706	714	721	728	735
599	743	750	757	764	772	779	786	793	801	808
600	815	822	830	837	844	851	859	866	873	880

$$\log_{10} e = .43429 \qquad\qquad \log_e 10 = 2.30259$$

FIVE-PLACE LOGARITHMS
(BASE 10)

N	0	1	2	3	4	5	6	7	8	9
600	77 815	822	830	837	844	851	859	866	873	880
601	887	895	902	909	916	924	931	938	945	952
602	960	967	974	981	988	996	*003	*010	*017	*025
603	78 032	039	046	053	061	068	075	082	089	097
604	104	111	118	125	132	140	147	154	161	168
605	176	183	190	197	204	211	219	226	233	240
606	247	254	262	269	276	283	290	297	305	312
607	319	326	333	340	347	355	362	369	376	383
608	390	398	405	412	419	426	433	440	447	455
609	462	469	476	483	490	497	504	512	519	526
610	533	540	547	554	561	569	576	583	590	597
611	604	611	618	625	633	640	647	654	661	668
612	675	682	689	696	704	711	718	725	732	739
613	746	753	760	767	774	781	789	796	803	810
614	817	824	831	838	845	852	859	866	873	880
615	888	895	902	909	916	923	930	937	944	951
616	958	965	972	979	986	993	*000	*007	*014	*021
617	79 029	036	043	050	057	064	071	078	085	092
618	099	106	113	120	127	134	141	148	155	162
619	169	176	183	190	197	204	211	218	225	232
620	239	246	253	260	267	274	281	288	295	302
621	309	316	323	330	337	344	351	358	365	372
622	379	386	393	400	407	414	421	428	435	442
623	449	456	463	470	477	484	491	498	505	511
624	518	525	532	539	546	553	560	567	574	581
625	588	595	602	609	616	623	630	637	644	650
626	657	664	671	678	685	692	699	706	713	720
627	727	734	741	748	754	761	768	775	782	789
628	796	803	810	817	824	831	837	844	851	858
629	865	872	879	886	893	900	906	913	920	927
630	934	941	948	955	962	969	975	982	989	996
631	80 003	010	017	024	030	037	044	051	058	065
632	072	079	085	092	099	106	113	120	127	134
633	140	147	154	161	168	175	182	188	195	202
634	209	216	223	229	236	243	250	257	264	271
635	277	284	291	298	305	312	318	325	332	339
636	346	353	359	366	373	380	387	393	400	407
637	414	421	428	434	441	448	455	462	468	475
638	482	489	496	502	509	516	523	530	536	543
639	550	557	564	570	577	584	591	598	604	611
640	618	625	632	638	645	652	659	665	672	679
641	686	693	699	706	713	720	726	733	740	747
642	754	760	767	774	781	787	794	801	808	814
643	821	828	835	841	848	855	862	868	875	882
644	889	895	902	909	916	922	929	936	943	949
645	956	963	969	976	983	990	996	*003	*010	*017
646	81 023	030	037	043	050	057	064	070	077	084
647	090	097	104	111	117	124	131	137	144	151
648	158	164	171	178	184	191	198	204	211	218
649	224	231	238	245	251	258	265	271	278	285
650	291	298	305	311	318	325	331	338	345	351

$\log_{10} e = .43429$ $\qquad\qquad$ $\log_e 10 = 2.30259$

FIVE-PLACE LOGARITHMS
(BASE 10)

N	0	1	2	3	4	5	6	7	8	9
650	81 291	298	305	311	318	325	331	338	345	351
651	358	365	371	378	385	391	398	405	411	418
652	425	431	438	445	451	458	465	471	478	485
653	491	498	505	511	518	525	531	538	544	551
654	558	564	571	578	584	591	598	604	611	617
655	624	631	637	644	651	657	664	671	677	684
656	690	697	704	710	717	723	730	737	743	750
657	757	763	770	776	783	790	796	803	809	816
658	823	829	836	842	849	856	862	869	875	882
659	889	895	902	908	915	921	928	935	941	948
660	954	961	968	974	981	987	994	*000	*007	*014
661	82 020	027	033	040	046	053	060	066	073	079
662	086	092	099	105	112	119	125	132	138	145
663	151	158	164	171	178	184	191	197	204	210
664	217	223	230	236	243	249	256	263	269	276
665	282	289	295	302	308	315	321	328	334	341
666	347	354	360	367	373	380	387	393	400	406
667	413	419	426	432	439	445	452	458	465	471
668	478	484	491	497	504	510	517	523	530	536
669	543	549	556	562	569	575	582	588	595	601
670	607	614	620	627	633	640	646	653	659	666
671	672	679	685	692	698	705	711	718	724	730
672	737	743	750	756	763	769	776	782	789	795
673	802	808	814	821	827	834	840	847	853	860
674	866	872	879	885	892	898	905	911	918	924
675	930	937	943	950	956	963	969	975	982	988
676	995	*001	*008	*014	*020	*027	*033	*040	*046	*052
677	83 059	065	072	078	085	091	097	104	110	117
678	123	129	136	142	149	155	161	168	174	181
679	187	193	200	206	213	219	225	232	238	245
680	251	257	264	270	276	283	289	296	302	308
681	315	321	327	334	340	347	353	359	366	372
682	378	385	391	398	404	410	417	423	429	436
683	442	448	455	461	467	474	480	487	493	499
684	506	512	518	525	531	537	544	550	556	563
685	569	575	582	588	594	601	607	613	620	626
686	632	639	645	651	658	664	670	677	683	689
687	696	702	708	715	721	727	734	740	746	753
688	759	765	771	778	784	790	797	803	809	816
689	822	828	835	841	847	853	860	866	872	879
690	885	891	897	904	910	916	923	929	935	942
691	948	954	960	967	973	979	985	992	998	*004
692	84 011	017	023	029	036	042	048	055	061	067
693	073	080	086	092	098	105	111	117	123	130
694	136	142	148	155	161	167	173	180	186	192
695	198	205	211	217	223	230	236	242	248	255
696	261	267	273	280	286	292	298	305	311	317
697	323	330	336	342	348	354	361	367	373	379
698	386	392	398	404	410	417	423	429	435	442
699	488	454	460	466	473	479	485	491	497	504
700	510	516	522	528	535	541	547	553	559	566

$\log_{10} e = .43429$ $\log_e 10 = 2.30259$

FIVE-PLACE LOGARITHMS
(BASE 10)

N	0	1	2	3	4	5	6	7	8	9
700	84 510	516	522	528	535	541	547	553	559	566
701	572	578	584	590	597	603	609	615	621	628
702	634	640	646	652	658	665	671	677	683	689
703	696	702	708	714	720	726	733	739	745	751
704	757	763	770	776	782	788	794	800	807	813
705	819	825	831	837	844	850	856	862	868	874
706	880	887	893	899	905	911	917	924	930	936
707	942	948	954	960	967	973	979	985	991	997
708	85 003	009	016	022	028	034	040	046	052	058
709	065	071	077	083	089	095	101	107	114	120
710	126	132	138	144	150	156	163	169	175	181
711	187	193	199	205	211	217	224	230	236	242
712	248	254	260	266	272	278	285	291	297	303
713	309	315	321	327	333	339	345	352	358	364
714	370	376	382	388	394	400	406	412	418	425
715	431	437	443	449	455	461	467	473	479	485
716	491	497	503	509	516	522	528	534	540	546
717	552	558	564	570	576	582	588	594	600	606
718	612	618	625	631	637	643	649	655	661	667
719	673	679	685	691	697	703	709	715	721	727
720	733	739	745	751	757	763	769	775	781	788
721	794	800	806	812	818	824	830	836	842	848
722	854	860	866	872	878	884	890	896	902	908
723	914	920	926	932	938	944	950	956	962	968
724	974	980	986	992	998	*004	*010	*016	*022	*028
725	86 034	040	046	052	058	064	070	076	082	088
726	094	100	106	112	118	124	130	136	141	147
727	153	159	165	171	177	183	189	195	201	207
728	213	219	225	231	237	243	249	255	261	267
729	273	279	285	291	297	303	308	314	320	326
730	332	338	344	350	356	362	368	374	380	386
731	392	398	404	410	415	421	427	433	439	445
732	451	457	463	469	475	481	487	493	499	504
733	510	516	522	528	534	540	546	552	558	564
734	570	576	581	587	593	599	605	611	617	623
735	629	635	641	646	652	658	664	670	676	682
736	688	694	700	705	711	717	723	729	735	741
737	747	753	759	764	770	776	782	788	794	800
738	806	812	817	823	829	835	841	847	853	859
739	864	870	876	882	888	894	900	906	911	917
740	923	929	935	941	947	953	958	964	970	976
741	982	988	994	999	*005	*011	*017	*023	*029	*035
742	87 040	046	052	058	064	070	075	081	087	093
743	099	105	111	116	122	128	134	140	146	151
744	157	163	169	175	181	186	192	198	204	210
745	216	221	227	233	239	245	251	256	262	268
746	274	280	286	291	297	303	309	315	320	326
747	332	338	344	349	355	361	367	373	379	384
748	390	396	402	408	413	419	425	431	437	442
749	448	454	460	466	471	477	483	489	495	500
750	506	512	518	523	529	535	541	547	552	558

$\log_{10} e = .43429$ $\qquad\qquad$ $\log_e 10 = 2.30259$

FIVE-PLACE LOGARITHMS
(BASE 10)

N	0	1	2	3	4	5	6	7	8	9
750	87 506	512	518	523	529	535	541	547	552	558
751	564	570	576	581	587	593	599	604	610	616
752	622	628	633	639	645	651	656	662	668	674
753	679	685	691	697	703	708	714	720	726	731
754	737	743	749	754	760	766	772	777	783	789
755	795	800	806	812	818	823	829	835	841	846
756	852	858	864	869	875	881	887	892	898	904
757	910	915	921	927	933	938	944	950	955	961
758	967	973	978	984	990	996	*001	*007	*013	*018
759	88 024	030	036	041	047	053	058	064	070	076
760	081	087	093	098	104	110	116	121	127	133
761	138	144	150	156	161	167	173	178	184	190
762	195	201	207	213	218	224	230	235	241	247
763	252	258	264	270	275	281	287	292	298	304
764	309	315	321	326	332	338	343	349	355	360
765	366	372	377	383	389	395	400	406	412	417
766	423	429	434	440	446	451	457	463	468	474
767	480	485	491	497	502	508	513	519	525	530
768	536	542	547	553	559	564	570	576	581	587
769	593	598	604	610	615	621	627	632	638	643
770	649	655	660	666	672	677	683	689	694	700
771	705	711	717	722	728	734	739	745	750	756
772	762	767	773	779	784	790	795	801	807	812
773	818	824	829	835	840	846	852	857	863	868
774	874	880	885	891	897	902	908	913	919	925
775	930	936	941	947	953	958	964	969	975	981
776	986	992	997	*003	*009	*014	*020	*025	*031	*037
777	89 042	048	053	059	064	070	076	081	087	092
778	098	104	109	115	120	126	131	137	143	148
779	154	159	165	170	176	182	187	193	198	204
780	209	215	221	226	232	237	243	248	254	260
781	265	271	276	282	287	293	298	304	310	315
782	321	326	332	337	343	348	354	360	365	371
783	376	382	387	393	398	404	409	415	421	426
784	432	437	443	448	454	459	465	470	476	481
785	487	492	498	504	509	515	520	526	531	537
786	542	548	553	559	564	570	575	581	586	592
787	597	603	609	614	620	625	631	636	642	647
788	653	658	664	669	675	680	686	691	697	702
789	708	713	719	724	730	735	741	746	752	757
790	763	768	774	779	785	790	796	801	807	812
791	818	823	829	834	840	845	851	856	862	867
792	873	878	883	889	894	900	905	911	916	922
793	927	933	938	944	949	955	960	966	971	977
794	982	988	993	998	*004	*009	*015	*020	*026	*031
795	90 037	042	048	053	059	064	069	075	080	086
796	091	097	102	108	113	119	124	129	135	140
797	146	151	157	162	168	173	179	184	189	195
798	200	206	211	217	222	227	233	238	244	249
799	255	260	266	271	276	282	287	293	298	304
800	309	314	320	325	331	336	342	347	352	358

$$\log_{10} e = .43429 \qquad \log_e 10 = 2.30259$$

FIVE-PLACE LOGARITHMS
(BASE 10)

N	0	1	2	3	4	5	6	7	8	9
800	90 309	314	320	325	331	336	342	347	352	358
801	363	369	374	380	385	390	396	401	407	412
802	417	423	428	434	439	445	450	455	461	466
803	472	477	482	488	493	499	504	509	515	520
804	526	531	536	542	547	553	558	563	569	574
805	580	585	590	596	601	607	612	617	623	628
806	634	639	644	650	655	660	666	671	677	682
807	687	693	698	703	709	714	720	725	730	736
808	741	747	752	757	763	768	773	779	784	789
809	795	800	806	811	816	822	827	832	838	843
810	849	854	859	865	870	875	881	886	891	897
811	902	907	913	918	924	929	934	940	945	950
812	956	961	966	972	977	982	988	993	998	*004
813	91 009	014	020	025	030	036	041	046	052	057
814	062	068	073	078	084	089	094	100	105	110
815	116	121	126	132	137	142	148	153	158	164
816	169	174	180	185	190	196	201	206	212	217
817	222	228	233	238	243	249	254	259	265	270
818	275	281	286	291	297	302	307	312	318	323
819	328	334	339	344	350	355	360	365	371	376
820	381	387	392	397	403	408	413	418	424	429
821	434	440	445	450	455	461	466	471	477	482
822	487	492	498	503	508	514	519	524	529	535
823	540	545	551	556	561	566	572	577	582	587
824	593	598	603	609	614	619	624	630	635	640
825	645	651	656	661	666	672	677	682	687	693
826	698	703	709	714	719	724	730	735	740	745
827	751	756	761	766	772	777	782	787	793	798
828	803	808	814	819	824	829	834	840	845	850
829	855	861	866	871	876	882	887	892	897	903
830	908	913	918	924	929	934	939	944	950	955
831	960	965	971	976	981	986	991	997	*002	*007
832	92 012	018	023	028	033	038	044	049	054	059
833	065	070	075	080	085	091	096	101	106	111
834	117	122	127	132	137	143	148	153	158	163
835	169	174	179	184	189	195	200	205	210	215
836	221	226	231	236	241	247	252	257	262	267
837	273	278	283	288	293	298	304	309	314	319
838	324	330	335	340	345	350	355	361	366	371
839	376	381	387	392	397	402	407	412	418	423
840	428	433	438	443	449	454	459	464	469	474
841	480	485	490	495	500	505	511	516	521	526
842	531	536	542	547	552	557	562	567	572	578
843	583	588	593	598	603	609	614	619	624	629
844	634	639	645	650	655	660	665	670	675	681
845	686	691	696	701	706	711	716	722	727	732
846	737	742	747	752	758	763	768	773	778	783
847	788	793	799	804	809	814	819	824	829	834
848	840	845	850	855	860	865	870	875	881	886
849	891	896	901	906	911	916	921	927	932	937
850	942	947	952	957	962	967	973	978	983	988

$\log_{10} e = .43429$ $\qquad\qquad \log_e 10 = 2.30259$

FIVE-PLACE LOGARITHMS
(BASE 10)

N	0	1	2	3	4	5	6	7	8	9
850	92 942	947	952	957	962	967	973	978	983	988
851	993	998	*003	*008	*013	*018	*024	*029	*034	*039
852	93 044	049	054	059	064	069	075	080	085	090
853	095	100	105	110	115	120	125	131	136	141
854	146	151	156	161	166	171	176	181	186	192
855	197	202	207	212	217	222	227	232	237	242
856	247	252	258	263	268	273	278	283	288	293
857	298	303	308	313	318	323	328	334	339	344
858	349	354	359	364	369	374	379	384	389	394
859	399	404	409	414	420	425	430	435	440	445
860	450	455	460	465	470	475	480	485	490	495
861	500	505	510	515	520	526	531	536	541	546
862	551	556	561	566	571	576	581	586	591	596
863	601	606	611	616	621	626	631	636	641	646
864	651	656	661	666	671	676	682	687	692	697
865	702	707	712	717	722	727	732	737	742	747
866	752	757	762	767	772	777	782	787	792	797
867	802	807	812	817	822	827	832	837	842	847
868	852	857	862	867	872	877	882	887	892	897
869	902	907	912	917	922	927	932	937	942	947
870	952	957	962	967	972	977	982	987	992	997
871	94 002	007	012	017	022	027	032	037	042	047
872	052	057	062	067	072	077	082	086	091	096
873	101	106	111	116	121	126	131	136	141	146
874	151	156	161	166	171	176	181	186	191	196
875	201	206	211	216	221	226	231	236	240	245
876	250	255	260	265	270	275	280	285	290	295
877	300	305	310	315	320	325	330	335	340	345
878	349	354	359	364	369	374	379	384	389	394
879	399	404	409	414	419	424	429	433	438	443
880	448	453	458	463	468	473	478	483	488	493
881	498	503	507	512	517	522	527	532	537	542
882	547	552	557	562	567	571	576	581	586	591
883	596	601	606	611	616	621	626	630	635	640
884	645	650	655	660	665	670	675	680	685	689
885	694	699	704	709	714	719	724	729	734	738
886	743	748	753	758	763	768	773	778	783	787
887	792	797	802	807	812	817	822	827	832	836
888	841	846	851	856	861	866	871	876	880	885
889	890	895	900	905	910	915	919	924	929	934
890	939	944	949	954	959	963	968	973	978	983
891	988	993	998	*002	*007	*012	*017	*022	*027	*032
892	95 036	041	046	051	056	061	066	071	075	080
893	085	090	095	100	105	109	114	119	124	129
894	134	139	143	148	153	158	163	168	173	177
895	182	187	192	197	202	207	211	216	221	226
896	231	236	240	245	250	255	260	265	270	274
897	279	284	289	294	299	303	308	313	318	323
898	328	332	337	342	347	352	357	361	366	371
899	376	381	386	390	395	400	405	410	415	419
900	424	429	434	439	444	448	453	458	463	468

$$\log_{10} e = .43429 \qquad \log_e 10 = 2.30259$$

FIVE-PLACE LOGARITHMS
(BASE 10)

N	0	1	2	3	4	5	6	7	8	9
900	95 424	429	434	439	444	448	453	458	463	468
901	472	477	482	487	492	497	501	506	511	516
902	521	525	530	535	540	545	550	554	559	564
903	569	574	578	583	588	593	598	602	607	612
904	617	622	626	631	636	641	646	650	655	660
905	665	670	674	679	684	689	694	698	703	708
906	713	718	722	727	732	737	742	746	751	756
907	761	766	770	775	780	785	789	794	799	804
908	809	813	818	823	828	832	837	842	847	852
909	856	861	866	871	875	880	885	890	895	899
910	904	909	914	918	923	928	933	938	942	947
911	952	957	961	966	971	976	980	985	990	995
912	999	*004	*009	*014	*019	*023	*028	*033	*038	*042
913	96 047	052	057	061	066	071	076	080	085	090
914	095	099	104	109	114	118	123	128	133	137
915	142	147	152	156	161	166	171	175	180	185
916	190	194	199	204	209	213	218	223	227	232
917	237	242	246	251	256	261	265	270	275	280
918	284	289	294	298	303	308	313	317	322	327
919	332	336	341	346	350	355	360	365	369	374
920	379	384	388	393	398	402	407	412	417	421
921	426	431	435	440	445	450	454	459	464	468
922	473	478	483	487	492	497	501	506	511	515
923	520	525	530	534	539	544	548	553	558	562
924	567	572	577	581	586	591	595	600	605	609
925	614	619	624	628	633	638	642	647	652	656
926	661	666	670	675	680	685	689	694	699	703
927	708	713	717	722	727	731	736	741	745	750
928	755	759	764	769	774	778	783	788	792	797
929	802	806	811	816	820	825	830	834	839	844
930	848	853	858	862	867	872	876	881	886	890
931	895	900	904	909	914	918	923	928	932	937
932	942	946	951	956	960	965	970	974	979	984
933	988	993	997	*002	*007	*011	*016	*021	*025	*030
934	97 035	039	044	049	053	058	063	067	072	077
935	081	086	090	095	100	104	109	114	118	123
936	128	132	137	142	146	151	155	160	165	169
937	174	179	183	188	192	197	202	206	211	216
938	220	225	230	234	239	243	248	253	257	262
939	267	271	276	280	285	290	294	299	304	308
940	313	317	322	327	331	336	340	345	350	354
941	359	364	368	373	377	382	387	391	396	400
942	405	410	414	419	424	428	433	437	442	447
943	451	456	460	465	470	474	479	483	488	493
944	497	502	506	511	516	520	525	529	534	539
945	543	548	552	557	562	566	571	575	580	585
946	589	594	598	603	607	612	617	621	626	630
947	635	640	644	649	653	658	663	667	672	676
948	681	685	690	695	699	704	708	713	717	722
949	727	731	736	740	745	749	754	759	763	768
950	772	777	782	786	791	795	800	804	809	813

$\log_{10} e = .43429$ $\log_e 10 = 2.30259$

FIVE-PLACE LOGARITHMS
(BASE 10)

N	0	1	2	3	4	5	6	7	8	9
950	97 772	777	782	786	791	795	800	804	809	813
951	818	823	827	832	836	841	845	850	855	859
952	864	868	873	877	882	886	891	896	900	905
953	909	914	918	923	928	932	937	941	946	950
954	955	959	964	968	973	978	982	987	991	996
955	98 000	005	009	014	019	023	028	032	037	041
956	046	050	055	059	064	068	073	078	082	087
957	091	096	100	105	109	114	118	123	127	132
958	137	141	146	150	155	159	164	168	173	177
959	182	186	191	195	200	204	209	214	218	223
960	227	232	236	241	245	250	254	259	263	268
961	272	277	281	286	290	295	299	304	308	313
962	318	322	327	331	336	340	345	349	354	358
963	363	367	372	376	381	385	390	394	399	403
964	408	412	417	421	426	430	435	439	444	448
965	453	457	462	466	471	475	480	484	489	493
966	498	502	507	511	516	520	525	529	534	538
967	543	547	552	556	561	565	570	574	579	583
968	588	592	597	601	605	610	614	619	623	628
969	632	637	641	646	650	655	659	664	668	673
970	677	682	686	691	695	700	704	709	713	717
971	722	726	731	735	740	744	749	753	758	762
972	767	771	776	780	784	789	793	798	802	807
973	811	816	820	825	829	834	838	843	847	851
974	856	860	865	869	874	878	883	887	892	896
975	900	905	909	914	918	923	927	932	936	941
976	945	949	954	958	963	967	972	976	981	985
977	989	994	998	*003	*007	*012	*016	*021	*025	*029
978	99 034	038	043	047	052	056	061	065	069	074
979	078	083	087	092	096	100	105	109	114	118
980	123	127	131	136	140	145	149	154	158	162
981	167	171	176	180	185	189	193	198	202	207
982	211	216	220	224	229	233	238	242	247	251
983	255	260	264	269	273	277	282	286	291	295
984	300	304	308	313	317	322	326	330	335	339
985	344	348	352	357	361	366	370	374	379	383
986	388	392	396	401	405	410	414	419	423	427
987	432	436	441	445	449	454	458	463	467	471
988	476	480	484	489	493	498	502	506	511	515
989	520	524	528	533	537	542	546	550	555	559
990	564	568	572	577	581	585	590	594	599	603
991	607	612	616	621	625	629	634	638	642	647
992	651	656	660	664	669	673	677	682	686	691
993	695	699	704	708	712	717	721	726	730	734
994	739	743	747	752	756	760	765	769	774	778
995	782	787	791	795	800	804	808	813	817	822
996	826	830	835	839	843	848	852	856	861	865
997	870	874	878	883	887	891	896	900	904	909
998	913	917	922	926	930	935	939	944	948	952
999	967	961	965	970	974	978	983	987	991	996
1000	00 000	004	009	013	017	022	026	030	035	039

$$\log_{10} e = .43429 \qquad \log_e 10 = 2.30259$$

APPENDIX IV

MATHEMATICAL REVIEW

A. Progressions

1. *Arithmetic progression*
   If a is the first term; l, the last term; d, the common difference; n, the number of terms; and s, the sum of n terms; then

$$l = a + (n - 1)d$$

   and

$$s = \frac{n}{2}(a + l).$$

2. *Geometric progression*
   If a is the first term; l, the last term; r, the common ratio; n, the number of terms; and s, the sum of n terms; then

$$l = ar^{n-1}$$

   and

$$s = a\frac{(r^n - 1)}{r - 1} = \frac{rl - a}{r - 1}.$$

3. *Infinite geometric progression*
   If a geometric progression has a common ratio $-1 < r < 1$, then the sum as n approaches infinity becomes

$$s = \frac{a}{1 - r}.$$

B. Summing powers of natural numbers

1. $1 + 2 + \cdots + n = \frac{1}{2}n(n + 1)$.
2. $1^2 + 2^2 + \cdots + n^2 = \frac{1}{6}n(n + 1)(2n + 1)$.
3. $1^3 + 2^3 + \cdots + n^3 = \frac{1}{4}n^2(n + 1)^2$.

C. Binomial theorem

$$(1 + x)^n = 1 + nx + \frac{n(n - 1)}{2!}x^2 + \frac{n(n - 1)(n - 2)}{3!}x^3 + \cdots.$$

This expression converges if n is a positive integer or if $-1 < x < 1$.

D. Series expansions

1. $e^x = 1 + x + \dfrac{x^2}{2!} + \dfrac{x^3}{3!} + \cdots$ for all x.

2. $\log_e (1 + x) = x - \dfrac{x^2}{2} + \dfrac{x^3}{3} - \dfrac{x^4}{4} + \cdots$ if $-1 < x < 1$.

E. Finite differences

1. $x^{(m)} = x(x-1)\dots(x-m+1)$.
2. $\Delta f(x) = f(x+1) - f(x)$.
3. Newton's advancing difference formula:

$$f(x+n) = \left[1 + n^{(1)}\Delta + \frac{n^{(2)}}{2!}\Delta^2 + \frac{n^{(3)}}{3!}\Delta^3 + \cdots\right]f(x) .$$

4. $\Delta x^{(m)} = m x^{(m-1)}$.

5. $\displaystyle\sum_{x=1}^{n} x^{(m)} = \frac{1}{m+1}\, x^{(m+1)}\Big]_{1}^{n+1}$.

6. $\displaystyle\sum_{x=1}^{n} a^x f(x) = \left[\frac{a^x}{a-1}\left\{1 - \frac{a\Delta}{a-1} + \frac{a^2\,\Delta^2}{(a-1)^2} - \frac{a^3\,\Delta^3}{(a-1)^3} + \cdots\right\}f(x)\right]_{1}^{n+1}$.

7. $hD \equiv \log_e(1 + \Delta)$,
   where D is the derivative operator and h is the interval of differencing.

Answers to the exercises

CHAPTER 1

1. a) $\frac{1}{3}(l^2 + 2t + 3)$.
   c) $2n + 1$.
3. a) $\frac{1}{2}n(n+1) - \frac{1}{2}t(t+1)$.
   b) $2(2^n - 2^t)$.
4. a) $\frac{1}{24}$.
   b) $\frac{1}{29}$.
5. a) .1.
   b) .1.
7. 106.1106.
8. a) $101.92.
   b) $100.00.
   c) $103.33.
10. a) 4.8%.
    b) $3\frac{1}{3}$ years.
11. $582.50.
13. $\dfrac{i - j}{1 + j}$.
14. $100[(1 + i)^{10} - (1 + i)^5]$.
15. $\dfrac{A(n-1)}{A(n)}$.
16. $1000(1 + i)^7 + 500v^8$.
17. $\dfrac{3 + \sqrt{5}}{2}$.
18. a) $\dfrac{d}{1 - dn}$.
    b) $\dfrac{i}{1 + in}$.
21. a) (1) $25.
       (2) $0.
       (3) −$25.
22. a) $108.70.
    b) $108.51.

23. $\dfrac{1}{n + 1}$.
24. a) $\frac{1}{25}$.
    b) $\frac{1}{30}$.
26. a) $100(1.015)^8$.
    b) $100(1.015)^{-40}$.
27. a) $100(.995)^{-24}$.
    b) $100(.995)^{120}$.
28. a) $\left(1 + mi^{\left(\frac{1}{m}\right)}\right)^{\frac{1}{m}}$
    $$= \left(1 - pd^{\left(\frac{1}{p}\right)}\right)^{-\frac{1}{p}}.$$
    b) (1) $100(.76)^{-.5}$.
       (2) $100(.76)^{2.5}$.
29. a) $4\left[1 - \left(1 + \dfrac{i^{(3)}}{3}\right)^{-\frac{3}{4}}\right]$.
    b) $6\left[\left(1 - \dfrac{d^{(2)}}{2}\right)^{-\frac{3}{3}} - 1\right]$.
32. $d < d^{(m)} < \delta < i^{(m)} < i$.
34. a) $\log_e a + 2t \log_e b + c^t \log_e c \log_e d$.
    b) Formula (1.22).
36. a) $6\left(e^{\frac{\delta}{6}} - 1\right)$.
    b) $-4 \log_e \left(1 - \dfrac{d^{(4)}}{4}\right)$.
37. a) (1) $\dfrac{i}{1 + it}$.
       (2) Decreasing.
    b) (1) $\dfrac{d}{1 - dt}$.
       (2) Increasing.

38. $e^{.01} - 1$.

39. $e^{.038}$.

40. $1 - 2^{-\frac{1}{4}}$.

41. $(.912576)^{-\frac{1}{4}} - 1$.

42. $100(1.02)^{20}(.93)^{-5}(.97)^{-10}$.

43. a) $(1 + r)^{\frac{n(n+1)}{2}}(1 + i)^n$.

    b) $(1 + r)^{\frac{n+1}{2}}(1 + i) - 1$.

44. b) $\dfrac{\delta^3}{3!} + \dfrac{\delta^5}{5!} + \dfrac{\delta^7}{7!} + \cdots$.

45. $\dfrac{\log_e i - \log_e \delta}{\delta}$.

47. a) $(1 + i)^{-2}$.
    b) $(1 + i)^{-1}$.

    c) $(1 - d)^{-\frac{m-1}{m}}$.
    d) $-v^{-1}$.
    e) $e^{-\delta}$.

48. a) $d + d^2 + d^3 + d^4 + \cdots$.
    b) $i - i^2 + i^3 - i^4 + \cdots$.

    c) $1 - \delta + \dfrac{\delta^2}{2!} - \dfrac{\delta^3}{3!} + \cdots$.

    d) $i - \dfrac{m-1}{2!\,m}i^2$
       $+ \dfrac{(m-1)(2m-1)}{3!\,m^2}i^3$
       $- \dfrac{(m-1)(2m-1)(3m-1)}{4!\,m^3}i^4$
       $+ \cdots$

    e) $d + \dfrac{d^2}{2} + \dfrac{d^3}{3} + \dfrac{d^4}{4} + \cdots$.

51. a) (1) $e^{at + \frac{1}{2}bt^2}$.
       (2) $e^{(a - \frac{1}{2}b) + bn}$.

    b) (1) $e^{\frac{a}{\log_e b}(b^t - 1)}$.

       (2) $e^{\frac{a}{\log_e b}(b-1)b^{n-1}}$.

52. 4%.

53. $\frac{5}{102}$.

CHAPTER 2

3. $159.30.
4. $150.68.
5. a) $275.
   b) $260.

6. $\dfrac{1}{\delta}[\log_e(s_1 + s_2 + \cdots + s_n)$
   $- \log_e(s_1 v^{t_1} + s_2 v^{t_1}$
   $+ \cdots + s_n v^{t_n})]$.

7. $\dfrac{\log_e 2}{\delta}$.

8. 36.4 years.
9. a) 14.0 years.
   b) No.

10. $\dfrac{2n^2 + n}{3}$.

11. 3.72%.

12. $\dfrac{\sqrt{19} - 4}{3}$.

13. $1\frac{1}{2}\%$.

14. $\dfrac{\log_e 2}{50}$.

15. 84.03 years.

16. $100(x^{12} + x^9 + x^6 + x^3 - 4)$.

17. $673.42.

18. a) .0400.
    b) .0469.
    c) .0452.

CHAPTER 3

1. a) $n + \frac{1}{2}n(n - 1)i$.
   b) $n - \frac{1}{2}n(n + 1)d$.
2. a) $a_{\overline{n}|} < n < s_{\overline{n}|}$.
   b) $i = 0$.

4. 442.48.
5. $1684.
10. 5.695.
14. $2389.72.

15. $3633.38.
17. a) $3256.88.
   b) $5403.15.
   c) $6959.37.
19. $v^{\frac{1}{2}}a_{\overline{7}|} = (a_{\overline{9}|} - a_{\overline{2}|})(1 + i)^{\frac{1}{2}}$.
21. a) $\dfrac{v^{n-1}}{i} = \dfrac{v^n}{d}$.
   b) $_{n-1}|a_{\overline{\infty}|}$.
   c) $_{n}|\ddot{a}_{\overline{\infty}|}$.
22. $100[(1 + i)^{30} - (1 + i)^{10}]$.
23. 4.
24. $\dfrac{k(k - 1)}{2!} i + \dfrac{k(k - 1)(k - 2)}{3!} i^2$
$$+ \cdots$$
25. $\ddot{a}_{\overline{n}|} + v^{n-1+k}\left[\dfrac{(1 + i)^k - 1}{i}\right]$.
26. a) $-s_{\overline{n}|}$.
   b) $-a_{\overline{n}|}$.
27. 9; $32.41.

28. 21; $146.07.
29. 20; $89.24.
30. 3.35%.
31. $\dfrac{4\sqrt{2} - 5}{7}$.
34. $\log_2 (n + 1)$.
35. a) 8.145.
   b) 8.230.
36. $\dfrac{(1 + i)^{\frac{1}{2}} P}{1 + 2a_{\overline{4}|i} + 2(1 + i)^{-4}a_{\overline{5}|i}}$.
37. 14.2.
38. 12.0.
39. 7.5%.
40. 280.
41. $\dfrac{2x - y}{x^2 + 2x - y}$.
43. $\dfrac{1000}{4a_{\overline{20}|} - a_{\overline{15}|} - a_{\overline{10}|} - a_{\overline{5}|}}$.
44. $6000.

CHAPTER 4

1. a) $\dfrac{100}{s_{\overline{4}|}} (s_{\overline{40}|} - s_{\overline{8}|})$.
   b) $\dfrac{100}{a_{\overline{4}|}} (s_{\overline{36}|} - s_{\overline{4}|})$.
2. a) $\dfrac{200}{s_{\overline{4}|}} (a_{\overline{176}|} - a_{\overline{32}|})$.
   b) $\dfrac{200}{a_{\overline{4}|}} (a_{\overline{180}|} - a_{\overline{36}|})$.
3. $\dfrac{500 \ddot{a}_{\overline{40}|} \ddot{a}_{\overline{2}|}}{\ddot{s}_{\overline{20}|}}$.
5. $300\dfrac{1 - (.995)^{120}}{1 - (.995)^6}$.
6. $10\dfrac{1 - e^{-.25}}{1 - e^{-.0125}}$.
7. 1.95.
8. $\dfrac{1 - v^{48}}{1 - v^{\frac{1}{2}}}$.
9. a) $761.06.
   b) $758.06.
10. $\ddot{a}_{\overline{n}|}^{(12)} = \dfrac{i^{(2)}}{d^{(12)}} a_{\overline{n}|}^{(2)}$.
11. $551.30.

14. a) .782.
   b) 1.279.
   c) 88.527.
   d) 88.745.
   e) 113.253.
   f) 113.532.
15. $\dfrac{1 - v^{36}}{1 - v^{\frac{1}{2}}}$.
16. a) $\displaystyle\int_0^n \dfrac{1}{a(t)} dt$.
   b) $\displaystyle\int_0^n \dfrac{a(n)}{a(t)} dt$.
17. $1 - \dfrac{1}{\delta} \log_e \dfrac{i}{\delta}$.
19. a) $\dfrac{\log_e (1 + in)}{i}$.
   b) $\log_e (1 + n)$.
21. 27.5 years.
22. $\dfrac{\log_e 20[1 - (1 - d)^{\frac{1}{2}}]}{\log_e (1 - d)}$.
23. 6%.
24. $6a_{\overline{20}|} + \dfrac{a_{\overline{20}|} - 20v^{20}}{i}$.

26. $\dfrac{a_{\overline{n}|}}{d}$.

28. $200 \dfrac{\ddot{a}_{\overline{10}|} - 10v^{10}}{d} \cdot \dfrac{a_{\overline{5}|}}{s_{\overline{20}|}}$.

30. \$7792.

31. \$1591.

33. *a)* $\dfrac{P}{is_{\overline{k}|}} + \dfrac{Q}{(is_{\overline{k}|})^2}$.

    b) $\dfrac{P}{i^{(m)}} + \dfrac{Q}{i \cdot i^{(m)}}$.

36. *a)* $\displaystyle\int_0^n (n-t)v^t \, dt$.

    b) $\dfrac{n - \bar{a}_{\overline{n}|}}{\delta}$.

37. 16,020.

38. 84.5.

39. *a)* $(2) - \dfrac{n(n+1)}{2}$.

    b) $(2) - \dfrac{n^2}{2}$.

43. $a_{\overline{29}|} + \dfrac{a_{\overline{28}|}}{s_{\overline{2}|}}$.

44. 74.9.

46. 40.

47. 5.124.

52. *a)* $\dfrac{q}{p-q}$.

    b) $\dfrac{2q}{p-q}$.

CHAPTER 5

1. *a)* $200a_{\overline{8}|} + 100a_{\overline{3}|}$.
   b) $(200a_{\overline{15}|} + 100a_{\overline{10}|} + 100a_{\overline{5}|})$.
        $(1+i)^7 - (400s_{\overline{7}|} - 100s_{\overline{2}|})$.
2. \$635.32.
3. \$1326.46.
4. \$675.02.
5. $400a_{\overline{12}|}$
    $(10,000 - 400a_{\overline{20}|})$.
    $+ \dfrac{(3a_{\overline{12}|} - a_{\overline{7}|} - a_{\overline{2}|})}{3a_{\overline{20}|} - a_{\overline{15}|} - a_{\overline{10}|} - a_{\overline{5}|}}$.
6. $\dfrac{1000a_{\overline{15}|} - 2500}{a_{\overline{13}|}}$.
7. $20,000 \dfrac{a_{\overline{15}|}(1+i)^2}{a_{\overline{20}|} a_{\overline{13}|}}$.
8. \$64.19.
9. $a_{\overline{n}|} - nv^{n+1}$.
11. 7th.
12. \$724.59.
13. 4%.
14. *a)* $i(a_{\overline{5}|i} + v_i^6 a_{\overline{10}|i})$.
   b) v_i^6 .
15. *a)* $(K - Ai)(1+i)^{t-1}$.
   b) Yes.
17. \$133.29.
20. *a)* \$60.
   b) \$40.
   c) \$35.
   d) \$65.
   e) \$565.

21. \$89.10.
22. \$222.14.
23. *a)* \$229.87.
   b) \$229.62.
24. \$7610.47.
25. *a)* 18, \$74.18.
   b) \$44.99.
26. $20(20 - a_{\overline{20}|}^{(2)})$.
27. \$1395.05.
28. \$1344.89.
31. \$7.82.
33. \$908.87.
34. $\dfrac{100x}{1 + .06x}$ where $x =$
    $s_{\overline{4}|.03}(1.02)^6 + s_{\overline{6}|.02}$.
35. $\dfrac{1000/[a_{\overline{10}|.05} + v_{.05}^{10}a_{\overline{10}|.04}]}{1 + .06[s_{\overline{10}|.03}(1.02)^{10} + s_{\overline{10}|.02}]}$.
39. 2.94%.
40. 4%.
41. $B + Bis_{\overline{t}|i} + (A - B)(1+j)^t -$
                   $Ps_{\overline{t}|t}$
42. 2.8659.
43. \$57.36.
44. *a)* \$757.19.
   b) \$826.40.
45. \$138.46.
46. $R \dfrac{a_{\overline{30}|.05} - a_{\overline{15}|.045}}{a_{\overline{20}|.045} - a_{\overline{15}|.045}}$.

47 $a)$ $\dfrac{30{,}000(1.04)^9 - \left(\dfrac{30{,}000}{a_{\overline{20}|.04}}\right)s_{\overline{9}|.04} - 5000}{a_{\overline{9}|.05}}$

$= \dfrac{\left(\dfrac{30{,}000}{a_{\overline{20}|.04}}\right)a_{\overline{11}|.04} - 5000}{a_{\overline{7}|.05}}.$

$b)$ $\dfrac{30{,}000(1.05)^9 - \left(\dfrac{30{,}000}{a_{\overline{20}|.04}}\right)s_{\overline{9}|.05} - 5000}{a_{\overline{5}|.05}}.$

CHAPTER 6

1. $912.24.
2. $1047.14.
3. $115.87.
4. $a)$ 3%.
   $b)$ 15.
5. $794.83.
6. $945.
10. $1 - \frac{1}{2}p$.
11. $20.
12. $8.50; $1091.50.
13. $65.43.
14. $574.39.
15. $19.80.
19. $1016.92; $1026.92.
21. $a)$ 5.15%.
    $b)$ 5.13%.
    $c)$ 5.14%.
22. 2.93%.
23. $a)$ $1085.84.
    $b)$ $895.35.
24. 5.37%.
25. $150 - 5a_{\overline{10}|.04}$.
26. $1220.74.
28. $110{,}400 - 800(5a_{\overline{16}|.05} - 2a_{\overline{4}|.05})$.
31. $1153.21.
32. $A = 105i^{(2)} - 4$.
    $B = 4$.

33. $1000v^{80} + \dfrac{40a_{\overline{30}|} + 10a_{\overline{70}|}}{s_{\overline{4}|}}$ at rate

    $\dfrac{i^{(4)}}{4}.$

34. $a)$ $100v^6 i + 6 - a_{\overline{6}|}$.
    $b)$ $a_{\overline{6}|} - 100v^6 i$.
35. $407.42.
36. Infinite.
37. $E \sum\limits_{t=1}^{\infty}\left[p_t \prod\limits_{r=1}^{t}\left(\dfrac{1 + k_r}{1 + i_r}\right)\right].$
39. $K' = v^{25}$.
    $C' = v^{10}$.
40. $100e^{-12\delta} + 5\,\dfrac{1 - e^{-12\delta}}{\delta}.$
41. $A = 3$.
    $B = -2$.
42. 11 years.
44. $a)$ $1019.27
        1014.45
        1009.64
        1004.82
        1000.00
    $b)$ $ 981.19
        985.89
        990.60
        995.30
        1000.00
45. $76.7616.
46. $1067.59.

CHAPTER 7

1. $a)$ $2,050,000.
   $b)$ $2,000,000.
   $c)$ $2,150,000.
   $d)$ $2,096,200.

2. 5.025%.

3. $I = iA + \displaystyle\int_0^1 n_t \cdot {}_{1-t}i_t \, dt$

$\qquad - \displaystyle\int_0^1 w_t \cdot {}_{1-t}i_t \, dt\,.$

4. \$943.

5. a) $\dfrac{ti}{1 + (1 - t)i}\,.$

   b) $\dfrac{(1 - t)i}{1 + ti}\,.$

7. a) $a_{\overline{n}|} = a_{\overline{n-1}|} + v^n\,.$
   b) $s_{\overline{n}|} = s_{\overline{n-1}|} + (1 + i)^{n-1}\,.$
   c) $(Ia)_{\overline{n}|} = (Ia)_{\overline{n-1}|} + nv^n\,.$
   d) $(Da)_{\overline{n}|} = (Da)_{\overline{n-1}|} + a_{\overline{n}|}\,.$

8. a) $\dfrac{n - a_{\overline{n}|}}{i}\,.$

   b) $\dfrac{\ddot{s}_{\overline{n}|} - n}{i}\,.$

   c) $\dfrac{n(1 + i) - 2\ddot{a}_{\overline{n}|} + nv^n}{i^2}\,.$

   d) $\dfrac{\frac{1}{2}in(n + 1) - n + a_{\overline{n}|}}{i^2}\,.$

10. (1) \$11,593.
    (2) \$5366.
    (3) \$5119.
    (4) \$8817 if wife is alive.
        \$2496 if wife is dead.
    (5) \$0.

11. \$10,686.
12. \$117.23; \$62.94.
13. a) \$1628.89.
    b) \$1638.23.
16. \$5.
17. 14.7%.
18. 34.5%.
19. 10.9%.
22. a) (1) \$1340.10.
        (2) \$1000.
        (3) \$250.
    b) (1) \$11,408.50.
        (2) \$10,000.
        (3) \$6875.

23.

t	D	B_t
0......		10,000
1......	4,000	6,000
2......	2,400	3,600
3......	1,440	2,160
4......	864	1,296
5......	296	1,000

24. a) \$1715.55.
    b) \$34,310.90.
25. 4.6%.

Index

This book has been set in 10 point Bodoni #175, leaded 3 points, and 9 point Bodoni #175, leaded 2 points. Chapter numbers are in 11 point News Gothic Bold and 18 point News Gothic, and chapter titles are in 18 point News Gothic. The size of the type page is 27 by 46 picas.